For

Charles and Velura White,
dedicated workers for
our beloved Faith in
Inglewood,
          with Bahá'í love
     and warmest wishes,
          Marion Yazdi
          18 August 1982

YOUTH IN THE VANGUARD

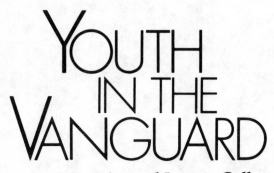

YOUTH IN THE VANGUARD

*Memoirs and Letters Collected
by the
First Bahá'í Student at Berkeley
and at Stanford University
by
Marion Carpenter Yazdi*

*The next generation will hunger for the
Beauty of His Presence, now so manifest
in our midst, and every little fragment
of word or deed concerning Him
will be their treasure.*

Isabella D. Brittingham

BAHÁ'Í PUBLISHING TRUST
WILMETTE, ILLINOIS

Library of Congress Cataloging in Publication Data

Yazdi, Marion Carpenter, 1902–
    Youth in the vanguard.

    Includes index.
    1. Yazdi, Marion Carpenter, 1902–   2. Bahaism—
Biography.   3. Bahaism—California—History.   I. Title.
BP395. Y39A39   297'.89'0924 [B]   82-6793
ISBN 0-87743-173-6   AACR2

Design by John Solarz

10   9   8   7   6   5   4   3   2   1

Printed in U.S.A.

In Memory of
Sheikh-Ali

Contents

Foreword by Publisher

She sported a bobbed hairdo and a serge pleated skirt; she tooled about campus and countryside in an Overland coupe nicknamed "Peter Pan"; on her ukelele she played such tunes of the day as "I'll Take a Box of Whitman's Chocolates"; a few of her friends were quite "bohemian." Yet with all these delightful accessions to the fads and fashions of collegiate life in the 1920s, Marion Carpenter [Yazdi] had a commitment that distinguished her from most of the coeds around her: she was a Bahá'í, and the center of gravity around which her life as a student revolved was the Bahá'í Faith. She received her inspiration and took her instructions from the then few published writings of Bahá'u'lláh, from the precious Tablets and accounts of 'Abdu'l-Bahá, and, after 1921, from the letters of Shoghi Effendi. Mrs. Yazdi's story harks back to a very different era when Bahá'í principles that now find acceptance in some quarters were startling. But any Bahá'í who has ever undertaken the often lonely though rewarding task of bringing the Faith to a community's attention, whether on a college campus or not, is bound to recognize himself or herself in these pages.

In telling her story of the early days of the Bahá'í Faith in

Berkeley and at Stanford University, Marion Yazdi has
drawn from a virtual "God's plenty" of sources: personal letters and documents; interviews; unpublished manuscripts;
notes of public lectures; unpublished talks and Tablets of
'Abdu'l-Bahá for which no approved translations yet exist;
verbal reports ("pilgrims' notes") of 'Abdu'l-Bahá's utterances that cannot be authenticated; unpublished letters and
cables of Shoghi Effendi for which original copies do exist; accounts in Bahá'í periodicals; newspaper articles; earlier
translations of Bahá'í writings, now superseded by new
translations; and authorized, published translations of
Bahá'í sacred writings.

The rich variety of source materials enables the author
to recreate the excitement and challenge of being a Bahá'í
during the earliest years of the Faith's existence in America.
But the differing nature of these materials, while being one
of the book's most appealing aspects, calls for a measure of
discrimination on the reader's part. Shoghi Effendi, in a letter written on his behalf, has cautioned us: "Bahá'u'lláh has
made it clear enough that only those things that have been
revealed in the form of Tablets have a binding power over
the friends. Hearsays may be matters of interest but can in no
way claim authority." Thus Mrs. Yazdi in writing and we in
editing have worked to make it clear which of the Bahá'í
writings quoted "have a binding power over the friends"
and which do not, which of the stories of 'Abdu'l-Bahá are
authentic and which should be regarded as pilgrims' notes.

Keeping this fundamental principle about Bahá'í texts
in mind, a very pleasurable and inspiring reading experience
awaits, for the reader will enjoy a glimpse into the devotion
of a group of Bahá'ís of an earlier and very special time, a
generation of Bahá'ís who laid the foundation for the future
expansion of the Cause of Bahá'u'lláh. As Marion Yazdi's
remembrances reveal beyond a doubt, those early believers
were motivated by a powerful, unyielding love for the Cause

of Bahá'u'lláh. Indeed, woven into her recollections of Berkeley and Stanford is the story of two loves—her profound love for the young man who became her husband and her quintessential love for the Bahá'í Faith.

Foreword by Ali M. Yazdi

To recall the early days of the Bahá'í Faith in Berkeley and at Stanford University is to look back at the time when a new Faith was taking hold in a new continent. The happenings in Berkeley and Stanford were but a part of the wider movement that came to life simultaneously in many parts of the United States and Canada.

How does a new religion prove itself? How is a new spiritual cycle initiated in this sophisticated and materialistic age?

From its beginning in 1844 the Bahá'í Faith suffered a baptism of fire in Persia and the Middle East. The people who responded to its call and were transported by its message went through the ordeals and upheavals that greet a new Prophet when He announces His Mission. The story of those early days following the declaration of the Báb in Shíráz, Persia, has been movingly told by Nabíl in *The Dawn-Breakers* and by Shoghi Effendi in *God Passes By*.[1]

That was the beginning of the Heroic Age of the Faith. It was an explosive period, full of turmoil and excitement, violence and cruelty, nobility and valor that shook the lives and the culture of the people of Persia and the whole Middle East. It continued through the ministry of Bahá'u'lláh, the

Prophet-Founder of the Bahá'í Faith, and that of His appointed successor, 'Abdu'l-Bahá, and came to a close with the ascension of 'Abdu'l-Bahá in 1921.[2]

Against this background unfolds the story of the early days of the Bahá'í Faith in the United States. The time was the beginning of the twentieth century; the setting, the American continent. A vigorous young nation was coming of age. The American people, confident and adventuresome, had created a material civilization that aroused the admiration of others everywhere. Though happy and optimistic, they began to feel the need of things spiritual. A number of them began to search actively for answers.

On the other side of the globe, in an old fortress-city on the eastern coast of the Mediterranean, there was a religious prisoner Who had spent the greater part of His life in hardship and confinement. The city was 'Akká; the prisoner was 'Abdu'l-Bahá. He had been entrusted by His Father, Bahá'u'lláh, with the mission of carrying on the work He had started. The whole world was His province. 'Abdu'l-Bahá was eager to undertake His weighty, bewildering, and dangerous assignment. There were renewed persecutions in Persia and treachery and intrigue in the Holy Land that aroused the Turkish authorities and endangered His life. But neither danger nor obstacles weakened His resolve or clouded His vision. The time had come to carry the Faith to the Western world. He turned His thoughts to America.

Thus began the inspiring and history-making relationship between 'Abdu'l-Bahá and the band of earnest seekers scattered over the United States of America. The story of this relationship and the chain of events that followed is told in Shoghi Effendi's God Passes By. To these early pioneers their study and espousal of the Faith was not an intellectual exercise; it was a personal experience that had a lasting impact on their lives and on their perspective of the world. It was an enlightening, exhilarating spiritual experience.

When Bahá'u'lláh assigned 'Abdu'l-Bahá His mission,

He conferred on Him a unique station—the station of Center of the Covenant.[3] Though not a Manifestation of God, He was divinely inspired; though human, He partook of the divine. His very appearance, His manner, His love betokened His power and His station. The early Bahá'ís felt they were in the presense of a living Man of God—the representative of a Manifestation of God in this day.[4]

The early believers in the San Francisco Bay Area were active members of the fledgling American Bahá'í community. They shared their feelings and worked hand in hand with others to spread the Bahá'í message. What kind of people were they? How did they go about their lives and their service to the Faith? Some of the answers are found in this book.

In the fall of 1920 a young girl, just graduated from high school, came to Berkeley to enter the University of California. Her name was Marion Carpenter. She had come from Santa Paula, eager, enthusiastic, full of youthful confidence in the future and in the opportunities offered by the Bahá'í Faith. She took part in all aspects of Bahá'í work, youth and adult, inside and outside the university. Later, in 1923, she entered Stanford University as a senior, graduated, and went on to get a master's degree.

In her work at both universities she came to know the old believers who lived in the Bay Area. She loved to hear them speak of their early experiences in the Faith and of 'Abdu'l-Bahá. The thought came to her that someday these people would not be there. Once they were gone, only memories would remain—vague, blurred, and incomplete. Someone had to keep a record, a firsthand account, giving a vivid, accurate, and detailed picture of these blessed people, of the way they sought and found the truth, of their efforts to share the news with others, of the friendships they formed, and of the joy of working under the guidance of 'Abdu'l-Bahá. She realized that the opportunity would soon be gone. She could not wait for that "someone." She would have to do what she could to preserve the precious remembrances. So she listened carefully and took notes when these old believers spoke in public. She sought their company and talked to them in private—and she took notes.

These notes, supplemented with research and comparison with other records, form the basis of this book. Looking back wistfully more than fifty years later, our author, Marion Carpenter Yazdi, wishes she had done more. It was a rich opportunity, but to her the harvest seems inadequate. Nevertheless, she is grateful for what little she has done and is eager to share it with her fellow Bahá'ís as a token of love and gratitude.

Future generations will be grateful for her efforts.

ALI M. YAZDI

Preface

People sometimes ask, "What was it like to be a Bahá'í youth in the time of the Master and the early days of the Guardian?"[1]

These pages will, I hope, convey something of the exhilaration and the joy of being among "the first to believe" in the Bahá'í Faith. I hope also my youthful letters may impart some of the intense and eager awareness I had of the blessedness of those early days.

It was a bounty beyond measure to receive, as I entered the University of California, a message from 'Abdu'l-Bahá outlining my course of study and vocation and to have, while at Stanford University, the advice and encouragement of the young Shoghi Effendi. All the manifold blessings of my life have emanated from the privilege of accepting the Faith of Bahá'u'lláh while still a child. I am profoundly grateful and humble.

I have had another reason for recording my remembrances of the early days of the Faith in Berkeley. It seemed to me important that a chapter be set aside in the annals of the Bahá'í Faith in the United States for the Berkeley Bahá'í story, for it is a community with a proud heritage. Berkeley was one of the first cities in America to have Bahá'ís, one of the few to have the distinction of a visit by 'Abdu'l-Bahá, and one of the earliest to establish a Local Spiritual Assembly. I wanted to pay tribute to the valiant little band of Berkeley believers whom I knew and loved and, since I am the last repository of memorabilia, to record the experiences they entrusted to me.

To all those who have generously contributed materials for *Youth in the Vanguard* I wish to express sincere appreciation.

To The Universal House of Justice I am deeply grateful for the verified and moving translations of Tablets of 'Abdu'l-Bahá concerning Ali M. Yazdi, which it has made expressly for this book.

Among the sources of information for the Berkeley section, in addition to my own recollections and letters, are my notes of talks with Kathryn Frankland, Ella Bailey, and Ramona Brown and of lectures by Ella Goodall Cooper; written statements by J. V. Matteson; an article by Lorne Matteson prepared for inclusion here; a passage from Dr. Yunis Khan's *Memories of Nine Years in 'Akká*, translated by Nura Mobine Ioas; the diary of Maḥmúd-i-Zarqání; letters of Lua Getsinger; and the September and October 1912 diary notes of Juanita Storch.

I am indebted to the following for some of the material found in the Stanford section: To Ella Cooper for her lectures and notes and Maḥmúd-i-Zarqání for his diary. To Dr. David Starr Jordan and my professors H. D. Gray and S. S. Seward, who were exceptionally kind and helpful to me during my days at Stanford, fall 1923 to fall 1925. To Joseph and Ruth Gates for permission to use excerpts of letters from Dr. David Starr Jordan. To Professor A. J. G. Guérard for permission to use excerpts of letters from his father, Albert Leon Guérard. To Ray Lyman Wilbur, Jr., for his kind help in identifying his father, Dr. Ray Lyman Wilbur, in the photograph with 'Abdu'l-Bahá, as well as for permission to use his own letter. To Gretchen Wulfing and Barbara (Bobs)

Probasco Bach, my contemporaries at Stanford, for the life-long friendships we formed and also for assenting to the references to them in this book, and to Bobs for the use of her letters. To Joyce Lyon Dahl, Marzieh Nabil Carpenter Gail, and Marion Holley Hofman, who, together with my brother Howard Carpenter, were my successors at Stanford, for their valuable accounts used here.

For permission to quote from letters and materials I am indebted to a number of people in addition to those named above: To Barbara West for the excerpt from the letter of her mother Ramona Brown; to Douglas Struven for the excerpts from the letters of Lua Getsinger; to Gretchen Wulfing for the quotations from the letter of her aunt Kathryn Frankland; to the Hand of the Cause of God Paul Haney for the letter from his mother Mariam Haney and for the excerpts from her article on Helen S. Goodall; to Marion Holley Hofman for the quotation from the report of her mother Grace B. Holley; to Sam Somerhalder for the quotation from the letter of his aunt Louise Bosch; to Marzieh Gail for the excerpt from the letter of her mother Florence Khánum; to Anita Ioas Chapman for the text of the memorial service for Howard Carpenter and the letter of her father Leroy Ioas; to Afsaneh and Faramarz Yazdani for use of their letters; to Robert and Bahia Gulick for excerpts from Ella Bailey's "Memories of 'Abdu'l-Bahá"; and to the Stanford University Archives for the use of excerpts from their letter.

I am under obligation to the following for the use of their photographs: Dorothy and William Frey for the photograph of the mayor and city council of Berkeley, 1912, and of Berkeley High School, 1912; Lorne Matteson for the photographs of his parents and for the photograph of the Bahá'í Juniors taken in 1920 or 1921; Bahia Gulick for a photograph of Ella Bailey; Masao Yamamoto for the photograph of Kanichi Yamamoto with his wife and twelve children; the Stanford University Archives for the photographs of Dr. David Starr Jordan, of the 1912 Assembly Hall, and of Xasmin

House; Molly King and also the Spiritual Assembly of the Bahá'ís of Palo Alto for the photograph of the Waverly Street house where 'Abdu'l-Bahá was entertained; Harmon Jones for the photograph of John Bosch's seventieth birthday celebration; Joyce Dahl for the photographs of herself and of Marion Holley Hofman; Afsaneh Yazdani for the photograph of the Spiritual Assembly of the Bahá'ís of Stanford University; the Los Angeles Bahá'í Archives for the photograph of 'Abdu'l-Bahá, 16 October 1912; to Shinji Yamamoto for the 1913 photograph of Kanichi Yamamoto and his family; and to the National Bahá'í Archives for the 1920 prize-winning photograph of 'Abdu'l-Bahá taken in Haifa.

I thank my friends, the devoted Berkeley Bahá'ís of today, for their enthusiasm for "the book"; Harmon Jones for "instant" documented answers to several puzzling questions; Shahla Piff, Dorie Markert, and Kristi Lofthus for help in typing.

I want to express my special appreciation to Dr. Betty J. Fisher for her warmth and good humor, no less than for her truly accomplished editing; and to Martha K. S. Patrick for her special part in helping to organize the material.

I take pleasure in giving credit to my dear children Robert Yazdi and Barbara Markert and to my sixth generation Bahá'í grandchildren—Dorie, Jim, and Molly Markert —for their very constructive ideas and assistance.

Above all, I want to acknowledge with abiding gratitude the foreword, the suggestions, and the encouragement of my beloved husband Ali M. Yazdi—always Sheikh-Ali to me. As long as he lived, he gave inspiration to every endeavor—and happiness to our years together in Berkeley.

MARION CARPENTER YAZDI

Part One

Early Days of the Bahá'í Faith in Berkeley
1898–1925

1

The Beginning, 1898–1912

Attending the University of California at Berkeley was a sudden decision for me; my heart had been set on entering Stanford. I had fulfilled the requirements and had the grades, but so had others. Women were "on quota" in 1920; only a few were admitted as freshmen, and I was not one of them.

A friend named Bob and I were seen off by my family in Santa Paula, or rather at a flagstop in Montalvo, as we boarded the Southern Pacific "Lark" for San Francisco. Bob was a University of California senior, and on the train he helped me fill out my program and described the excitement of life at "Cal." He also asked me about my religion. I was surprised to discover that as a boy he had heard 'Abdu'l-Bahá speak in Denver in 1912.

It was midnight when we climbed the long flight of steps to the hillside house of the Franklands in Berkeley, but the lights were all on. I was expected. Kathryn and Alec and their daughter Helen greeted me warmly as if I were a member of the family.

At the door I said good-bye to Bob, who said he would call me. During the year he did come over to talk, and we had dinner together or went to the Half Hour of Music at the Greek Theater. I invited him to hear Jináb-i-Fáḍil in the spring.[1]

I was eager to meet the Bahá'ís. Kathryn Frankland was already a friend. Ella Goodall Cooper and Helen S. Goodall, from San Francisco, and Kathryn had come as Bahá'í teachers to Southern California and had visited in my parents' home. I met Ella Bailey soon after my arrival and then Berdette and J. V. Matteson, Kanichi Yamamoto and his family, Frances Allen, and Ramona and Joe Bray.

How different they were; yet they shared a remarkable bond. They had all been in the company of 'Abdu'l-Bahá just eight years before during His visit to the Bay Area. To each one of them He had shown His special tender concern. For Him they had steadfast love and complete devotion. The meeting with Him had made each "joyful, active, aglow with zeal and wonderful."[2] I was fascinated to hear their stories, to retell which I must go back to the beginning of the Faith in California.

In 1942 I heard Ella Cooper at the Geyserville Bahá'í School speak on "Early Days of the Cause in the West."[3] She was well qualified to make such a presentation, as she and her mother were among the very first to join the Bahá'í Faith in California and were largely responsible for its rapid growth throughout the state. Ella said:

> The Message came to the West in 1898 through Dr. Edward and Lua Getsinger. They came to California and visited Mrs. Phoebe Hearst in her country home near San Francisco.[4] Mrs. Hearst was interested and invited her friends to hear Lua give a series of lessons which led up to a climax called "the Pith." . . .
>
> Mrs. Emogene Hoagg lived in San Francisco.[5] She couldn't wait for the lessons and camped on the Getsinger's doorstep every day to learn more. She was the first confirmed believer.[6]

Mrs. Helen S. Goodall and her daughter Ella had become intensely interested in the Bahá'í Faith when Ella's friend, Miss Helen (Nellie) Hillyer, told them of it in the summer of 1898. Helen Hillyer had heard the Message from Ann Apperson, a niece of Mrs. Hearst.[7] Mrs. Goodall and Ella attended Lua's classes in Phoebe Hearst's penthouse in San Francisco. They "felt the truth before the end of the classes."[8] Because Mrs. Hearst was leaving with a party (which included the Getsingers) on a pilgrimage to visit 'Abdu'l-Bahá in 'Akká, classes were no longer to be available in California. Mrs. Goodall and Ella went to New York, resolved, if possible, to find a teacher. They joined a group at

HELEN S. GOODALL
one of the earliest Bahá'ís in California
and the mother of the Bahá'í communities of the
San Francisco Bay Area, at the home
of Marion Carpenter's parents in Santa Paula, California,
circa 1915

the home of Arthur Pillsbury Dodge where a humble Syrian believer, Anṭún Ḥaddád, gave lessons daily through an interpreter. Ella has said, "From him we learned the Message and accepted fully and at once."[9]

While in New York Ella Goodall and Helen Hillyer were invited by Mrs. Hearst to come to Egypt and make the pilgrimage from there.[10] In order not to attract attention the party of fifteen pilgrims, the first Westerners to visit 'Abdu'l-Bahá in prison, had to go to 'Akká in small groups. After arrangements were made and permissions were received, Helen and Ella arrived in March 1899 with the last group of the first pilgrims from the West.[11]

Mrs. Goodall had been ill while in New York, but she returned to Oakland in February 1899 and started teaching immediately. At first the classes were not held regularly, and there were no experienced teachers and no books to study. When 'Abdu'l-Bahá said that devotional meetings would be a means of attracting believers, these were also held.

Weekly teaching meetings began as early as 1903 in the Goodall home at 1537 Jackson Street, Oakland.[12] They were beautiful affairs, for loving attention was paid to detail. The atmosphere was warm and friendly, and there were flowers in abundance and delicious refreshments, sometimes served in the garden. Presiding over these afternoon teas were the radiant hostesses, Mrs. Goodall and Ella, assisted by Emogene Hoagg. In 1904 Ella married Dr. Charles Miner Cooper; although they lived in San Francisco, and later Mrs. Goodall also, Ella and Helen continued to sponsor the Oakland meetings for many more years.

To one of these gatherings in 1904 a relative of Mrs. Hearst, Mrs. Anna Monroe (who herself held meetings in Berkeley but never became a Bahá'í), took Mrs. Woodson Allen (Frances Orr Allen) and her fifteen-year-old daughter, Ramona. In later years Ramona often spoke of this occasion; she described it to me in a letter:

ELLA GOODALL COOPER
the daughter of Helen S. Goodall, was one
of the earliest Bahá'ís in California.

The first time I saw Moto [Kanichi Yamamoto, the first Japanese Bahá'í in the world], he opened the door of the Goodall home to my mother, a friend (deceased), and myself. It was in 1904. I was greatly impressed by his beaming smile of welcome. Then Mrs. Goodall and Ella Cooper came to greet us with their heavenly smiles. That was the first time my mother and I heard of the Faith. During the afternoon as they spoke of 'Abdu'l-Bahá I accepted Him.[13]

She told me her mother took a little longer to become a believer, and her father followed.

The Allens were the first Bahá'ís in Berkeley. Dr. Woodson Allen, a well-known physician, was active in civic affairs and served as president of the Berkeley Board of Education from 1902 to 1905. Until 1905 the Allens lived in Berkeley in a house that still stands on the north side of Ashby Avenue and Lorena. Returning to Berkeley in 1907, after the earthquake, they built a house at 2718 Webster Street, where Bahá'í meetings were held.

Early in 1908 after a second pilgrimage to 'Akká, Ella Cooper invited Ramona to bring her girl friends to tea to hear about the Bahá'í teachings. A group was formed called "The Peach Tree." Among the members were Marie Barr (Bray), Edith Woodward (Loomis), Helen Barr (Tice), Betty Vent, and Ramona. The class was continued by "Mother Peach" [Ella Cooper] for many years, and a number of the girls became Bahá'ís.[14]

In 1911 Ramona gave the Message to Joseph G. Bray, a young printer and publisher, who accepted it almost at once. Five years later Ramona and Joe were married. They lived for a time in Berkeley, where their children Barbara (West) and Allen grew up.[15]

Later in her life Ramona became a Knight of Bahá'u'lláh during the Ten Year Crusade when she lived on the island of Majorca and in a number of European cities, including Salzburg—always teaching the Faith from the hotels where she resided.[16] She returned to California at the end of 1963 and lived in La Jolla until she passed away on 23 February 1975.

Ella M. Bailey became a believer in Berkeley during this early period, probably in 1905. She was teaching elementary grades at McKinley School when she first heard about the Bahá'í Faith from Mrs. Rosa V. Winterburn, who spoke to a Berkeley teachers' group.[17] Lua Getsinger instructed Ella Bailey further in the Bahá'í teachings, and she became an outstanding and devoted believer, an inspiration to everyone who knew her during her long life in Berkeley.[18]

As long as they lived, Helen Goodall and Ella Cooper were guiding lights for all the believers in northern California. Their radiance and charm lent distinction to every Bahá'í occasion. I adored them both with all my heart, and it was like being in fairyland to visit them. Mariam Haney wrote in an unpublished article that to honor and perpetuate the memory of Helen Goodall is to

> experience once more the fervor and exaltation of life as lived then—life which was fundamentally wholesome and expressive of spiritual beauty.
>
> As we think of Mrs. Goodall we remember not only a kind friend and sincere Bahá'í but a real mother, the mother of the Bahá'í group in San Francisco and all the cities of the Bay area. In fact, 'Abdu'l-Bahá Himself addressed her as the "spiritual mother of this confirmed Bahá'í community."[19]

In one of many Tablets Mrs. Goodall received from 'Abdu'l-Bahá He said:

> I desire for you a new confirmation at every moment, and wish for you the wonderful providence and assistance, so that city (San Francisco) may become a lamp and you the light shining through it.[20]

The Goodalls' Oakland home was the headquarters for the Bahá'ís of Northern California; Mr. J. V. Matteson said of it in 1928:

All were welcome in that Bahá'í home—that palace of God. Such spiritual feasts. We met 'Abdu'l-Bahá there. [We met] Mr. Thornton Chase, Mr. Howard MacNutt, Lua Getsinger, Mrs. [Isabella D.] Brittingham. . . .
And material feasts. We gathered there 150 strong in beautiful parlors banked with floral decorations.
But Mrs. Goodall did not forget us when we went to our homes. She knew when the poor were in need—and she sent them aid.
She was not unmindful when there was sickness, and a nurse was sent.[21]

The first Nineteen Day Unity Feast in the West was held on 21 March 1908 at the Jackson Street house.[22] 'Abdu'l-Bahá had instructed Mrs. Isabella D. Brittingham to go to California to teach the Faith and inaugurate the Unity Feast. Bahá'ís attended from Berkeley, Oakland, Fruitvale, Alameda, San Francisco, San Mateo, and Geyserville. They were seated at one long table profusely decorated with flowers. Following 'Abdu'l-Bahá's example, Mrs. Goodall, assisted by Mrs. Cooper and Mrs. Brittingham, served the guests. According to Mariam Haney's account:

There was no chatter or worldly conversation at this Feast, only the reading of the Holy Utterances and an account of a pilgrimage to 'Akká. Nothing like the secluded calm of the place had ever before been experienced. It was in a small degree similar to that felt in the presence of the Master in 'Akká. When the time came to leave, Mrs. Goodall stood at the door, smiling as she distributed the flowers, a few to each friend. Though not a word was spoken, everyone departed feeling intensely the spirit which had bound the hearts together. The blessedness of that Feast became clear when, in July, a Tablet was received from 'Abdu'l-Bahá in which He wrote: "'Abdu'l-Bahá with His heart and soul was present at your Naw-Rúz Feast. He associated and took part in your happiness, joy, and harmonious union. Therefore thank ye God that ye had such a Friend and Caller; notwithstanding the distance of thousands of miles, He was present in spirit at your Feast of Love."[23]

Many early teachers came to Berkeley and spoke in the Allen home. These included Thornton Chase, the first American Bahá'í, a convert to the Faith in 1894; the "immortal" Lua Getsinger, "mother teacher of the West"; Isabella Brittingham, a forceful teacher and writer who traveled widely for the Cause in the United States; Hyde and Clara Dunn, who pioneered to Australia; Helen S. Goodall, one of the most "prominent" among those who "consecrated their lives to the service of the newly proclaimed Covenant"; Ella Goodall Cooper, charismatic, radiant, an inspiration to everyone; Ali-Kuli Khan, Persia's chief diplomatic representative to the United States, speaker, and translator; and Martha Root, "the foremost Hand raised by Bahá'u'lláh" after 'Abdu'l-Bahá's passing, and the "Leading Ambassadress" of Bahá'u'lláh's Faith.[24]

Lua Getsinger was especially well known by the early Berkeley Bahá'ís. She enjoyed spending weekends with the Allens; friends were invited and she would speak to them with great sincerity and charm. While on a teaching trip throughout California in 1911 to prepare for a possible visit by 'Abdu'l-Bahá, she spoke before a Berkeley writers' group.[25] On 17 April 1911 she wrote a friend:

> We [Dr. Amínu'lláh Faríd and I] have been to San Francisco—Oakland, Berkeley, Alameda, and Fruitvale and other little suburban places—about the Bay teaching and talking on the Cause. . . . Mrs. Goodall and her daughter Mrs. Cooper were very kind to us while there and made it very pleasant as well as easy to get about for they have a very fine Automobile which was at our disposal. . . .[26]

On 1 September she wrote again, elated over the response: "A great wave of interest is sweeping over the Country up and down this Coast just as Abdul Baha said it would—and He now writes that thus far is only the beginning."[27]

2

'Abdu'l-Bahá's Visit to Berkeley, 9 October 1912

Excitement was mounting among the Bahá'ís who lived in the San Francisco Bay Area in the fall of 1912. The friends gathering in from up and down the coast were also in a state of such intense and happy anticipation as nothing in life could ever again evoke. 'Abdu'l-Bahá was coming to San Francisco. The disappointment they had felt when word had first been received that His teaching tour in America would be confined to the East Coast and Midwest was now forgotten. Despite His age, and His health ravaged by forty years in a Turkish prison, 'Abdu'l-Bahá, the Servant of God, had responded warmly to the entreaties of the California Bahá'ís. He was now en route, lecturing to crowds and inspiring individuals along the way from Minneapolis, St. Paul, Omaha, and Lincoln to Denver and Salt Lake City.[1]

Juanita Storch, a seventeen-year-old art student in Fruitvale (East Oakland), captured for all time in notes she kept the changing emotions of the days preceding 'Abdu'l-Bahá's decision to visit the West Coast and then of His arrival. On 9 September 1912 she recorded: "It is nine o'clock, and all the friends are having a nineteen-day prayer at this time so that they may create a strong magnet for 'Abdu'l-Bahá, so I must stop writing." On 11 September she had good news to report: "'Abdu'l-Bahá is coming. He is on His way from the East." A meeting at Mrs. Goodall's on 12 September sharpened the anticipation: "He has left the Eastern half of the United States for our beloved West. He sent His love to all of us." But there was still a time for waiting and new disappointments. A 23 September 1912 newspaper reported that 'Abdu'l-Bahá would arrive in San Francisco the following day. Juanita wrote simply, "We are all happy." But on 24 September she had to say that "The paper was ahead, for we have neither seen nor heard a thing. After supper I ran over to the Mattesons to see if they had heard, but they had not."

More days passed before the Mattesons did bring, on 1 October, the long-awaited news that 'Abdu'l-Bahá would arrive the next day and that the Bahá'ís would "see Him tomorrow evening." Even so, the wait continued. Juanita's mother telephoned her at school on 2 October to say that the train had not arrived. The eagerly anticipated meeting was cancelled.

But on 3 October Juanita had a different story to report:

> Everything was so beautiful this morning. Some birds were singing in the big Acacia tree in our garden; the doves were cooing, the plants were so fresh and the slanting rays of the sun fell on the path ways. It was truly a New Day and the air was filled with peace.
>
> Some one came up the side pathway . . . so Nyxie, our little dog, gave his welcome and announcement at the side gate. Mrs. Matteson was the Bahá'í friend who had come to ask if we were going to Mrs. Goodall's in the afternoon for the regular meeting. Then Mrs. Matteson gave us the joyous news, and the doves in the garden seemed to echo it. 'Abdu'l-Bahá arrived last night and would be at Mrs. Goodall's this afternoon to meet us all.
>
> I was so happy I could hardly get ready.[2]

'Abdu'l-Bahá had, indeed, arrived in California early in the morning of 3 October. Dr. Frederick D'Evelyn, who with

Helen Goodall, Ella Cooper, and Mr. and Mrs. W. C. Ralston was chosen to meet Him, has described the epic moment of His appearance and the hours preceding:

> The trans-continental passengers to San Francisco leave their train at Oakland, and are ferried across the Bay to their journey's end. Arriving there, they disembark and follow the wharf to a long corridor, terminating on the "Main Street," here their friends are permitted to meet them.
>
> It was October 2nd, 1912, a day of great expectancy in San Francisco. The furnished home prepared for Abdul Baha was garnished, swept and beflowered. All arrangements were complete. Slowly the hours seemed to pass. Eventide came, and with it, disconcerting reports of delay. Telegrams confirmed the reports, while telegrams to railway headquarters brought the discomforting news that schedule time had been abandoned, and no time of arrival was hazarded. Close on mid-night a telegram from Abdu'l-Baha instructed friends not to await His arrival, "send only one friend to depot." . . .
>
> Securing two taxis we left for the Ferry. Arriving there we ascertained the sections may possibly arrive about 1.30 a.m. The night deepened, the Ferry [Building] was deserted. The lights of the city waned. . . . The ever dimly lighted corridor became still darker and still more gloomy and lonely. But we were awaiting the Master. At 1.40 a.m. the siren announced the incoming of a belated ferry-boat. Some minutes later, the slide at the end of the corridor was upraised. A few, very few emerged. They reached the street, still no evidence of the Master. What, if he was not there? The half lowered slide seemed a sort of possibly confirmatory evidence. By this time, a night patrol man, we of the taxi party and a red-capped porter constituted the entire population of the corridor. The red-cap we assumed had come over the Bay, so addressing him we enquired had all the passengers of both sections come over? His reply was negative. Still hoping, we ventured to enquire—were there any unusual looking people on board? Yes, he replied, there is a very old gentleman with strange dress and several other strangers with Him. This was reassuring. Once again we hoped and centred our gaze upon

the far end of the corridor. Some minutes later Abdul Baha appeared, walking slowly, calmly, majestically, followed by his secretaries. Forgetful of boundary lines, uncovering, we advanced to meet him. He drew near more rapidly and with outstretched arms he embraced us, uttering a salutation followed by the English words—"Very good; very Good." Abdu'l-Baha was in San Francisco: Leading the way to the side-walk where the taxis awaited us, one was naturally desirous after seating Abdu'l-Baha, to attend to the welfare of his staff. But it was not to be, for saying something to his staff, he, through an interpreter, desired that we should seat ourselves beside him. The strange, great, new thing awed one into silence. But Abdu'l-Baha, with a perceptible note of pleasure, a victorious gladsomeness in his voice as if a long-hoped for moment had been attained—said, "Speak to me." But how could one speak, what could one say—was it not the birthing of a moment—from which henceforth even time must find its dating, and eternity its reckoning?

Ere long we reached the home, made ready by true, loving and expectant friends. Rare indeed was the reverential welcome extended to Abdu'l-Baha. Orient and Occident had met. Supper was served, prepared by Persian friends, then resident in San Francisco. Truly a never to be forgotten communion! . . .

. . . Abdu'l-Baha reached San Francisco, the west—the sun had set, the lamps were lightless, the people slumbered and slept. The Center of the Covenant, Bearer of the Message, came and uttered the call of the Kingdom of God. "Be confident, have no doubt about it, this banner of Baha'u'llah will be unfurled waving towards all religions. The anthem of the Oneness of the world of humanity will confer a new life upon all the children of men."[3]

Later that same morning President David Starr Jordan came to pay his respects to 'Abdu'l-Bahá and invite Him to speak at Stanford University. Then 'Abdu'l-Bahá was interviewed by a correspondent of the *San Francisco Examiner* and gave His famous "welcome" to California at the Goodall home in Oakland.[4] His schedule was crowded with public addresses and private interviews throughout His twenty-three day sojourn in California.

When the Master came to Berkeley on the evening of 9 October, there were no banner headlines to herald that unique occasion. Several brief newspaper announcements, two of them front page, had appeared:

Berkeley Daily Gazette, 3 Oct. 1912, p. 1
ABDUL BAHA TO SPEAK IN BERKELEY

Abdul Baha, leader of the Bahai movement and universal peace advocate, arrived in San Francisco yesterday after attending the truth conferences in the east.[5] Baha is arranging for a talk in Berkeley, which will probably be given in the Greek theater. He has established headquarters at 1815 California street, San Francisco.

Berkeley Daily Gazette, 5 Oct. 1912, p. 5
ABDUL BAHA TO SPEAK.

Abdul Baha, leader of the Bahai movement, will talk at 7:45 tomorrow evening at the First Congregational church in Oakland. Baha is arranging for a meeting in Berkeley.

The Sun and Letter, 9 Oct. 1912, p. 1
ABDUL BAHA HERE TOMORROW NIGHT

Abdul Baha, Persian prophet and leader of the Bahai movement, will speak at the high school auditorium at 8 oclock [*sic*] tomorrow evening.[6] The theme for the lecture has not been announced, but it is expected that it will be on Baha's general subject, "The Peace of the Nation and the Unity of Religion."

Oakland Enquirer, 9 Oct. 1912, p. 6
ABDUL BAHA TO SPEAK ON FAITH
"Prophet of Peace" to Be Heard in Berkeley

. . . will deliver an address in the auditorium of the Berkeley high school, corner Allston way and Grove streets, tonight. . . .

'Abdu'l-Bahá was the guest of the City of Berkeley when He spoke at the high school auditorium, Wednesday, 9 October 1912, at 8:00 p.m. He was invited by the socialist mayor, J. Stitt Wilson, who called on Him soon after His arrival in San Francisco. Wilson had been taught extensively about the Bahá'í Faith by Lua Getsinger. A minister who had gone into politics, he was a remarkable scholar and spoke many languages, including Hebrew and Greek; Mary Hanford Ford, the author of *The Oriental Rose*, thought he was one of the most interesting men she had ever met.

According to Maḥmúd's Diary, Wilson arrived at 'Abdu'l-Bahá's San Francisco residence on 5 October for the evening meeting.

The mayor of Berkely [*sic*] was announced. He questioned the Beloved on economic problems. The master gave salutary answers to all of his questions. In conclusion, He said, "We must try to bring about everlasting happiness for mankind. . . . In general society is like an army which needs an organization composed of generals, captains, lieutenants and men. The grades of responsibility are essential and the difference of ranks in service is a necessity. Just as a family needs for its perfection elders and youngsters, master and mistress, servants and attendants, likewise society needs organization. However, it must be under such laws as will insure comfort and happiness for all in their different ranks. . . .

The Mayor asked, "Will these things be realized soon?" The Master replied, ". . . they will prevail without fail, although they will be brought about gradually. . . . if these ills be allowed to become chronic, their cure will be difficult and they will end in a revolution."

He gave an account of the unity and self-sacrifice of the friends of the East and expounded various phases of the true economic laws which He wrote at Dublin.

The Mayor was so impressed that he could not help giving vent to his sincere admiration. . . . He invited the Beloved to an important meeting that was to be held in the city that night. But as this meeting had political affairs as its objective, the Beloved tendered an apology.[7]

Unsuccessful efforts were made to arrange for 'Abdu'l-Bahá to speak at the University of California as He had at Stanford University on 8 October.[8] Ella Bailey told me that Bishop Parsons of the Episcopal Church in Berkeley (a friend of Ella's who had read Bahá'í literature) wanted 'Abdu'l-Bahá to speak in his church; however, the Episcopal Board ironically declined to offer Him an invitation because the rules allowed no one to speak in the church who "did not believe in Christ."[9] Mrs. Woodson Allen was able to secure the auditorium of the Berkeley High School that was available for gatherings of public interest.[10] 'Abdu'l-Bahá's talk there was the "only public address" He gave in Berkeley, though He did speak to a small literary group, the Berkeley Short Story Club, to which Mrs. Allen belonged.[11]

BERKELEY HIGH SCHOOL
where 'Abdu'l-Bahá gave a public address on 9 October 1912. This building is no longer in existence.

A large, representative crowd of people came to hear 'Abdu'l-Bahá on the evening of 9 October. They were not just curiosity seekers, Mrs. Allen told me, but intelligent, thoughtful men and women from the community. Also present were many Bahá'ís who had traveled some distance to meet with Him at Mrs. Goodall's home in the afternoon and later to hear Him talk in Berkeley. Maḥmúd wrote in his Diary that "Multitudes of people poured into His presence to hear His life-giving words. . . ."[12]

Mayor Wilson had planned to preside at the meeting, but his congressional campaign was just opening, and he was unable to attend. Mr. Herman I. Stern, a member of the Board of Education, introduced 'Abdu'l-Bahá with these earnest remarks:

> It is a distinguished honor, as well as a pleasure, to be selected to introduce our guest, our eminent visitor, 'Abdu'l-Bahá.

MAYOR J. STITT WILSON (left) and BERKELEY CITY COUNCIL, 1912
Mayor Wilson, a Socialist, invited 'Abdu'l-Bahá to give a public address at Berkeley High School as a guest of the city of Berkeley, California.

We are familiar with the commonplace remark that the East is given to contemplation and the West to action; the East to mysticism and the West to exact science. We are western—ultra-western and ultramodern on this Pacific Coast—yet there is a universal and an eternal element that we share with all races and nations. We have learned and mastered a great many little things exactly, but I am afraid we have neglected the one big thing. We are, therefore, glad to welcome a man from the far East who comes with the old message, with the one thing needful:

"Thou shalt love the Lord thy God with all thy heart, and with all thy soul, and with all thy mind.

"This is the first and great commandment.

"And the second is like unto it, Thou shalt love thy neighbour as thyself.

"On these two commandments hang all the law and the prophets."

We are, perhaps, more interested in the second than in the first, especially in this time of great social unrest, when we are seeking and reaching out for better social relations, for social justice, for more love for our fellowman in our actual business.

I know very little about our visitor. I have become interested in his work through friends and have read some of the Bahá'í literature. I understand that his chief work is endeavoring to unify all religionists, to uphold the one element that is common to all religions—the spiritual, the moral and the social. I understand that he comprehends the science as well as the social problems of the West, and so his message certainly is welcome to us. In the Parliament of Religions, in connection with the Chicago World's Fair, there was a beginning made in this direction. The Bahá'í message of peace seems to be a response to the prayers that went up from the representatives of all the religions of the earth at that time, and I feel honored in being permitted to welcome 'Abdu'l-Bahá in the name of the city of Berkeley, whose guest he is.[13]

'Abdu'l-Bahá gave a forceful and logical presentation on reality in which He related truth to the basic needs of hu-

'ABDU'L-BAHÁ
talking to Indian students attending the University of California,
at the Goodall home, 1537 Jackson Street, Oakland, California,
12 October 1912

manity today. Unfortunately, the original Persian text has not been found to date. An as yet unauthenticated translation is in the Berkeley and the National Bahá'í Archives.[14] A few passages from 'Abdu'l-Bahá's address are quoted here for the first time as a matter of interest:

> . . . the center of reality is focalized in great souls among men. There are souls who confer life upon the world of humanity, who are the first educators of mankind, who rescue men from the abyss of ignorance and cause them to attain to sublime degrees of knowledge. For example, His Holiness Christ was a center of reality.
>
> All the Manifestations of God were centers of reality. They were like the sun. Though it has various dawning-points, it is still the same sun, and he who gazes at that sun will recognize it whatever may be its dawning-point.
>
> Likewise, he who is a lover of truth, or reality, will recognize the Sun of Reality by its effulgence, regardless of its dawning-point.
>
> One of the dawning-points of the Sun of Reality was Moses. Another was Abraham. Another was His Holiness Christ. Another was Muḥammad. Another was the Báb. Another dawning-point was Bahá'u'lláh.
>
> The people of truth, or reality, are characterized by their recognition of the Sun of Reality reflecting through these different dawning-points, while the people of traditional beliefs are characterized by their recognition of only one dawning-point of the Sun of Reality. For example, the people of Moses have confined their gaze to the Mosaic dawning-point, and though the Sun of Reality appeared also from the dawning-point of Christ yet the Jews have not recognized that light.
>
> The people of truth, or reality, are not lovers of dawning-points. They adore the Sun of Reality itself, and they will recognize it wherever it may appear, whether in the East or in the West. They do not consider the bounty of God as limitable, but as a continuous bestowal, for were it limited it would denote imperfection, whereas the bounty of God is

everlasting. The grandeur of God is everlasting. The sovereignty of God is everlasting.

Sovereignty presupposes subjects, a treasury, an army, and if we say that there was a time when God was not possessed of His creation, or when the Sun of Reality was not shining, or if we say that the time may come when there will be a cessation of the bounty of God, or that the Sun of Reality will not shine, such statements are contrary to the nature of the Sun of Reality, because the sovereignty of God is everlasting. God has always possessed creation, and forever will possess creation, and everlastingly will there be the divine Manifestations. . . .

'ABDU'L-BAHÁ
with Bahá'ís attending the Feast on 16 October 1912
at the Goodall home in Oakland. Hiroshi Yamamoto is
sitting on the lap of Juanita Storch (front row, center).

The reality of divinity is manifest in all things, even as the sun is manifest in all phenomena. All earthly phenomena owe their existence and their development to the sun. The bounty of the sun reaches all. The light of the sun shines upon all the earth. It shines upon the trees and upon the plants. It shines upon the mountains and upon the ocean. It shines upon the animal and upon man. In short, the rays and heat of the sun permeate all phenomena. Not a single thing is bereft of the effulgence of the sun.

Likewise, the light and power of the Sun of Reality become effective in each phenomenon according to its capacity. Thus each phenomenon, especially man, is a sign of God's power. Man is the greatest sign, because he is the consummate phenomenon. Man is like a mirror in which is reflected the Sun of Reality with all its radiance.

When we use the word *man* we refer primarily to the greatest examples of mankind—the noblest men; that is to say, the perfect members of humanity. We do not mean those men who are men in form but animal in character, who are bereft of reason, who are acquainted only with folly, and are submerged in the sea of materialism. When we use the appellation *man* we signify thereby a perfect man, a man who is created in the image and likeness of God, a man who is a reflector of God's light and guidance, a man who is an educator of his fellow kind, a man who is a discoverer of the mysteries of God, a man who is a manifestor of the mercy of God, a man who is an advocate of the oneness of the world of humanity. He is *man*. [15]

After the meeting, Ella Cooper was waiting with her big limousine and liveried chauffeur to take the Master to San Francisco. Instead, 'Abdu'l-Bahá chose to ride with Georgia Ralston in her little electric car. The two of them in that diminutive auto followed the luxury car out of Berkeley. [16]

How wonderful it must have been to be with Him and to have experienced that night another of His triumphs in the service of His Father's Cause.

3

The Faith Gathers Momentum, 1912–1925

After 'Abdu'l-Bahá left California on 26 October 1912, regular meetings to teach the Bahá'í Faith increased in Berkeley. In the spring of 1915, with encouragement from 'Abdu'l-Bahá, several San Francisco area Bahá'ís served as the planning committee for the first International Bahá'í Congress held in San Francisco from 19 through 25 April. Mrs. Goodall, Mrs. Cooper, Georgia Ralston and her husband W. C., and Dr. Frederick D'Evelyn planned an impressive series of public meetings and other events for the Congress, which was held under the auspices of the Panama-Pacific International Exposition.[1] The Berkeley Bahá'ís attended the Congress, the Convention of the Bahá'í Temple Unity, the week of public meetings, and the Official Reception given to the Congress by the Directorate of the Exposition.[2]

They and the other Bahá'ís at the meetings traveled to Mrs. Goodall's home in Oakland for the Ridván Feast, called by Mary Hanford Ford "The most charming event of the Bahai Congress at San Francisco. . . ."[3] Mrs. Ford reported that

> When all were seated Mrs. Goodall greeted them in a few touching words, in which she told how Abdul-Baha had

walked through her rooms, and up and down the broad
stairway repeating, with that wonderful smile of his, "This is
my house, this is *my* house!" Her description brought to every
mind the vivid recollection of Abdul-Baha's presence in
America, and seemed to place him bodily among the guests,
so naturally every one was happy.[4]

The arrival of the Franklands in Berkeley in 1916
marked the beginning of a new and exciting chapter in Berkeley Bahá'í history.[5] Kathryn Frankland had become a believer in Chicago in 1901 and her husband Alec, a year later.
In Berkeley they lived on Hearst Avenue for a short time before moving to 1199 Spruce Street, where their home re-
sembled a Bahá'í center for many years.[6]

There was never anyone quite like Kathryn. She
worked for the Faith with energy and ability. The more
difficult the task the more ingenuity she brought to it. She
served from morning until night. Both young and old con-
fided in her. She was beautiful in appearance and spirit, and
was the kindest person imaginable.

Alec Frankland was a generous-hearted, true believer.
He was something of an inventor, and he had a great store of
jokes and pranks. He was proud of Kathryn and served
through her. He liked to see her fashionably dressed; and, as
advertising manager for the *Berkeley Daily Gazette,* he would
sometimes bring home a surprise outfit from one of his good
accounts. I remember sadly a Friday night in 1922 when Kathryn and I were called home from the San Francisco meeting
by the sudden death of Mr. Frankland.

Kanichi Yamamoto and his family, devoted friends of
the Franklands, came to Berkeley in 1919.[7] Mrs. Goodall had
left Moto in charge of her home in Oakland in 1909 when she
moved to San Francisco after her husband's death. In 1918
the house went into other hands; Moto visited Japan, then
took up landscape gardening, and came to live in Berkeley
where his ever-increasing family of delightful children could
learn the Bahá'í teachings from Mrs. Frankland. Always firm

KANICHI YAMAMOTO
the first Japanese Bahá'í (standing), photographed in 1913
shortly after 'Abdu'l-Bahá's departure from California.
Seated, left to right: Hiroshi; Shinji; Masao; and Ima, Kanichi's first wife

in his faith, he lived in Berkeley the rest of his life (except for the brief period when he and his family were relocated during the Second World War).[8] He was the first Japanese Bahá'í in the world, having become a believer in Honolulu in 1902.

The Mattesons lived in Berkeley from about 1919 to 1926.[9] They had become Bahá'ís when they were neighbors of the Franklands in Fruitvale—Berdette in 1903 and J. V.

J. V. MATTESON

three years later. Mr. Matteson I remember as a distinguished-looking man, an effective and witty speaker, and a talented architect. Mrs. Matteson was a serene, radiant person, motherly and lovable. Lorne, their son, a bright and likable boy, was already a staunch member of the Berkeley Bahá'í Juniors (as youth groups were known) when I met him in 1920. Later he graduated from Berkeley High and went to the university. He now lives in Hayward with his wife, Eleanor.

In 1919 the Franklands received a Tablet from 'Abdu'l-Bahá regarding the little group that was forming:

> It is apparent that you have returned to Berkeley. I beg of God that this will have valuable results and conduce to the spread of the divine teachings. Think not of your own capacity; think of the confirmations of God. If as it is fitting you engage in

BERDETTE MATTESON

serving the Kingdom you will see that the confirmations from the unseen world will continually come, and that their light will wax greater day by day. Think not of the smallness of the group which you have gathered; through sincerity of purpose it will grow. Then strive to increase your efforts and the purity of your purpose, so that like unto a magnet you may attract divine confirmations.[10]

The Berkeley Bahá'ís elected Emogene Hoagg and Georgia Ralston, both of San Francisco, as their delegate and alternate respectively to the Twelfth Annual Bahá'í Convention held in New York City, 26–29 April 1920.[11] (At that time duly accredited delegates and alternates did not need to live in the cities they represented.) Delegates from Berkeley and sixty other localities voted unanimously that year for the Bourgeois Temple design.

In the fall of 1920 my parents wrote Kathryn Frankland that I was entering "Cal." Mrs. Frankland telegraphed immediately, "Marion must come straight to us." So it was that I became the first Bahá'í to attend the University of California. I had been a Bahá'í since I was about twelve, but when I was fourteen, I experienced a deep confirmation, to which a little pencil-written diary attests. Now seventeen, I eagerly joined the Berkeley Bahá'ís and their manifold activities, which my letters to my parents describe in great detail.[12] The University of California was an entirely new world after Santa Paula High; opportunities beckoned in every direction. The vast and beautiful campus, the hordes of students pouring out of, and into, large buildings, excited rather than intimidated me. The Bahá'í Faith was foremost in my life; I wanted to prepare to teach it.

Everything was grist for my mill. I signed up for the *Daily Cal* and a potpourri of courses I now find hard to explain: Astronomy I—all I recall is something about "the obliquity of the ecliptic"; English IA taught by Professor Chauncey Wells—*Leaves of Grass*, American Literature, and Professor Wells' comments, still cherished, on my themes;

KATHRYN FRANKLAND
became a Bahá'í in 1901. She helped
establish the first Spiritual Assembly of the
Bahá'ís of Berkeley in 1925.

Appreciation of Art taught by Eugen Neuhaus with his text, *Painters, Pictures, and the People;* Great Books with famous Charles Mills Gayley in Wheeler Auditorium, overflowing with students; Public Speaking with Professor Vonneumeyer, who asked a lot of questions after I spoke on the Bahá'í Temple; and Sanskrit Literature, taught by Arthur William Ryder, well known for his lectures on the Bhagavad-Gita and his translation of a hundred little verses called *Women's Eyes.* [13]

I wore a white serge pleated skirt and a navy blazer; my hair was bobbed and marcel waved like every woman student's. Greenwich Village was the theme for parties, and my friends and I wrote free verse.

Two girls in the Sanskrit class were quite bohemian. They often came with me to the Bahá'í Juniors. Once they invited me to an "evening." The room was crowded with students and nonstudents, all of whom seemed quite tense. I panicked when they sang, "We'll never let the red flag fall," and read the Communist Manifesto as if it were Holy Writ. It turned out that the object of the meeting was to free three prisoners from San Quentin! I found at the end of the evening that my "friends" had picked up dates for themselves and for me. Scared stiff, I was escorted home by a "Commie," the Greatest Name in my heart.

I had better luck with social service at the YWCA. There were several openings for service, and I chose weekly visits to the California School for the Deaf and Blind on Waring Street. I took groups of deaf children for walks and played games with them, but my hope was to spread the Faith. The blind children were adorable and responsive. They were ecstatic over my new beaver fur; it made the rounds of our circle to be petted and hugged while I told them stories, often about 'Abdu'l-Bahá. The authorities gave me permission to take groups of the children to Bahá'í Juniors from time to time; it was a responsibility for me, but they enjoyed the classes.

Sorority rushing at the University of California in the Roaring Twenties, just as now, was filled with dates, dances, and glamor. It was fun to be invited to join a congenial group of girls, but I weighed the matter and decided to fly free. Mother responded to my decision:

> I was glad when you wrote that you had about decided not to join the ———. You have a wonderful place at Mrs. Frankland's, homey and good, and she is one of the older firm Bahá'ís, and it is a rare opportunity to be with her and be trained in the teachings. I consider that as valuable to you as your university work.[14]

When I arrived in Berkeley in 1920, Mrs. Frankland was getting ready to leave on her first pilgrimage with her close friends Helen Goodall, Ella Cooper, and Georgia Ralston.[15]

ELLA COOPER, HELEN GOODALL, KATHRYN FRANKLAND
(left to right) photographed while on a teaching trip
to Southern California around 1914

My heartfelt, girlish letter to 'Abdu'l-Bahá written 29 August went with them:

> O Master:—
> Now that Thy heavenly servants Mrs. Goodall, Mrs. Cooper, and Mrs. Frankland are going to Thy Holy Presence, I am writing this supplication that perchance a Tablet may be revealed in answer.
> Grant that I may be self-renouncing and that I may love everyone. May I be able to withstand tests and may I always be happy.
> While attending college, may I fit myself to be of great service to the Cause of Bahá'u'lláh. In what vocation may I best serve as a herald of the Kingdom?
> O 'Abdu'l-Bahá is it Thy Will that Mother and I should go to see Thee? This is our utmost desire!
> Grant that my father and sister may come to know Thee and to love Thee.[16]

Three months later I was awed to receive a message from 'Abdu'l-Bahá, which Mrs. Frankland mailed me with this note:

> I have mentioned you to our dear Lord and also prayed for you at the Holy Tomb.
> It was not possible for the Master to reveal separate Tablets to the friends, so He gave us a number of messages which we took down while He spoke. . . .
> Isn't it wonderful to have the Lord of the earth tell us just what to do? It relieves us of all responsibility in deciding.[17]

That message, which was to have a profound effect on my life, read:

> Message from Abdul-Baha
> To Miss Marion Carpenter
> Give her My loving greeting.
> I hope that you will become absolutely detached from the material world and be protected from tests.

'ABDU'L-BAHÁ
with resident believers and pilgrims from California outside the Tomb of the Báb, October 1920.
Front row, seated, left to right: Mírzá Ekbal, Emogene Hoagg, Georgia Ralston, Helen Goodall, 'Abdu'l-Bahá,
Elizabeth Stewart, Ella Cooper, Kathryn Frankland. Hájí Muḥammad Yazdi, the father of Ali Yazdi, is standing on the
extreme left. Mírzá Hussein, an uncle of Ali Yazdi, is standing behind Emogene Hoagg. Saichiro Fujita is standing
behind Ella Cooper.

I beg of God that you will be kind to all human beings. You must endeavor in your studies. Take the course in Education (literature) so that you may be able to write *very* well.

I hope that you and your mother may make the visit, but at present it is not possible.

I hope that your father and sister will become converted to the Cause.

November 20, 1920
Haifa, Palestine[18]

It was a thrilling experience for the Berkeley Bahá'ís when Mrs. Frankland returned and told us of the thirty days—21 October to 21 November—spent in the presence of the Master. Various clubs asked her to speak on her trip, and a magazine published an article by her, as well as many pictures taken with the camera I had lent her for the pilgrimage.[19]

While in Haifa, Mrs. Frankland had become acquainted with a Persian Bahá'í, Ḥájí Muḥammad Yazdí; Mrs. Cooper had known him from her two earlier pilgrimages, and Mrs. Goodall had met him on her trip with Ella in 1908. When the party, on their return trip, stopped in Boston on Christmas Eve, they met his son, Sheikh-Ali Yazdi, who had arrived from Germany a month before. Kathryn's enthusiastic description of that twenty-one-year-old believer, so well informed on the Faith, made me very anxious to meet him. Here was a young man who not only was "of an accepted family at the Threshold of God," but who had been the subject of letters of recommendation from 'Abdu'l-Bahá Himself referring to him as "the distinguished son of Ḥájí Áqá Muḥammad, . . . a sensible and cultured young man of good behavior," traveling to America "to complete the courses of sciences and arts which he has been studying in Berlin."[20] Never could I have imagined that in 1926 we would be married!

Sheikh-Ali came to the University of California, Berke-

ALI M. YAZDI
known to the early Bahá'ís as Sheikh-Ali, the name given
him at birth by 'Abdu'l-Bahá, married Marion Carpenter
on 31 August 1926. Shoghi Effendi prayed that the union
would be ''a living testimony to the harmony and
fellowship which the Faith of Bahá'u'lláh has established
between the East and the West.''

Ali Yazdi, third from the left, and Bahá'í friends from the American Syrian Protestant College, fall 1919. Aboard the S.S. *Hellovan* on the Adriatic en route to Germany for a year of graduate studies.

Ali Yazdi and Marion Carpenter

Ali and Marion

Ali Yazdi, 31 October 1921, shortly after arriving
in Berkeley, California

ley, in the fall of 1921. He was warmly welcomed and immediately loved by all the believers.

I first saw Ali across the room at a Cosmopolitan Club meeting in Stiles Hall on campus. He was young in years for a graduate student in civil engineering but poised and confident. I still remember his face—the natural "suntan," expressive golden brown eyes, and the most engaging smile in the world. He cut a dashing figure in the traditional yellow "cords" and Stetson "sombrero" then worn by senior and graduate students.

Those were the days of Rudolph Valentino and "The Sheik," and here was a handsome, Persian Bahá'í youth with dash and charm and the name Sheikh-Ali! I soon found Ali to be a strong, exemplary Bahá'í, an intelligent and purposeful student, and a delightful young man with an original and winning sense of humor. We became fast friends. Now there were two Bahá'í students on campus.

Together we attended all the Bahá'í events of the Bay Area. We looked forward to taking the Key Route train and the ferry across San Francisco Bay for the public meetings in California Hall at which Ella Cooper, Leroy Ioas, and Dr. D'Evelyn spoke. But our special joint project was bringing friends and contacts to the Berkeley Bahá'í Junior meetings. It was terribly exciting!

Bahá'í children and youth had been almost unknown to me in Santa Paula. In Berkeley I was happy to find Mrs. Frankland's Sunday class of Bahá'í children: Hiroshi, Shinji, Masao, Michiaki, and Fumiko Yamamoto; Eleanor and Marion Cooper, nieces of Dr. Cooper; Lorne Matteson; Helen Frankland; and others. During my freshman year I was drawn into teaching this delightful group, and I also brought my college friends. The following year, after Ali arrived, many college students attended.

In those days the term "Bahá'í Juniors" included children and older students as well, and that is what we were called. Youth groups and college clubs did not exist at that time. As secretary of the Berkeley Bahá'í Juniors, I wrote a report for the *Magazine of the Children of the Kingdom* describing the diversity of our thriving group:

> The Bahai Junior Group of Berkeley is very much alive! Under the guidance and careful cultivation of Mrs. Frankland it is blossoming like a beautiful flower-garden.
>
> This group has in it boys and girls of varied ages and nationalities, Americans, Persians, Filipinos, Germans, Egyptians, Japanese, a Russian-French girl, a Turk and a little Hindu boy.
>
> It is like the garden of many-colored flowers which Abdul Baha says is more beautiful than the garden with no variety of color.[21]

We all, of whatever age, gave talks. At one of the afternoon meetings Michiaki, the youngest member, explained the Bahá'í principles; everyone smiled when he said, "The equality of men and women means that men and women should be united." Some of the Berkeley Juniors gave

BAHÁ'Í JUNIORS, 1920–21
Front row, left to right: Michiaki, Masao, and Shinji Yamamoto
Back row: Phillip Rood, Hiroshi Yamamoto, Helen Frankland,
Lorne Matteson, Margery Carpenter

"wonderful" addresses at the Teaching Conference and Congress of the Western States, held in San Francisco 24–26 November 1922.[22] There Berkeley children and youth "told about their meetings and feasts and delivered the Message, and demonstrated beyond doubt that the future of the Cause depends upon their training. . . ."[23] After the Junior meetings we often stayed on at the Franklands for Persian dinners, music, and dancing. We were, indeed, "joyful, active, aglow with zeal. . . ."[24]

On campus Ali and I worked with the Cosmopolitan Club, an international organization that existed before International House was established. Many friends for the Faith and contacts for the Junior meetings were made among the foreign students, who were responsive to the teachings and grateful for Bahá'í hospitality.[25] I served on the executive

BAHÁ'Í JUNIORS, 1920
the Berkeley Bahá'í youth group with Kathryn Frankland.
Front row, left to right: Hiroshi Yamamoto; Masao Yamamoto;
Marion Cooper, niece of Dr. C. M. Cooper; Michiaki Yamamoto;
and Shinji Yamamoto
Back row: Mahmud Amerie; Eleanor Cooper, niece of Dr. Cooper; Marion
Carpenter; Mr. Y. Milad; Helen Frankland; Mrs. Kathryn Frankland

board as program chairman, which made it possible to present Bahá'í speakers; Jináb-i-Fáḍil, Louis Gregory, other Bahá'ís from across the country, as well as Bahá'ís from the San Francisco area, spoke there to enthusiastic audiences.

In the early 1920s Martha Root spoke to a large class at the University of California. I remember that the professor was annoyed that she had talked about the Bahá'í Faith, and he expressed his displeasure to Mrs. Frankland, who had made the arrangements. When Martha heard of the reproof, she made an appointment at once to see the professor. She did not leave his office until she had made amends, and he was friendly once again.

A few years later Martha also spoke at the new International House. Of this meeting she wrote:

Cosmopolitan Club "College Night" Program
Marion Carpenter (center), program chairman of the Club, and Ali Yazdi, after his arrival in 1921, where both members of the Cosmopolitan Club. Many of the students involved in this production took part in Bahá'í activities. Louis Gregory, Jináb-i-Fáḍil, and Kathryn Frankland gave lectures on the Bahá'í Faith at Berkeley under the auspices of the Cosmopolitan Club.

I found too that the atmosphere in International House in the University of California was distinctly cosmopolitan. Many scholars of international repute are counted among the members of the faculties and there is a constant flow of visiting professors and lecturers from both Occidental and Oriental countries. The student group is distinctly international in character. I found in my two lectures there and in a general lecture in the university, that forty national and cultural groups were present in this great university situated at one of the main gateways to the United States.[26]

Uppermost in my mind was my desire to inform people in a winning way about Bahá'í principles. Little was known about the Faith; it was still new, with no institutions and only a handful of believers. When we spoke of the Cause, no one would say, as we hear so often nowadays, "I saw your House of Worship in Wilmette," or "I visited the Bahá'í gardens in Haifa," or "My cousin is a Bahá'í."

One day while reading my sister Margery's *Survey* of 1 October 1921, I came upon an article by William L. Chenery about a Mr. Urbain Ledoux, "Mr. Zero: The Man Who Feeds the Hungry."[27] The author described the man who was feeding thousands of people in Boston Commons as a "Bahaist, a member of a Buddhist sect, the end of whose religion is a pursuit of nothingness by merging individuality with the infinite." I wrote a letter to the editor, and when it was printed it was fun to see that Bertha C. Hyde (Kirkpatrick) had also rushed to the defense of the Faith.

THE BAHAISTS

TO THE EDITOR: May I take the liberty of correcting a statement in a recent issue of the SURVEY [see the SURVEY for Oct. 1, page 15]: "Mr. Ledoux is a Bahaist, a member of a Buddhist sect the end of whose religion is a pursuit of nothingness by merging individuality with the infinite."

I am sure you will be glad to be more correctly informed in regard to the Bahai movement for it stands for the things for which the SURVEY is working. . . . The Bahais believe "that mankind must love mankind, that universal amity must be practiced; that dead dogmas must be thrown away; that we are at the threshold of the Era of Independence; that we must forget prejudice and that universal love must become the dominant note of the Twentieth Century."

The Bahai faith is "Trust in God. Be kind to their fellow men; fill the world with the spirit of love. The spirit of faith in a Bahai is very strong. His trust is in the grace of the Holy Spirit."

Bahaism is not at all a Buddhist sect, but a new religion or religion renewed, the spirit of the age, embodied in a great religious movement which though small and misunderstood at present is destined to bring brotherly love into the world and overcome racial, economic and religious prejudice, through the power of the Holy Spirit.

Bahais were active in carrying out the Convention for Amity between the colored and white races in Washington last May.

I trust I have not overstepped my privilege in bringing information regarding this great movement to your attention.

BERTHA C. HYDE.

TO THE EDITOR: . . . The Bahai Movement was founded over sixty years ago by Baha'o'llah when he announced the dawn of a new age when brotherhood and peace should reign in the world. The twelve basic principles which he laid down all centered about the "oneness of mankind." But the principles he advocated were too universal for the limited minds of his contemporaries and his life was passed in persecution and imprisonment.

That the Bahai religion is an all-inclusive movement can best be proved by the words of Abdul Baha, the present leader: "The Bahai revelation is not an organization. The Bahai cause can never be organized. The Bahai revelation is the spirit of this age. It is the essence of all the highest ideals of the century. The Bahai cause is an inclusive movement; the teachings of all religions and societies are found here. Christians, Jews, Buddhists, Mohammedans, Zoroastrians,

Theosophists, Freemasons, Spiritualists, etc., find their
highest aims in this cause. Socialists and philosophers find
their theories fully developed in this revelation."

MARION B. CARPENTER.[28]

Suddenly, catastrophic news reached the Berkeley
Bahá'ís—the Master had ascended. It is impossible to convey the impact of that devastating announcement. I, for one,
had never really thought there could be a time without
'Abdu'l-Bahá. To me He was life itself and immortal in this
world.

But the announcement was true. A non-Bahá'í friend
telephoned to tell me he had read in the paper that 'Abdu'l-
Bahá had passed away. It was the first I had heard; I could
not answer. I cried all day; at night my sister, worried,
begged me to find Sheikh-Ali. He was in our usual place at
the university library, but neither of us could speak. We
were totally bereft, stricken.

Mrs. Frankland wrote a long, impressive article on
'Abdu'l-Bahá, which was published in the Berkeley Daily
Gazette on 12 December 1921.[29] It included descriptions of
His life, travels, and teachings; an account of her pilgrimage
the year before; and the beautiful picture of 'Abdu'l-Bahá she
had taken in Haifa.

As I noted in my letters home in January 1922, the Berkeley Bahá'ís welcomed the news of Shoghi Effendi's appointment by 'Abdu'l-Bahá as Guardian of the Faith.[30] The
first letter from the Guardian to the Berkeley Bahá'ís was
written on 7 January 1923:

> The beloved of the Lord and the handmaids of the Merciful in
> Berkeley, Calif., U.S.A.
> Care of the members of the Spiritual Assembly.
> Dear Friends!
>   I need not tell you how pleased I feel at this moment when
> I enter into correspondence with the loved ones of 'Abdu'l-
> Bahá in that city, who I am sure, fired with the spirit of service

and teaching which His passing has kindled in every heart, are striving to proclaim His Word and promote His Teachings in that great country.

The services you have rendered and are still rendering in the Path of God, the accounts of which have been reaching the Holy Land, have served to renew my unshaken confidence in those faithful children of 'Abdu'l-Bahá to whom He has shown abundant favors in the past and from whom He expects an undying devotion to the service of His Cause.

No need for me to remind you of the assurance He has so repeatedly given in His tablets to His friends in America as to the glorious triumphs that await every believer, who with determination, selflessness and ardor, arises for the diffusion of the Light of this Divine Revelation throughout the world. And we, who witness from every quarter the crying need of humanity, what nobler service can we render, than to raise the call of Yá Bahá'u'l-Abhá—a call which amid the rising tumult of so many conflicting sects and creeds can alone assure to distracted mankind the reign of true felicity and lasting peace.

Remembering you in my prayers at the Holy Shrines,
I am your brother and co-worker,
(signed) Shoghi
Haifa, Palestine,
January 7th, 1923[31]

The Berkeley Bahá'í Library, known as the Chester Rasmussen Bahá'í Junior Library, had its beginning in 1924. The Bahá'í books of that time, together with a sizable bookcase with glass doors, were given as a memorial to her son by Mrs. Rasmussen, a dear believer of modest means.

In 1919 'Abdu'l-Bahá had revealed a very moving Tablet to Mrs. Rasmussen on the death of her son, which said in part:

That beloved child addresses thee from the hidden world, thus: "O thou kind mother! Thank divine Providence that I have been freed from the narrow and gloomy cage and, like unto the birds of the meadows, have soared to the divine world. . . . Following this separation is everlasting association. Thou shalt find me in the heaven of the Lord, immersed in an ocean of light.''[32]

After the library had been established in Chester's memory, Mrs. Frankland received the following letter from Shoghi Effendi through his secretary with a section in the Guardian's own handwriting:

My dear Bahá'í sister,

It gave our dear Shoghi Effendi much joy to read your interesting and encouraging letter and he is looking forward with great hopes to see the spread of the Cause in the Western States as never before. Indeed whenever we remember how much our dear Master spoke of that country and what a great deal He expected from every pioneer worker there, we feel assured that the glorious days He foretold are not far distant. Our Guardian wishes you all to realize what a stirring pleasure it is for him to cooperate with you in the promulgation of the Cause we all adore and it gives him great joy to help you and give you his advice in the task you have so gladly chosen.

In respect to the little library for the Juniors in memory of Mrs. Rasmussen's dear son, Chester, he wishes me to write you of his deep pleasure in its establishment; and he feels that her son who now dwells in realms more holy, will have his name remembered forever by all the children who will use that little library. The fact that Mrs. Rasmussen has had to save that sum from her little earnings will certainly add a touch of true self-sacrifice to that library.

It might interest you to know that we already have a very large group of Western friends here in Haifa and how we would wish everybody could come over.

The members of the family all join me in sending you our very best wishes and heartfelt regards.

I am
yours in His service
(signed) Soheil

My spiritual sister:—
I assure of my deep affection and ardent prayers for the success of
your spiritual activities. Convey to Mrs. Rasmussen my high appre-
ciation of her noble, self-sacrificing efforts. I remember her most ten-
derly at the Three Holy Shrines. Your true brother,
(signed) *Shoghi*[33]

In the spring of 1925 the San Francisco and Berkeley
Bahá'ís initiated a three-day Conference for World Unity,
held at the Palace Hotel in San Francisco, 20–22 March. Mrs.
Frankland served on the Committee on Arrangements, Dr.
David Starr Jordan of Stanford University served as honorary chairman, and Jináb-i-Fáḍil was among the many distinguished speakers.

In the summer of 1923 Ali left Berkeley to take a civil
engineering position with the Southern Pacific Railroad
Company in Sacramento first, and later in the Sierras. In
1925 he moved to San Francisco and worked in the chief
engineer's office. In the fall of 1923 I transferred to Stanford
Univerity. There I received my bachelor's degree, worked
toward a master's degree, which I completed in 1928, and
held weekly Bahá'í meetings on campus for over two years.[34]

Ali and I were married on 31 August 1926 and returned
to make our home in Berkeley.[35] Except for the years we
pioneered in Merced, California, we lived in Berkeley until
1978, raising our two children, Robert and Barbara, and
serving the Cause as best we could.

4

Letters Home, 1920–1923

*Recently I discovered a cache of my letters to my parents when
I lived in Berkeley and attended the university. Excerpts from some
of those youthful letters convey, I think, a feeling of the exhilaration
and blessedness of being a Bahá'í student in the early twenties.*

August 1920

From where I am sitting up in my room [at the Franklands, 1199 Spruce Street] I can see the Bay and the Golden
Gate. The sun is shining on the water, and the scene is perfectly glorious! Today it is warm and clear. They say that
summer begins up here about the first of September.

Yesterday was the most gloriously grand day imaginable. We, Helen [Frankland], Marg [Carpenter, my sister],
and I, left here at ten o'clock in the morning. Upon arriving
in the City we were taken in the limousine to the hall for the
exhibition dancing. After that, our party of nine, which included besides us three, Mrs. Cooper, Mrs. Frieda Cooper,
Eleanor and Marion Cooper and two other nieces of Mrs.
Cooper (Dorothy and Helen Cooper), was taken by Henry
[Keeling, the Goodall's Bahá'í chauffeur] to Mrs. Goodall's
where we had lunch. Mrs. Goodall is a dear old lady and as

sweet as she can be. She spoke very nicely of you, Mother, and asked to be remembered to you. She said that Aunt Julia [Mrs. Edgar Wilson, my father's aunt in Kimberly, Idaho, who became a Bahá'í through my mother] had written to her and had sent her a letter to take to 'Abdu'l-Bahá.

We had a wonderful lunch, with all sorts of style, and it took us about an hour and a half to eat. For the first course we had a delicious shrimp salad in tomatoes. Next we had fried chicken and rice (which came in on a handsome big silver platter), gravy, sweet corn, tea biscuits, jelly. For dessert we had the grandest strawberry shortcake with whipped cream, mints, and bonbons. Then we had black coffee. Isn't that a good-sounding menu?

After lunch all of us but Mrs. Goodall were taken to the Orpheum. The program was fine. The most special part of it was the midgets' performance. There was a whole troop of these cunning, tiny people in different scenes.

This morning I wrote a letter to 'Abdu'l-Bahá and gave it to Mrs. Frankland to take with her. She is extremely busy.[1]

August 1920

Just got back from the meeting in San Francisco. They have a beautiful big hall which Mrs. Goodall rents (Mrs. F[rankland]. told me). The Assembly is large—about one hundred believers around the Bay.[2] Mrs. Cooper spoke on the Mashriqu'l-Adhkár. She told the story about Mr. Bourgeois. . . . While walking in the foothills of Santa Barbara one evening, uplifted spiritually, he beheld the vision of this wonderful building. He tried to hold the vision but it vanished. Several years passed while he endeavored to find the origin of the inspiration. At last he found it in the Bahá'í Message which he received in the east. When he heard of the aim to have a Mashriqu'l-Adhkár, he knew that he had had the vision of it.

August 1920

Helen and I have just been reading our prayers and *The Hidden Words* before going to bed. We are doing it each night. Tonight a Miss [Ella] Bailey, a Bahá'í, called up Mrs. Frankland and told her she thought I could get a place at the house that she has charge of, the Brae Mar. It is rather a select place with a lot of girls. Mrs. Frankland would like me to stay here, I think.

18 August 1920

Mrs. Frankland is very busy now getting ready. Yesterday there was a meeting at her house which I got home just in time to attend. Next Tuesday evening she is planning to have a big meeting at her house and have Dr. D'Evelyn speak.

I am eating so much up here. I thought probably I would not want anything because I liked our food so much. Quite the contrary.

19 August 1920

I am going to lend Mrs. Frankland my Kodak to take with her to Haifa. Won't that be a lovely trip for it? I am tickled to death to have it go.

Tonight we are going over to San Francisco to the meeting. It is going to be kind of a surprise (?) for Mrs. Frankland and Mrs. Cooper and Mrs. Goodall. Mrs. Frankland will be going two weeks from tomorrow. They have built a little house on their side lot and are going to sell it to pay her way.

Fall 1920

I want to tell you about the meeting in San Francisco Friday night. We got there at half past eight and thought that we would be late, but we found that they were waiting for

Mr. and Mrs. Bosch to come. Mrs. Bosch spoke informally about their work on the Island of Tahiti, which was very successful. She said it had taken them seven years to accomplish in Geyserville what they had done there in seven months.

Mrs. Bosch is much younger or seems much younger than her husband who is quite an elderly man.

Fall 1920

We had such a lovely meeting here last night with thirty people, half of them new. Three of my friends were present. A Persian bishop of a church in San Francisco came. He signed the petition against the persecution of the Bahá'ís in Russia by the Bolsheviks. Mrs. Frankland gave a lovely talk. She was much pleased over the success. Have you heard about the trouble in Chicago to get the grant to build the Temple? I don't know the details, but a Presbyterian missionary is making some difficulties.[3]

November 1920

I just got through giving a short speech in English class on the Teachings of Bahá'u'lláh. When I finished, the professor asked me to repeat the name. He said it was a very good example of an extemporaneous speech and asked if the Bahá'í Teachings had anything to do with Tagore! I was much pleased to be able to give a tiny bit of the Message to thirty-five people who had never even heard the name, I suppose.

January 1921

Well, Mrs. Frankland is here again, and it is certainly good to have her home. Next Wednesday night there is going to be a feast in the City for just the Bahá'ís, and Mrs. Cooper is going to give a talk on the more intimate part of the visit.

January 1921

Oh what a wonderful meeting it was! If you could only have been there. I don't see why I should have all the good things and opportunities. Mrs. Cooper is so inspiring, and she is such a dear. I wonder if she ever does anything unkind or selfish. The talk was beautiful! She told of the difference in the prison life of 'Abdu'l-Bahá as she saw it when she was there before [1908] and what the life is now. She gave many little incidents of 'Abdu'l-Bahá's sympathy and unceasing labors for others. She said that He did not look a day older than when He was in America, and that in spite of His seventy-six years. He just seems to sweep into a room—His presence is so inspiring. I do so long that you will be able to come up and hear it all. It is the next best thing to going oneself.

14 January 1921

Friday night Miss Bailey came to dinner, and afterward Mrs. Frankland read some of her Haifa notes to us. They straightened up a lot of things for me, and there is certainly no quibbling with words as to the Japanese question and many others.

'Abdu'l-Bahá said that we should be very kind to the Japanese and that they should not be shut out of California, and, although regulations should be made, they should be allowed to own land. I was certainly glad to hear it. The notes are wonderful and cover a large number of questions.

This afternoon I went up to the State Institute for the Blind. I went alone today, and so I had a chance to tell the children some stories about 'Abdu'l-Bahá and His love. You would be surprised to know how rabid even these children have been taught to be about the Japanese, etc.

February 1921

We are going to have the Tuesday night meeting here

now. I am looking forward to tomorrow. Mrs. Cooper invited Helen and me to luncheon, and then afterward we are going shopping with her to get things for the Valentine party that I wrote you about. Isn't that lovely?

February 1921

We had a delightful time at Mrs. Cooper's. The luncheon was delicious and beautifully served. We had

Artichokes and mayonnaise
Toast and two kinds of bread

Wonderful steak
Stuffed baked potatoes
Mashed squash
Hot biscuits

Tutti-fruiti and assorted cakes

Some luncheon was it not for four people? Mrs. Goodall, Mrs. Cooper, Helen, and me.

At two o'clock we got in the car, and Henry took us (Mrs. Cooper, Helen, and me) downtown to meet Mrs. Frankland, and we went to get some things for the party. . . . You should see the lovely Dennison stuff we have to make our costumes. Mrs. Cooper has engaged the St. Francis Hotel for the Naw-Rúz Feast. Isn't that perfectly lovely? Jináb-i-Fáḍil will be here, and so it will be a big gathering.[4]

Mrs. Frankland was preparing us for the shock the other night! Jináb-i has a false tooth which he takes out and puts in his pocket while he eats! Now you will be prepared too.

February 1921

I had a lovely time at the Valentine party yesterday. I came home Friday night planning to rush in and make my dress, when I found Mrs. Frankland had already made it. I was certainly relieved because I had been dreading it. Helen and I dressed alike, and our costumes were very cute. The decorations were like fairyland. . . . For refreshments we had ice cream, assorted tiny cakes (pounds of them), loads of candies, and fancy punch. There were about thirty guests.

Dr. Cooper came up afterward to the studio where it was held, and I met him.

February 1921

Mrs. Frankland is very busy getting ready for Jináb-i-Fáḍil. She already has one sure opening and many other possibilities. He has been asked to a luncheon of the International Committee at the University to speak on "The Resources of Persia." The luncheon will be held at the Faculty Club. The members of the Committee are such men as President Barrows, Dean Probert, Professor Noyes, and other big professors. It will be a fine opening, especially as Jináb-i is prepared to speak to people of the highest intellect. Professor Breitwiezer is going to get openings for him to speak before some of his largest classes.

Mrs. Frankland is planning to have a dinner with a caterer, to relieve her of the responsibility, and invite some professors and their wives, Dr. D'Evelyn, and Mrs. Cooper.

February 1921

They are sending out programs for the Jináb-i-Fáḍil lectures. I am making a list of those I want to send them to. I have seventeen so far and will probably think of others. Mrs. Frankland received a letter from Fujita tonight saying that the Master had been ill in bed with a cold for a week, and although better was still in bed.[5]

Tomorrow I am going to the Blind Institute. I want to do a lot of studying ahead too, so I will have more time during the Fast and can hear Jináb-i-Fáḍil.

It has been decided not to have the Naw-Rúz Feast at the St. Francis Hotel because it would cost $3.00 a plate. It is the plan now to have it at the Bellevue. Mrs. Frankland said Mrs. Cooper and Mrs. G. are going to pay part of the expenses, and then it will be so much for each person; $1.00 or $2.00, I imagine.

Monday night is going to be a play at the Hillside Club—Bernard Shaw's "You Never Can Tell"—and the Franklands are going to take Helen and me. It is a very dress-up affair, and so I may wear my evening dress!

20 February 1921

Mrs. Frankland has secured six fine openings for Fáḍil in Berkeley now. . . . I told her about the Cosmopolitan Club, and he has been asked to speak before it at Stiles Hall. Last semester when I was reporting on the "Cal" staff, I came in touch with one of the members when I was getting a report, and he gave me his card. It was through him that Mrs. Frankland got the date. I was tickled to be of some little help.

5 March 1921

My costume party was a great success. Mrs. Frankland lent me a funny old white dress with a train that originally belonged to Mrs. Cooper.

I am enclosing some pictures of 'Abdu'l-Bahá's carriage and the prison of Bahá'u'lláh. You remember hearing of 'Abdu'l-Bahá's carriage, don't you? I never imagined it was such a funny old carryall. He rides in this and gives the Cunningham car [a gift from Mrs. Goodall and Mrs. Cooper] to the pilgrims and others to use, unless He has to get to a place quickly.

March 1921

They had about a hundred posters printed to put in the

store windows in Berkeley to advertise the meeting at the High School tonight. There was a mistake made in the day—Friday being put instead of Thursday. Mrs. Frankland went down to the office and printed off slips to paste over the error, and I did the pasting. They are making a big effort to advertise this meeting because it will not be before any organized gathering. I have five girls promised to come.

March 1921

Yesterday I was upstairs in the big room of the library (U.C.) with Mary and Jewel studying. There was a buzz in the room, and I looked around and saw Fáḍil and Aḥmad [Sohráb] with Professor Priestly who was showing them around. I told the girls to look and see them, and they did. They made me so exasperated! They showed no interest; it is like talking to stones to talk to them. That was the first glimpse I had of Fáḍil, and it was very fleeting.

March 1921

Friday night the reception at the Clubhouse (Hillside Club) was simply lovely. The place was decorated like a big living room with Persian rugs, floor lamps, easy chairs, and beautiful flowers. There was music, and afterward Fáḍil spoke. Some very interesting questions were asked, and Fáḍil answered them so beautifully. Professor Breitwiezer (Head of the Dept. of Education at U.C.) asked about his (Breitwiezer's) idea of establishing an international university which would not be under the control of any one country. (He is very broad-minded, and Mrs. Frankland is going to have him for dinner Wednesday night together with several other people, making twelve in all.)

After the talk Helen and I presided at the punch bowl. We both wore our white net dresses. Everything was lovely, and I certainly enjoyed it.

March 1921

This morning I went with Mrs. Frankland over to the City to hear the talk on "The Seven Valleys." It was most glorious and inspiring. It uplifts one spiritually just to listen to Jináb-i-Fáḍil speak in Persian and watch the sweet expression on his face. Tonight he is to be here for dinner, and others are invited. Miss Bailey is staying here. She has been sick, and Mrs. Frankland brought her up here to take care of her. She is getting better now.

After dinner we will all go to Wheeler Hall to the Cosmopolitan Club. The place has been changed from Stiles Hall because it was not big enough. I will be able to attend twelve of the lectures.

Mrs. Frankland calls me just in time for breakfast (the Fast), and everything is all ready when I go down. She feeds me well and is great on dietetics. She tears around from morning until night. She gets up and has her breakfast early, and then gets Mr. Frankland's and mine.

March 1921

I have been to three meetings this week and am going to another tonight. Wednesday Mrs. Frankland had the lovely dinner I wrote you about. . . . Helen and I served. Afterward we went to the auditorium in Cal Hall, U.C. [California Hall, University of California], where Fáḍil lectured. Professor Breitwiezer introduced him very nicely, and the talk which Fáḍil gave was beautiful: "Education in Persia and the Modern Movement."

Thursday I went with Mrs. Frankland and a friend to Oakland where Fáḍil spoke at the Ebell Club to the Writers' Club. There was a big crowd, and it was quite an affair. It is wonderful how Jináb-i-Fáḍil understands each audience. Mr. Keeler, the poet, gave a little talk afterward in appreciation and told how he had been inspired by 'Abdu'l-Bahá when he met Him in London.

March 1921

At the Camera Shop here in Berkeley they put enlargements of their prize pictures in the window. The two for this week were taken with my camera: one of 'Abdu'l-Bahá (it is beautiful), and one of the party in Egypt on camels [and a donkey] at the Pyramids. The one of 'Abdu'l-Bahá has His name under it, and it attracts quite a bit of attention.

March 1921

Monday night will be the big Feast at the Hotel Bellevue. There will be 250 people there—Bahá'ís and their guests.

This is the picture I wrote you about which was the prize enlargement at the Camera Shop. You may cut it down if you like so that it leaves 'Abdu'l-Bahá alone. I think it is the most beautiful picture of 'Abdu'l-Bahá that I have ever seen, and I just love it. The secretary has given Him a paper to sign, and 'Abdu'l-Bahá is reaching for the pen.

22 March 1921

I am certainly the most fortunate child to be here amongst such wonderful friends! For Sunday, Mrs. Goodall hired a beautiful seven-passenger Cadillac limousine and driver and asked Jináb-i-Fáḍil, Aḥmad, the Franklands, and me to go on a wonderful drive together to the Blossom Festival at Saratoga. . . . It will be a day that I will always remember.

Last night, the Feast was another big event, and it was a wonderful and inspiring experience. Unfortunately it rained, and one could not wear one's nicest things. After we got several blocks away from the house, Mrs. Frankland remembered that she had left the lovely corsage of buds which a blind lady, who is becoming a Bahá'í, sent her for the Feast. I told her I would go back for it and come on the next ferry, and finally Mrs. Frankland let me go.

'ABDU'L-BAHÁ
The prize-winning photograph of the Master reaching for a
pen to sign the Tablet a secretary has given Him to read,
November 1920, Haifa. Taken by Kathryn Frankland with
Kodak of Marion Carpenter.

The dining room of the hotel where the Feast was held was most beautifully decorated in all the spring flowers, bushels and bushels of them—hyacinths, jonquils, fruit blossoms, sweet peas, and many others. I have never seen such artistic bouquets as the masses of flowers on the tables. At each place was a lovely card with the words of 'Abdu'l-Bahá printed in gold: "The Cause of Bahá'u'lláh is the same as the Cause of Christ. . . . The spring of this year is the same as the spring of last year."

The delicious four-course dinner was elaborately served. Then we turned our chairs around and listened to the musical program—a wonderful harpist and two vocalists. Mrs. Cooper was in charge and introduced Fáḍil who gave a splendid talk on Naw-Rúz. It was a real Bahá'í Spring Festival as the invitations called it.

A prize-winning photograph
taken with Marion Carpenter's Kodak at the Sphinx, November 1920.
Left to right, mounted: Georgia Ralston, Kathryn Frankland, Ella G. Cooper

Fall 1921

I told you Mrs. Cooper was going to speak at the Cosmopolitan Club, but her mother is not well (they have two nurses for her), and so she couldn't. The plan now is to have Mrs. Frankland speak on November 19.

15 November 1921

The Cosmopolitan Club was asked to put on a variety show for College Night. Many of the participants were regular attendants at the Bahá'í Junior Class.

November 1921

Mrs. Frankland spoke at the Cosmopolitan Club on "The Ideals of the New Age." I was surely glad to have her. She was sick with tonsilitis, but she came anyway. She was in bed yesterday when we went to the Junior meeting, and so Ali took charge.

2 December 1921

These seem like very lonesome days [since the ascension of 'Abdu'l-Bahá], but still there is no reason why we should feel so. The Beloved is with us now just as much as when we had His physical presence.

Sheikh-Ali, one of my Persian friends, the one who is a graduate student here, was terribly stricken with the news.[6] His father is in Haifa, and it is going to be very hard for all the Bahá'ís there who have depended so much upon 'Abdu'l-Bahá. Tomorrow night is to be the Memorial meeting.

15 January 1922

Margery, Lorne Matteson, and I were on the committee for the Feast today and I was in charge. I had for the subject "The Divine Art of Living"—how the Bahá'í life differs from any other life. We must *act* in accordance with the Teachings of Bahá'u'lláh. . . . To label ourselves is not enough.

Lorne read a paper that he had written on "Deeds" with excerpts from *The Hidden Words*. He is a sophomore in high school.

Then Ali gave a speech on "'Abdu'l-Bahá's Life as an Example." Margery planned and fixed most of the refreshments. Just think, there were thirty-seven present! The most we have had yet. There were several Germans, Persians, a Turk, an Egyptian, Indian (Hindu), Japanese, and Americans. There was a Christian Scientist practitioner and Catholics, Jews, Muhammadans, and representatives of other religions. We had a flute and piano duet, vocal solos, and, besides, Helen and I sang "Softly His Voice." Don't you think it sounds like a lovely meeting? It really was beautifully spiritual, I think. I always want you present though.

On my way home from the Junior meeting today I stopped at Miss Bailey's and she told me news that had been received from Haifa and some details concerning [the passing of] 'Abdu'l-Bahá. A wonderful letter came from Mrs. Bosch [in Haifa] just in time to be read at the Memorial meeting. . . .[7] Shortly before the ascension, 'Abdu'l-Bahá told His eldest daughter that He was dying. . . . Mrs. Bosch said that everything was so spiritual that she was completely changed and could never be the same person again. . . .

17 January 1922

I have some good news for you! A cablegram was received from the Greatest Holy Leaf which said that 'Abdu'l-Bahá's Will had been opened, and Shoghi Rabbaní had been appointed Head of the Cause and Head of the House of Justice.

It seems that 'Abdu'l-Bahá sealed His Will about two weeks before His death and then said to send to England for Shoghi Effendi. They asked if they should cable, and the Master said no, to write.

Shoghi Rabbání is about twenty-four years old. Mrs. Frankland said she didn't think there would be a dissenting voice because everyone loved him so much.

Ali was here to dinner tonight. He knows Shoghi very well, and he told me some interesting things about him.[8]

31 January 1922

Mrs. Goodall knows of 'Abdu'l-Bahá's ascension now. Mrs. Cooper was reading her some Christmas cards and read a reference to that by mistake. She seemed to take it all right though.[9]

February 1922

Mrs. Goodall died Saturday night. Everyone had been expecting it. When she went to Haifa the last time, 'Abdu'l-Bahá told her that she had done more than her share. How few could He say that of!

Last night it rained quite hard, but I went to San Francisco to the memorial meeting for Mrs. Goodall. It was a most beautiful meeting, and I would not have missed it for a great deal. Dr. D'Evelyn was in charge. Tablets written by 'Abdu'l-Bahá to Mrs. Goodall were read, and the history of her life, which has been compiled for the *Star of the West* and which is to be placed in the archives in Washington, was read.[10]

Mrs. Goodall was a Methodist and heard the Message from Lua Getsinger (1898) after she had come to California, when she lived in Oakland.[11] 'Abdu'l-Bahá called her the Mother of the Assembly of 'Abdu'l-Bahá. When 'Abdu'l-Bahá was in Chicago at the time of the Convention, Mrs. Goodall was there. He said, "There are many gems hidden in the earth. Mrs. Goodall is one of these gems. At present her value is not known, but later it will become manifest. . . ."

Mrs. Cooper was at the meeting and afterward distrib-

Students from the University of California at Berkeley.
Left to right: Mahmud Amerie, Shukri Hussein, Ali Yazdi

Marion Carpenter, Spring 1922

Margery Carpenter,
the author's sister

Marion, 1922

Helen Frankland (left)
and Marion Carpenter

Turkish student who attended
Bahá'í classes (left) and Ali Yazdi

uted the daffodils from the three big baskets to all the friends. When Mrs. Goodall had the wonderful meetings at the Oakland home, of which everyone here speaks, she always had beautiful flowers from the florist, and they were divided among those present.

February 1922

Saturday afternoon I went to Mrs. F[rankland]'s to meet Mr. [Louis] Gregory.[12] There were quite a number of the Berkeley friends there, and we had a nice talk with him. He is so splendid and surely a real Bahá'í.

Margery came later and brought Mrs. Seely, a dear blind person who heard the Message shortly before Mrs. F. went to Haifa. . . .

Mrs. F. had a delicious dinner for eleven, and afterward we left for the Cosmopolitan Club. Margery took some of us down in the car. . . . The President of our club was sick, and so I was in charge of the whole thing, introducing the speakers and everything. It was sort of fortunate in a way because of course I loved to introduce Mr. Gregory. The meeting turned out highly successful all around, I think, and Mr. Gregory's talk was great. He said so much in such a comparatively short time. Everyone was quite pleased.

March 1922

I am keeping the Fast, of course. There are a good many of us here in Berkeley who are fasting: Sheikh-Ali, Mrs. F., Helen, Lorne Matteson, and probably others.

Spring 1922

I am sending you a little booklet telling of 'Abdu'l-Bahá's funeral service.[13] It is quite remarkable for Christians, Jews, and Muhammadans to give such glorious eulogies to the Lord of the Earth. So much had been said by them in appreciation of the Master that nothing necessary remained to be said by the Bahá'ís themselves.

21 March 1922

Last Sunday I read the Will of 'Abdu'l-Bahá at Mrs. Frankland's after the Junior meeting. She was going to have the Mattesons and the Brays—the other Berkeley Bahá'ís— come in the afternoon to hear it, but I couldn't wait, and so read it to myself. It is surely very precious and wonderful. How very clear it is. There cannot be any misinterpretation.

Next Sunday the Berkeley Juniors will have their Naw-Rúz Feast. I am going to ask our nice landlady and Harriet and Eva. Margery is going to make the ice cream for it— pineapple milk sherbet. Different ones are to read on Naw-Rúz and on Happiness. Maḥmúd is going to tell about the Persian New Year's Festival, and Mr. Assadi is going to chant a Persian prayer that has just been received from Mr. [Dr. Ḍíyá] Baghdádí.

After the Feast the youngsters and the older people can go home, and the rest of us will have a little dance. Doesn't it all sound nice?

Last Wednesday night Ali took me to a wonderful concert—the San Francisco Symphony Orchestra, which was here in Berkeley.

Riḍván 1922

Our Riḍván Feast was at 4 o'clock. The three Persian boys were in charge, and it was perfectly lovely. There must have been forty people; some came from San Francisco. After all the grown-ups had gone, we young people had a sort of party. We had an awfully good time. It was the last time we could be all together for fun because exams are almost upon us. Before we left Mrs. F. gave us more "eats"— fried egg sandwiches, tea, and cake. When I came home, I had to put in some good licks at study.

14 May 1923

A week ago he [Ali] sent a beautiful big bouquet of roses to me. . . .

My letters home from the University of California stop at this point; for in 1923, having completed my junior year, I left Berkeley. In the fall of the same year I would enter Stanford University as the first Bahá'í student. My dear Ali left for his new engineering job with the Southern Pacific Railroad far away in the High Sierras, but letters, books, and boxes of roses kept our attachment growing and deepening until we were married three years later.

5

"Cause Welcomes Berkeley Assembly"

Kathryn Frankland must go down in history as the spiritual mother of the Berkeley Bahá'í community. It was she who gathered the flock together, arranged the dinners and festive occasions, and created the Bahá'í atmosphere. She also inspired action.

In the fall of 1925 new believers arrived in Berkeley: James and Carmen O'Neill; Carmen's son, Elmer Dearborn; and her mother, Mrs. Dearborn.[1] The four had accepted the Faith in Sacramento, where they had been taught by Ali Yazdi and the Kuphals. After this family moved to Berkeley, the roll of adult believers probably included the following: Frances Allen, Ella Bailey, Kathryn Frankland, Kanichi Yamamoto, J. V. and Berdette Matteson, James and Carmen O'Neill, and Mrs. Dearborn.

Ali ferried across the Bay from San Francisco one evening early in October at Kathryn's invitation. He was impressed by the Bahá'í spirit as the Berkeley friends discussed a telegram from the National Spiritual Assembly asking for suggestions for raising $400,000 to build the first story of the House of Worship.[2] Ali wrote to me about the evening:

We had a very nice dinner with *fried* chicken and rice as the main feature. I was hungry and the chicken was delicious; so I enjoyed the meal.

Then we had the meeting. Mr. and Mrs. O'Neill of Sacramento were present. Mrs. O'Neill, on seeing me, ran into the room, and said, "I am going to kiss Mr. Yazdi," but I smiled, and held back my head; so she grabbed my hands and kissed them several times. She has proved to be a real believer, and I hope she stays firm. Rather unconventional, but she will get over that.

It was a beautiful meeting . . . and there was a true Bahá'í spirit in the air. Mr. Matteson has grown spiritually; so much so that he is an inspiration. His suggestion was to follow the Teachings and for everyone to give the "hokuk." The suggestion was unanimously adopted, and everyone showed such a beautiful spirit that I was glad I had come.[3]

The Bahá'ís of Berkeley, San Francisco, and the entire Bay Area always had worked together harmoniously as one unit. Now the Berkeley membership had reached the point where a new Assembly was called for. Under the direction of Mrs. Frankland, the Spiritual Assembly of the Bahá'ís of Berkeley was organized quickly and quietly with Ella Bailey as its chairman. The results were triumphantly announced.

There were immediate repercussions. San Francisco was horrified! It had not been prepared for this "breaking away" without notice; there was no procedure in those days for the formation of new Local Spiritual Assemblies. This great milestone for the Faith in Berkeley was, at the time, a ridiculously painful experience.

Ali, who lived in San Francisco but attended meetings on both sides of the Bay, was surprised, to say the least, to learn that his name was on the new list of Berkeley members! With a great deal of love, tact, and good humor, he helped heal the wounds. An amusing letter he wrote me shortly after the Local Assembly was formed tells the story:

Now don't laugh and I'll begin.

Last night I called Mrs. Frankland and asked her if she was going to hear Mrs. Cooper's talk. No she wasn't, and furthermore she wanted to see me badly. "Well, what's the trouble?" Couldn't tell me over the phone.

We met at the hotel lobby, and went in for dinner. Query from me about the mystery. Unfolding: "You know, Ali, you and I are dissenters!"

Sheikh-Ali laughs at this, laughs heartily, thinks it is a good joke. Rather disappointing! He evidently was expected to get mad, furious, vow terrible revenge, but he doesn't. He laughs! . . .

I took it all as a joke. I felt like being happy and didn't want to have a grudge against anybody. . . .

Still I *was* a little brokenhearted to see those Bahá'ís so terribly set against each other. And I had pictures of me at the Sunday afternoon meeting [in San Francisco] shunned, ignored, and discarded. A dissenter! (My name was on Mrs. Frankland's list of the Berkeley members.) But I was happy when I went in; I had a nice smile on my face (couldn't suppress it). It worked wonders! I was not shunned or discarded. Most of the friends were really glad to see me; among these Mrs. Wedde, Mrs. Cooper, the Ioases, etc. I was generous with my praises and "nice little things" and that went big. For instance, I told Mrs. Cooper that her talk was delightful, and added, "your accent exquisite and your appearance very sweet." Joy! Ali, Ali!—"You look very nice," I repeated. (She *did*—Paris gown.) She beamed! Then I raved to Mrs. Wedde about her baby (it is the sweetest tot). Again radiance, gratitude. And so on and so forth. . . .

Gee, I wish I could get these Bahá'ís together and have them act as Bahá'ís and not like silly children. You'd be surprised how *childish* most people are (that includes me!).

And now . . . aren't you proud of me?! You may think "much ado about nothing," but gee, it looked awful for a while, after listening to Mrs. Frankland's reports.[4]

Mrs. Frankland wrote Haifa to inform Shoghi Effendi of the formation of the new Spiritual Assembly. On 21 November 1925 she received a cablegram in reply:

Received at
2104 Allston Way
Tel. Berkeley 5794
Berkeley, Calif.
SF26BR⟨RCJX⟩ 11

Halifax Nov 20 1925

LCO
Frankland
1199 Spruce St Berkeley-Cal
CAUSE WELCOMES BERKELEY ASSEMBLY
Shoghi
1107 AM Nov 21 1925[5]

Then a letter from the Guardian followed:

Haifa
Nov. 24—25

Mrs. K. Frankland
1199 Spruce Street
Berkeley, Calif.
U.S.A.

My dear Bahá'í sister,

Your letter of Oct. 25th written to our beloved Guardian Shoghi Effendi has arrived and rejoiced his dear heart with its good news.

He has instructed me to write this acknowledging the receipt of your letter and conveying to you his loving greeting together with his appreciation for your devoted services in Berkeley and San Francisco.

As to whether your assembly in Berkeley is recognized by our Guardian or not, he wishes that you all should remember his instruction that in every locality where the number of adult and declared believers is nine or exceeds nine, they have the right to stablish a Spiritual Assembly, and as this is the case in Berkeley, surely your Spiritual Assembly is recognized by him.

The members of the Holy Household join him in sending

you love and greeting and assure you of their prayers for you and the other friends in Berkeley.

> Your humble brother,
> *(signed)* 'Azízu'lláh S.
> Bahádur

My dear fellow-worker:

Your magnificent services, your patient endeavors, your great devotion to the Cause of God will ever be remembered with gratitude and joy. May our Beloved reinforce your efforts and fulfill your fondest hopes.

> *Your brother and*
> *well-wisher,*
> *(signed) Shoghi*[6]

Despite the initial brouhaha, newspaper announcements headed "Baha'i Assembly to Meet" now appeared in the *Berkeley Daily Gazette* twice a week—23 October, 27 October, 30 October, and so on. The new Spiritual Assembly was fully functioning.

6

Sketches of Some Early Berkeley Bahá'ís

ELLA BAILEY

Ella Bailey and I first met in the fall of 1920. She was the housemother at Brae Mar, a girls' living group near the university. She suggested I come to live in the house, but I was already staying at the Franklands. Sometimes, however, I would stop by Brae Mar to talk with her. She was a lovable person, shy, gentle, kind, with a special gift for entering into the joys of young people.

Later she also became a dear friend to Ali and to all the members of our family. Many recollections of her thoughtfulness come to mind. After Ali and I were married in 1926, she insisted we spend part of our honeymoon in her apartment atop High Court. She herself took a vacation at that time and gave us the key to the attractive studio where she lived. We spent a week or ten days there while we found our first "home" in Berkeley. Later Ella, Kathryn Frankland, and the Bahá'í Juniors gave us a large welcoming reception there, which she made a beautiful and happy affair.

At Geyserville School in 1927 Ella stayed in the little cabin by the Big Tree with Mrs. Cooper. Anxious about a family that had arrived hungry, she said she could cook an omelet if Mrs. Cooper would go to the store and buy some eggs—two for each person. When Mrs. Cooper returned, she had only one egg each, for Julia Culver, a health expert and ahead of her time, would not let her get more.

Ella Bailey appreciated, praised, and encouraged in others the good qualities she herself possessed. She told my brother at that same session of the school, "Howard, it was worth coming to Geyserville if for no other reason than to watch your mother taking care of people and making them happy." When Howard died before he was thirty, it was Ella Bailey who asked if she could have a yellow rosebush planted on his grave.

In 1944, on her eightieth birthday, we took Ella to my parents' home in Berkeley for an afternoon party. My sister brought Mrs. Cooper from San Francisco. It was a special family time.

One afternoon the next year I visited Ella in her cozy room at the Berkeley Women's City Club. She had never talked much about herself before, but that day she related incidents from her early life and her experiences with 'Abdu'l-Bahá. I took paper from my handbag and wrote down her words. The following account includes what she said that day, as well as sections from her unpublished "Memories of 'Abdu'l-Bahá."

Ella's father, Lewes Newton Bailey, was descended from early colonial settlers, the Richardsons; the city of Richmond, Virginia, was named for one of his forebears. Her mother was Almira Gray, whose father was of Scotch origin; it was rumored, but not confirmed, that her mother's mother was a descendant of the Indian princess Pocahontas.

When Lewes Bailey was sixteen years old, he was sent south for his health. At the time of the Civil War he fought on the side of the South and saw Sherman's march to Atlanta. During the war he became very ill with yellow fever and wrote a letter to his family. His father and brothers sent back a scathing letter denouncing him as a traitor and indicating that he would be better dead than serving in the Confederate army. After the war he went into mining—"rich today and down tomorrow." He was intelligent and honest.

Ella was born in Houston, Texas, on 18 December 1864. When she was three years old, the Bailey family moved from Texas to San Diego County in California. On the way she was stricken with polio, and both legs were paralyzed so that she was unable to walk. After they arrived in California, her parents did all they could for her, often bringing home a new doctor. Ella missed being active with other children. One day her mother carried her to her little red chair placed next to a sandbox where a few children were playing. She recalled, "Oh! how I longed to be in there playing with them."

In time she overcame the paralysis in her left leg, but the right foot was turned over, and she wore a heavy leg brace and a built-up shoe all her life. Although she suffered from a serious lameness, she always tried to walk briskly and to go everywhere.

Ella graduated from a normal school (now known as a teacher's college) and first taught in a one-room school near her father's mine. One of the trustees had a son in her school and visited the opening day. He encouraged her and called her Ella. When she attended the funeral of one of her pupils, the family was so touched that they said they hoped many would come to her funeral! There were often dances at the school—beautiful waltzes of the sun, moon, and stars done in a large circle. Because she could not dance, the children broke confetti-filled eggs over her head. From the beginning she was a successful and greatly loved teacher.

Ella Bailey came to Berkeley alone, probably as early as 1900, to find work so she could send her brother to college. She told me that

> To get a teaching position I found I had to interview seventeen different people—board members and directors of this or that. Imagine me limping around! I ate a steak to get up my

ELLA BAILEY
became a Bahá'í in Berkeley around 1905.
A Knight of Bahá'u'lláh, she died in Libya at the age
of eighty-eight and was elevated by Shoghi Effendi to the rank of
the martyrs, "shedding forth luster American Bahá'í Community
consecrating fast awakening African continent."

strength. Then I hired a horse and buggy and made the rounds. There was an opening in Oakland, but the superintendent was so mad that I applied that he could have kicked me down the stairs; he said I wasn't fit with my lameness to stand up before a class.

I was happy when the superintendent of the Berkeley schools came and told me I could teach in Berkeley—sixth grade at McKinley. After awhile I became ill from fatigue. Mr. Biedenbach, the principal, asked what he could do to make the work easier. I asked for a lower grade and was given first and second; my physical culture class was given to another teacher, and I helped her in my own way. My students were the best trained in the school![1]

Soon it was possible for Ella's brother Newton to come to the university. He worked for the wealthy Witters— helping with their horses and garden. Their son Dean was the same age, and the family wanted the boys to do everything together. They saw Sarah Bernhardt at the Greek Theater and went with Mr. Witter to races and sports events.

Ella first heard of the Bahá'í Faith around 1905 and became one of the earliest believers in Berkeley. Taught by Lua Getsinger, she became a close friend of Mrs. Helen S. Goodall, who treated her as a daughter. She and Mrs. Goodall had wonderful and intimate talks about the teachings in a summer house set in beautiful gardens behind the Oakland home. Mrs. Goodall and Mrs. Cooper always looked after Ella's welfare as long as they lived.

Since it was not expected that 'Abdu'l-Bahá could come West, Ella decided to travel to Chicago to see Him, as did Mrs. Goodall, Mrs. Cooper, and John Bosch. She recalled: "I had a terrible case of neuritis. I tried to call a doctor. He was going to the City and said he would see me when he came back. I said, 'I won't be here then because I am going to see 'Abdu'l-Bahá.' Mrs. Cooper helped me dress and sent the car for me."[2]

She has recorded her experiences with the Master:[3]

'Abdu'l-Bahá stayed at the Plaza Hotel while in Chicago and we were fortunate to get accommodations in the same hotel. There were throngs of people, who had come from everywhere to see 'Abdu'l-Bahá.
. . . Mrs. Goodall took me with her to see Him. He greeted me by saying that He was happy to see me with my spiritual mother. . . .
He kept repeating my name as He looked off into space. But He put into my name every possible emotion. That was the wonder of it. . . . He repeated, "O, Ella Bailey, Ella Bailey . . . I love Ella Bailey."
It meant to me as if He had said in plain words, "My child, you are going to suffer; you are going to have a great deal of sorrow. . . ." In those few words He gave me all the emotions of a lifetime—He gave [me] suffering, but with it He gave me faith and strength. . . .
After that first meeting, I saw Him repeatedly on the platform and with groups of people. One evening I caught a glimpse of Him when He looked very tired . . . from the . . . constant demands. . . . This vision of Him preyed upon my mind all night, and I felt I had to see Him again to reassure myself.
The next day, I went early . . . to see Him. . . . Although it was not yet four, I saw that someone else was already waiting at His front door, so I went to the rear door. There I was met by one of the Bahá'ís who knew me and let me in.
I was ushered into a room where He was sitting alone. I had heard that He did not approve of a weeping woman. He preferred self-control. Therefore I was determined to keep myself under control so as not to appear weak before Him.
As I went into that room, 'Abdu'l-Bahá looked at me and smiled, His eyes just dancing. There are no words to express the things that 'Abdu'l-Bahá could tell you with His eyes. They went clear through me and back to my spine. I felt as if He knew everything about me including my every thought. He knew all about what I was being put through. Before I

knew it I was on my knees, with my head on His knee, weeping away. . . . There was no reproach. There was just complete understanding. He said He loved me, and it was shown me. . . .

When 'Abdu'l-Bahá was in Oakland, there was a special meeting in the Goodall home on Jackson Street [on 12 October] in order that He might greet the children. Mrs. Cooper and I were both thrilled by the way 'Abdu'l-Bahá treated the children in Chicago. We said to each other, "Just wait till we get back home, and 'Abdu'l-Bahá comes out there. We'll get the children ready to meet Him."

The children were grouped in a circle in the big parlor, and we thought their singing was wonderful. There were small chairs for them.

The Goodalls had invited many people, and the rooms were full. There was a niche on one side with a raised seat in it. I got in that niche, and I could see all around the room. I was so interested in the people present. There were many guests of prominence and many children in addition to the Bahá'ís.

Dr. Cooper's youngest brother's wife was there with their first baby. The baby was very young, and the mother was very shy—so shy that Mrs. Cooper had had to use unusual persuasion in order to get her to the gathering. This shy young mother was seated with her baby away at the back of the room, behind everyone. The people in front amused me. Every mother wanted her child in front where 'Abdu'l-Bahá would see it. . . . One couple yanked their child around to sit straight in her little chair.

There were great open doors at the entrance. 'Abdu'l-Bahá came in through these open doors and looked over the concourse of people and made some remarks. His remarks, of course, were always helpful and always something fine about the children. Then He spoke a little to the parents, especially the mothers. With all the fancily dressed children around, He didn't seem to see them particularly. He walked down the room over to the shy little woman, 'way over in the corner at the back of the room, and lifted up her baby. He walked up and down the room, talking and crooning to it, and I thought I had never in my life before seen such gentleness and tenderness. I have never seen such real love for a child as He expressed. . . . That was one of the dearest pictures I have ever seen—the picture of 'Abdu'l-Bahá walking back and forth in that room crooning to that little baby. . . .

In the latter part of 'Abdu'l-Bahá's visit in Oakland, He asked permission to give a feast in Mrs. Goodall's home [which was held on 16 October].[4]

The entire lower floor was thrown open and tables were set up and beautifully decorated with flowers. At the same table with me, at the rear of the drawing room, was Mrs. Cooper's cousin, Allie Downing Robinson. She was newly married to a very nice-looking young man. 'Abdu'l-Bahá walked around among the tables talking to us and telling us

ELLA BAILEY
at right with a group of friends.
Left to right: Dr. Howard Carpenter, Ruth Williams,
Marzieh Carpenter, Velma Linfoot, and others

of the way we should live. . . . He stopped behind Mr.
Robinson, put His hand upon his shoulder, took His other
hand and ruffled his hair and smiled as only 'Abdu'l-Bahá
could smile.

'Abdu'l-Bahá went on through the rooms, and everybody
who wanted to do so had a chance to speak with Him. He
stopped by every table and addressed everybody. He made
everyone feel welcome. He sometimes picked a flower to give
to someone.

After He had gone all around among the tables, He went
up on the landing of the stairway and stood there. And O,
how I longed to have that picture. Behind Him was a beautiful stained glass window. He had a spray of flowers . . . in
His hand. He gave us a talk on the life we should live and the
spiritual values.

. . . He spoke at the Jewish synagogue in San Francisco
[on 12 October].[5] That was a memorable day. That was another mental picture that I always have of 'Abdu'l-Bahá. He
didn't stand where the speaker usually stands in the
synagogue. The building was finished inside with dark redwood. 'Abdu'l-Bahá was wearing a light-colored abá and
made a very striking picture as He stood in front of a dark
redwood pillar.

When the first Local Spiritual Assembly was formed in
Berkeley, Ella served as its chairman. Throughout the years
she was a member of the Local Assembly and of the teaching
committee.

In July 1953 at the age of eighty-eight she left Berkeley
to teach the Faith in Libya. She flew from San Francisco to
Tripoli. There she passed away in the government hospital
on 26 August not long after her arrival. She lies buried in the
Italian Municipal Cemetery, Hamaggi.

The Guardian paid tribute to her in a cable to the Inter-
continental Teaching Conference at New Delhi. ''Irresistibly
unfolding Crusade sanctified death heroic eighty-eight-
year-old Ella Bailey elevating her rank martyrs Faith shed-

ding further luster American Bahá'í Community consecrating soil fast awakening African continent."[6]
He further honored Ella on 29 March 1954 in a cable referring to eight American pioneers.

(This) triumphant soul [Marion Jack] (is) now gathered (to the) distinguished band (of her) coworkers (in the) Abhá Kingdom: Martha Root, Lua Getsinger, May Maxwell, Hyde Dunn, Susan Moody, Keith Ransom-Kehler, Ella Bailey (and) Dorothy Baker, whose remains, lying (in) such widely scattered areas (of the) globe as Honolulu, Cairo, Buenos Aires, Sydney, Ṭihrán, Iṣfáhán, Tripoli (and the) depths (of the) Mediterranean (Sea) attest the magnificence (of the) pioneer services rendered (by the) North American Bahá'í community (in the) Apostolic (and) Formative Ages (of the) Bahá'í Dispensation.[7]

KATHRYN FRANKLAND

Kathryn Frankland was a pioneer and trail blazer.[8] She had the boldness, the faith, the indomitable spirit, and the restless drive of a pioneer. Yet she was little in size, attractive in appearance, physically frail, and gentle in manner. She was kind and loving and easily won people's confidence—always ready to help, to encourage, to inspire. Early in life she found her goal and never deviated from it. She worked for it tirelessly, incessantly, and with great joy. In her work she made many devoted friends all over the United States and in many parts of the world.

Kathryn Sherman Frankland was born on 20 January 1872 in the little town of Richland Center, Wisconsin. Her mother was a Universalist and very broad-minded; she felt that creeds should not obscure the underlying reality. Her father's family were Presbyterians. They were very religious and great believers in prayer, but they were serious people, almost austere. Richland Center was isolated and dull. Life there was too confining for a lively, spirited girl like Kathryn; she would often go to her little attic bedroom and pray for release.

When the opportunity came to visit her sister in Mitchell, South Dakota, she felt like a bird released from its cage. During the visit she met a young traveling salesman by the name of Alec Frankland. After a brief courtship they were married on the day after her twenty-first birthday. Her family was shocked. Her sister fainted when she heard the news. Her mother did not write to her for six months. Undaunted, Kathryn went back to Richland Center to see her mother before a year went by; she knocked on the door and said, "Here is your new son-in-law."[9] The Shermans all forgave Kathryn and accepted Alec as part of the family.

The young couple moved to Chicago in the 1890s. For a while they lived near the fairgrounds where the great Columbian Exposition had been held. In 1901 Alec Frankland became a newspaperman; Kathryn took a kindergarten teaching course at the University of Illinois. That year something happened that was to affect her deeply and shape her whole life.

One day, when Kathryn came home from school, she became engaged in an unusual conversation with a music teacher named Mrs. Johnson, who lived in the same apartment house. "They say there is a Prophet in the world," announced Mrs. Johnson, "and if you write to Him and express any wish, it will be granted! There is a teacher on the West Side, and he speaks through an interpreter."[10]

This surprising announcement of a Prophet of God actually living on earth haunted Kathryn. She wanted to know more about this new Prophet to Whom she was strangely drawn.

When she decided to inquire, she found that the Prophet's writings were numerous but that they were in Persian or Arabic. Few translations were available. Fragmentary copies were scarce and eagerly sought. Her neighbor, Mrs.

Johnson, gave her a copy of Bahá'u'lláh's message to the Christians. She took it to her room and read: "O Concourse of the Son [Christians]! Are ye hidden from Myself because of My Name?"[11] As she read she could not restrain her tears. Then and there she knew she believed. She was transformed.

More than ever she wanted to learn. She attended the semiprivate gatherings where Persian teachers sent from the Holy Land explained the beliefs, the principles, and the history of the new Faith. The more she learned, the more convinced and enthusiastic she became. She held meetings in her home, and once, when the teacher was absent, she took charge. To be one of the few to know of the Prophet of God for this age filled her with awe and happiness.

Kathryn loved children but had not been able to have any of her own. A deep yearning for a child was in her heart when she wrote to 'Abdu'l-Bahá to declare her faith. In 1902 the reply came in the first of many Tablets she was to receive from 'Abdu'l-Bahá:[12]

> *O thou maid-servant of God!*
> It is incumbent upon thee to turn thyself wholly to the kingdom of God, to sever thyself from aught else but Him, to be filled by the love of God, to put on the garment of sanctity and continence, which is free from worldliness, to [become] transfigured in the mantle of the gifts of the kingdom of God and to be a great sign among the maid-servants of God; that the Supreme Concourse may send out through thee a fragrance by which hearts may be cheered and spirits rested.
> Give this Truth to every pliable soul that thou mayest deem ready to harken unto the voice of God; for this is better unto thee than the earth and that which is thereupon.

At first she was stunned with disappointment, as she had expected a different answer. Then gradually, as the message reached her heart, she recognized the mission that had been assigned to her. It was a divine summons to teach, to spread the Glad Tidings. This became the goal of her life, and long before the end a host of "spiritual children" called her "Mother Frankland."

Her husband was watching her. Occasionally he would say, "You need some more of that religion."[13] Now that he was advertising manager for a Chicago newspaper, the managers' wives would meet for whist parties, and Kathryn would tell them about the Bahá'í Faith. One day another manager asked Alec, "Say, Frankland, what about this religion your wife has?" With a twinkle in his eye Alec replied, "I don't know, but by golly it's helped my wife!"[14]

Kathryn wrote to 'Abdu'l-Bahá with an unexpressed longing that her husband become a Bahá'í: "Master, do you know what is in my heart?"[15] From 'Abdu'l-Bahá came these words:

> Be confident in the bounty of thy Lord. Verily He will make thee a manifest example and an evident proof for the attainment of His Kingdom in this glorious century. . . .
> . . . The Spirit knoweth the spirit, the Spirit addresseth the spirit and the Spirit associateth with the spirit.[16]

In one year Alec became a Bahá'í. Now the Franklands served the Faith together.

Since Bahá'í teachers were needed in California, Kathryn and Alec moved west in 1903 and settled in Fruitvale (now part of Oakland). There they met Helen Goodall and Ella Cooper; the J. V. Mattesons, who soon became Bahá'ís; and Kanichi Yamamoto.

Shortly after Kathryn became ill in 1903, a thirteen-year-old Japanese boy in knee pants came to the Franklands and asked to work for $1.50 a week. His name was Saichiro Fujita, and they called him "the little squirrel." While working for them, he went to school and did the housework and washing. He was small, but his mistress was smaller, and he would carry her down to the garden.

While Mrs. Isabella Brittingham, a traveling Bahá'í teacher, was a guest of the Franklands, Fujita declared that he was a Bahá'í, thus becoming the second Japanese believer in the world.[17] This marked the beginning of a long life of service that later took him to Haifa, where he served from 1920 until his death in 1976.

From Fruitvale the Franklands moved to Los Angeles, then to Glendale. In 1909 they and Helen, their newly adopted baby, went to live in Mexico City as the first resident pioneers in Mexico. There they received 'Abdu'l-Bahá's first and only Tablet about teaching in that country.[18]

When 'Abdu'l-Bahá visited California in 1912, the Franklands were living in their Tropico (Glendale) home. Kathryn was suffering from poor health, but nothing could prevent her from going to San Francisco to attend the meetings at which He spoke. On one occasion, in San Francisco in

KATHRYN FRANKLAND
talking with Mark Tobey outside the Bahá'í House of Worship
in Wilmette, Illinois, during the National Bahá'í Convention,
1–4 May 1947

the parlor at 1815 California Street, 'Abdu'l-Bahá took two little girls, one of them Helen Frankland (the other, Cable Hunt), in His arms and held them while He talked: "I longed very much to see you all," (then to the children) "to see you and to kiss you. All My endeavors are for the purpose that you may be happy."[19]

In June 1916 the Frankland family settled in Berkeley. Their home at 1199 Spruce Street was the center for many joyous gatherings. The Yamamoto children went to the Bahá'í Junior classes there. A young people's group of high school and college students also met at the house on Spruce Street. Many lasting friendships were made.

A few years after becoming a believer, Kathryn had asked for permission for herself and Alec to make the pilgrimage to Haifa. The reply had been, "Postpone this matter until some other time."[20] Then in 1920, just a year before the passing of 'Abdu'l-Bahá, she repeated her request:

> For nineteen years this maid servant has longed to make the pilgrimage to the City of her Beloved, and to worship at the Threshold of the Holy Tomb of Bahá'u'lláh. . . . O, my Master, her heart continues its longing and it begs of Thee, if it is according to Thy supreme wisdom, to make this the time to visit the Sacred Spot and to stand in the Holy Presence.[21]

Permission was granted. Together with Mrs. Goodall, Mrs. Cooper, Mrs. Ralston, and Mrs. Hoagg, Kathryn was a guest in the home of 'Abdu'l-Bahá for thirty days. He gave these early, dedicated believers many important teachings, saying,

> This is the Lord's Supper. . . . Now we have gathered in this spot through the grace of His Holiness, Bahá'u'lláh. . . . In the same way that we are gathered at this table, we hope that we shall be gathered at the table in the Kingdom of Abhá. . . . His Holiness, Christ, gathered His disciples one evening at supper and bestowed upon them His teachings

because it was near the time of His crucifixion. He gave them as much as was necessary.[22]

In 1922 Alec Frankland died suddenly while Kathryn was attending a meeting in San Francisco. Kathryn, who had always been protected, found herself without support. She joined the staff of Equitable Life, bought a car, learned to drive, and became one of the company's most successful agents.

In 1925 she helped establish the first Spiritual Assembly of the Bahá'ís of Berkeley. When the first Seven Year Plan was announced by Shoghi Effendi in 1937, Kathryn wholeheartedly devoted herself to it and worked continuously toward its goals.

In 1944, at the age of seventy-two, when most people

KATHRYN FRANKLAND
a stalwart, indefatigable pioneer

retire from active life, she embarked on a new and strenuous project. She again offered to teach the Faith anywhere in the United States where there were few or no Bahá'ís. With limited funds and failing health, her back encased in a steel brace, she went from city to city, and from state to state, staying months here, years there, but always teaching, consolidating, and building new Spiritual Assemblies: from Albuquerque, New Mexico, to Little Rock, Arkansas; to San Antonio, Texas; to Louisville and Lexington, Kentucky; to Austin, Texas; to Great Falls, Montana; to Nebraska, Oregon, Arizona, North Dakota; then back to California—to Chula Vista, Riverside, Sacramento, Bakersfield, and, finally, Berkeley.

At the age of eighty-seven she was granted permission to see Shoghi Effendi and to visit again the holy shrines. While she was making preparations for her journey, news came of the sudden death of Shoghi Effendi. She was grief-stricken, disappointed, and disheartened. Hearing of this, the Hands of the Cause at Haifa sent her a special invitation to make her tragically interrupted pilgrimage.

She responded eagerly. Alone, frail, and with failing eyesight, she flew to the Holy Land and prayed at the sacred shrines. On the way home she went to London and prayed at the tomb of her beloved Shoghi Effendi.

She served faithfully to the end. On Sunday, 4 November 1963, shortly before her ninety-second birthday, she died peacefully in her sleep.

KANICHI YAMAMOTO

By 1902—ten years after the ascension of Bahá'u'lláh—Thornton Chase, an American, had become the first from the Western world to believe in Him; Robert Turner, the first American Negro to become a Bahá'í; Thomas Breakwell, the first Englishman; and Hippolyte Dreyfus, the first Frenchman. To Kanichi Yamamoto, a twenty-three-year-old "youth of God," came the never-ending honor of being the first Japanese believer in the world.[23]

As a young man Kanichi left his parents in the rural village of To-saki in the prefecture of Yamaquchi, Japan, and set out for a new world. He was industrious, self-reliant, earnest, and adventuresome. Although brought up a Buddhist, he had become a devout Christian.

In Hawaii on his way to America he found employment in the home of Mr. and Mrs. William Owen Smith. Their son Clarence had returned with Agnes Alexander to the Islands from Paris where they had attended the meetings of May Bolles and had accepted the Bahá'í Faith. Living with the Smith family was Elizabeth Muther who helped "Moto" with his English. When she herself became a Bahá'í, her first thought was to speak to Yamamoto. Agnes Alexander recorded the story:

> . . . the power of 'Abdu'l-Bahá's Tablet to her [E. Muther], and her own earnest prayer, brought about a great event in the spiritual world, as God used her as His instrument to confirm the first Japanese Bahá'í. . . .
>
> . . . When she asked him [Kanichi] how he knew that it was the Truth, he answered by putting his hand to his heart, and said he knew there.[24]

Elizabeth Muther described the circumstances of Moto's wholehearted acceptance in a letter written 8 September 1902:

> I want to tell you of my great joy in being led to give the Message to Moto. . . . After I became a believer I felt that sometime I might tell Moto. I thought of him on Maui and prayed that his heart might be prepared to receive the Truth. . . . Although it was a little difficult to give him the Message because of his imperfect knowledge of English, yet God helped me so that he understands perfectly and is re-

joicing in the knowledge of His Truth. I have just had a little talk with him and he told me how happy he was and that he expects to write his letter to the Master this evening. He seems fearful lest something may happen to the Master before his letter may reach Him. . . . I feel that he will be a power for good among the Japanese here. He has a very even temper and winning disposition and seems to have many devoted friends. . . . "Oh Miss Muther, I am so happy!" he said in parting, "and I can only say, Oh God! How hast Thou honored me to have made me Thy servant!"[25]

When Kanichi wrote to 'Abdu'l-Bahá, he was so deeply affected that he composed the letter four times but still thought he had not adequately expressed his thoughts in English. Finally, Elizabeth told him to write in Japanese, for she felt sure the Master would understand. He wrote then in his own language, humbly confessing his belief in the Manifestation of God and asking for ability to teach the people of his native land. When he received a Tablet from 'Abdu'l-Bahá in reply, Moto felt he had been fully answered.[26] In February 1903 he received a second Tablet: "Verily, I pray my Lord to teach thee a language and writing of the Kingdom which will satisfy thee, so as to dispense with all things; for that spiritual writing and instructive tongue are eloquent, clear, laudable, legible, read by the tongue and preserved in the heart."[27]

In the early days of the Bahá'í Faith in Honolulu there was no home where that first group of the Pacific could meet. Agnes Alexander, Clarence Smith, Elizabeth Muther, and Kanichi Yamamoto took the trolley to Pacific Heights and there on the hilltop read prayers and Tablets.

Moto stayed six months in the Islands to learn more of the Bahá'í teachings. In the spring of 1903 he left for Oakland, California, where he became the butler in the home of Mrs. Helen Goodall. Mrs. Goodall wrote to the friends in Hawaii soon after his arrival:

It seems wonderful to me how the Spirit has taught Moto
as he does not understand English very well. . . .

. . . he is very happy and goes about the house as if he
were walking on air, especially if a believer comes to see us,
or we have a meeting.[28]

The early gatherings, presided over by Mrs. Goodall
and her daughter Ella, assisted by devoted Yamamoto, were
happy affairs indeed. Moto opened the door and greeted
each guest with a beaming smile.

In 1904 Kanichi wrote to 'Abdu'l-Bahá, again in
Japanese. We are fortunate to have an account of the receipt
of that letter in 'Akká. The Master's secretary, Dr. Yúnis
Khán-i-Afrúkhtih, records in "Memories of Nine Years in
'Akká" that the only word of Mr. Yamamoto's message he
could read was the signature! He translated an accompanying letter from Helen Goodall and gave it to 'Abdu'l-Bahá together with the Japanese letter. The Master said to him jok-
ingly, "Well, do you not know Japanese?" The secretary
bowed and replied, "No, Master, I hardly know English."
'Abdu'l-Bahá smiled and said, "Then what shall we do with
this letter?" Dr. Afrúkhtih answered, "Just do with it as you
did with the others [from Yamamoto]." The Master said,
"Very well, I will turn to Bahá'u'lláh, and He will tell Me
what to say."[29]

Accordingly, on 4 August 1904 'Abdu'l-Bahá revealed a
Tablet and an English translation was sent to Moto:

> O thou who art the single one of Japan and the unique one of the
> extreme Orient!
> That country hath been deprived of the divine breath until
> this time; now, God be praised! thou art initiated in the mys-
> teries. . . .
> Thou hast been earthly, I hope that thou wilt become
> heavenly. . . .
> Do not wonder at the favor and bounty of the Lord. By the

favor of God, how often a drop hath become undulating like a sea, and an atom hath become shining like the sun![30]

A few months after this Tablet was received, Mrs. Goodall wrote to Agnes and Elizabeth, "Moto is a beautiful believer and carries [out] the Master's wishes in his every day life—so patient and faithful. He is surely unique as the Master called him in his last Tablet. . . . It was a miracle that the Master knew what Moto's letter contained when it was written in Japanese. He answered all his questions."[31]

The familiar words of 'Abdu'l-Bahá on marriage were revealed in a Tablet to Yamamoto: "As to the question of marriage, according to the law of God: First you must select one, and then it depends upon the consent of the father and mother. Before your selection they have no right of interference."[32]

Moto was married to a young lady named Ima in 1908 in the ballroom of the Oakland home. An elaborate American wedding was given by the Goodalls; all the Bahá'ís and the Japanese friends of the couple were invited. Ramona Allen Brown told me, "Mother reported that the decorations, the bride's dress and all the appointments were as lovely as could be made possible, as though for a member of the family. My mother found the beautiful gold wedding ring favor in her piece of wedding cake." After the ceremony, according to Ella Cooper, Moto said to his bride, with characteristic humor, "I don't want you to be like a Japanese wife, always bowing. I want you to be like an American wife and boss me!"[33] Agnes Alexander notes that "Five boys and a daughter were born to this union. After this wife's death in 1919, Mr. Yamamoto married her sister [Tame] with whom he had six children. . . ."[34]

When Mrs. Goodall's husband died in 1909, she moved to her daughter's home in San Francisco but kept the Oakland house open for meetings with Moto in charge. Forty ladies and one man (John Bosch) came to these gatherings;

KANICHI YAMAMOTO

known to his friends as "Moto" (seated, center) with his second wife Tame and twelve children, 14 November 1937. Hiroshi, Shinji, and Masao were living in the Goodall home at the time of 'Abdu'l-Bahá's visit in 1912.
Front row, left to right: Chiyoko, Tame, Tamaye, Kanichi, William Koreaki, Wataru, Eiji, Yoshio
Back row: Michiaki, Shinji, Hiroshi, Masao, Goro, Fumiko

one of them wrote of Moto: "He looked forward to these meetings, and it was his great pleasure to prepare the tea, hot biscuits, and cakes which were always served. . . . he and his wife and children were very dear to the Bahá'ís."[35]

When 'Abdu'l-Bahá was in California, several memorable events took place in the Oakland home: His first talk on 3 October, the children's gathering with the Master on 12 October, and the Feast given by 'Abdu'l-Bahá on 16 October. Moto and Fujita served together with special love and radiance.[36] While the Master stayed in San Francisco at 1815 California Street, Moto lived there and served Him. 'Abdu'l-Bahá greatly loved Kanichi's three little boys. He held them on His knee, talked to them, and gave them special names: Hiroshi, the oldest, He called Ḥasan; Shinji He called Ḥusayn, and Masao, Farok.

Moto arranged for 'Abdu'l-Bahá to address the Japanese YMCA at the Oakland Japanese Independent Church, which gave the Master special joy because the members were Orientals. The women brought their babies for His blessing. Frances Allen noted that "to the Japanese friends he showed great favor."[37]

After Helen Goodall's Oakland home passed into other hands in 1918, Moto made a trip to Japan, then took up landscape gardening, and moved to Berkeley in 1919. It was very important to him that his five children attend Kathryn Frankland's Berkeley Bahá'í Junior classes. I met the Yamamotos in 1920 when I came to the University of California and helped teach those delightful youngsters. Moto enjoyed hearing Hiroshi, Shinji, Masao, Fumiko, and Michiaki recite the prayers and the Hidden Words and give talks.

After Pearl Harbor, when the Japanese were being rushed to relocation camps, the Yamamotos telephoned to say good-bye. They had just a few hours to pack. Moto's attitude was cheerfulness itself: "The W.P.A. is moving us. Isn't that wonderful! We can take our own clothes. Everything is fine. Hiroshi and Shinji can stay and come later. Perhaps we can be pioneers like Mrs. Frankland!" I remarked on his courage and optimism. He replied, "Bahá'u'lláh and 'Abdu'l-Bahá were forty years in prison; so we can't mind this!" To Fumiko, his daughter, I said that we would pray for their safety and comfort. She expressed her gratitude: "Now I know we will be all right!"[38]

When Moto returned to Berkeley after the war, we were relieved and happy to have him with us again. He always served the Berkeley friends; in times of need he was there with help, concern, and flowers.

Kanichi Yamamoto passed away on 1 May 1961. His children, all successful in business and the professions, came from several parts of the country. Shinji asked me to conduct a Bahá'í service for the family. 'Abdu'l-Bahá, long before, had provided an appropriate epitaph: *"O thou who art the single one of Japan and the unique one of the extreme Orient!* . . . thou wert a roving bird, thou hast reached the divine Rose-garden. . . ."[39]

BERDETTE MATTESON

Berdette Northrop began her life in the early California of stagecoaches, rugged pioneers, and adventurers; in the ninety-seven years of her life she saw it become a modern, bustling state.[40] She became a believer in the early days of the Bahá'í Faith in the West and lived to see the new religion grow strikingly in size and maturity. Berdette was born in 1873 in Stockton in the San Joaquin Valley. When she was twenty-three years old, she married J. V. Matteson. They moved to San Francisco and then to Fruitvale, now part of Oakland. There J. V. went into the real estate business, and the two settled down in that peaceful and growing community. Then something happened that was to change the course and character of their whole life.

In 1903, a couple walked into their real estate office—a

man with a mandolin and a frail woman with a guitar. "Do you have a rose garden?" they asked.[41] The young wife was ill with bronchitis, and she yearned for a rose garden!

J. V. sold them a house with a garden next door to his own house. When the newcomers moved in, they had no furniture and very few possessions of any kind. Their names were Alec and Kathryn Frankland. They had come from Chicago, and they were destined to become lifelong friends of the Mattesons.

Berdette was puzzled and attracted by this unusual couple. She watched Kathryn as she sat in her yard, writing. She went over, and they chatted. What was it that Kathryn was constantly writing? "Notes. Copying notes from the Writings of 'Abdu'l-Bahá." Who was 'Abdu'l-Bahá? "He was the son of Bahá'u'lláh, the Prophet of God for this day and the Founder of a new Faith for all mankind." Together they would read from the Tablets, "Soon will you see the signs of spring."[42]

J. V. became concerned about his wife's falling under the influence of these strangers with "strange" ideas. He tried to discourage her from going over, but Berdette wanted to know. Before accepting or rejecting, she wanted to know more. She felt a desperate need for a new spiritual light.

Few books had been translated into English. There were mostly carbon copies of typed notes that were eagerly passed from person to person. She read them avidly. Quickly, the magnitude of the new Message and its beauty became apparent. It spoke of the unity of religion under one God, of the high station of man and of his vast potential, of a new surge of the spirit, of economic and social justice, of the unification of the human race into an all-inclusive common-wealth, of the establishment of a new world order where peace and progress will prevail. These were the basic princi-ples of the Bahá'í Faith.

Why weren't people flocking to join this noble Faith? Vision and courage were required. A few disciples always lead the way. Others follow. As the need becomes acute, more people follow. Berdette had that vision and that courage. She joined the new Faith with all her heart. Three years later, her husband, convinced, also became a follower of Bahá'u'lláh.

In 1912 Berdette heard the news of the arrival of 'Abdu'l-Bahá in New York. She longed to see Him. Before long her wish was granted when 'Abdu'l-Bahá came to California, spoke in Oakland and San Francisco, and met with groups and individuals in every walk of life. All who

BERDETTE MATTESON

came in contact with Him were deeply impressed by His magnetic personality, His keen intellect, His sympathetic understanding, and boundless love.

Thereafter, J. V. and Berdette were very active in serving their beloved Faith and in sharing its Message and its teachings with all who showed interest. They worked together, scattering joy and hope wherever they went. Yet they were different in temperament and in manner: he, extroverted, jolly, witty, talented, equally at ease on the speaker's platform and in social gatherings; she, quiet and unassuming, kindly, diligently working in the background, bringing out others, and greeting everyone with a smile. Her beautiful smile radiated warmth and happiness. It spoke louder than a thousand speeches. Her smile and her serenity were characteristic of her personality.

They had two children, Dr. J. Vance Matteson (who now resides in Los Angeles) and Lorne Matteson (who lives in Hayward), and several grandchildren and great-grandchildren.

In 1958 J. V. passed away. Berdette staunchly carried on, maintaining her sweetness and serenity throughout the following years, sustained by her deep faith. Her spirit stayed young. When she was ninety-one years old, while in a convalescent hospital, she embarked on a new hobby— making ceramic tile designs. Her mind stayed clear almost to the very end.

At the age of ninety-five, two years before her death, she broke her leg. In the hospital she discovered, to her delight, that her nurse, Ruth Collier, was a Bahá'í. The warmth and cheer between the two attracted the attention of the other patients. When asked why there was this friendship between the two, Berdette answered with her familiar smile, "We are both Bahá'ís." Berdette Matteson died 25 January 1971. Her radiance affected all around her to the very end of her long and beautiful life.

J. V. MATTESON

Jesse Vance Matteson was born in 1875 in Murphys, California, an 1849 gold-rush town.[43] His father, T. J. Matteson, had come around the Horn by sailing ship in 1849, had mined gold briefly, and stayed on as a civil engineer and the operator of stagecoaches running between the railroad terminal at Milton and the Calaveras Big Trees.

The family moved to Stockton, California, in time for J. V. to complete his formal education at a business college. In Stockton he met and married Berdette Northrop. Their first home was in Angel's Camp, near Murphys. But "the City," San Francisco, attracted them. Hence they moved to a flat facing Golden Gate Park, where their son, J. Vance, Jr., was born. J. V. worked downtown as a bookkeeper.

Soon J. V.'s restless, enterprising spirit led him to take up real estate sales in Fruitvale, then a fast-growing suburb of Oakland. Among his clients were Alec and Kathryn Frankland, from Chicago, who found their dream home "with a rose garden" next door to J. V. and Berdette.

There in 1903 Kathryn told Berdette about the Bahá'í Faith. Although there was little literature available, much of it carbon copies of letters from 'Abdu'l-Bahá, Berdette accepted the teachings immediately. J. V., an active churchgoer, first opposed, then questioned, and finally accepted the Faith. In this process he developed a conviction that enabled him to withstand the bitter opposition of family and friends during the coming years.

J. V. rode the tide of suburban expansion, became the proprietor of the Fruitvale Lumber Company, and was active and well known in business and social circles. He built a new hilltop home on Sunset Avenue, where their second son, Lorne, was born in 1908.

In this home, which featured a circular dining table seating nineteen persons, weekly Bahá'í meetings presented such well-remembered Bahá'í teachers as Thornton Chase, Lua Getsinger, Roy Wilhelm, George Latimer, Grace Ober, Dr. D'Evelyn, Hyde Dunn, Howard MacNutt, Mason Remey, Charles Haney, Ella Robarts, and John and Louise Bosch. The peak of activity at the Mattesons' was the celebration of the Feast of Riḍván on 28 April 1912, attended by some eighty believers from the entire Bay Area, with a program led by Thornton Chase.

Later that year J. V. and Berdette were among the fortunate Bahá'ís who met 'Abdu'l-Bahá on many occasions during His visit to San Francisco and Oakland. J. V. recorded his remembrances of one of those meetings:

> It was my great privilege to meet 'Abdu'l-Bahá several times when He came to California in 1912.
> While ministering to us at a feast in the home of Mrs. Helen S. Goodall, He stood behind a young man who was seated at one of the tables, and with His hands on his shoulders, spoke of youth in this Cause. I felt that it was wonderful to have His touch, and I bowed my head and [silently] asked for such an experience. Then, as if He had heard my voice, He walked to the back of my chair and placed His hands on me and continued to speak.
> A Tablet that I had previously received from 'Abdu'l-Bahá said: "I know in what condition thou art."
> I knew now that He even knew my thoughts.[44]

A recession swept away J. V.'s business in 1908, and by November of 1912 even the hilltop home was taken away. In the succeeding years the Mattesons were to experience the literal meaning of the verse "poverty is followed by riches, and riches are followed by poverty."[45] J. V. turned his talents to residential design and construction, summer resort development, the management of a factory that built pipe organs for the silent movies, and the building of a sawmill, among other things.

Throughout their lives the Mattesons' faith, optimism,

and patience never wavered; they continued to serve and teach the Bahá'í Faith in every way they could. In 1925 J. V. and Berdette were among those who formed the first Spiritual Assembly of the Bahá'ís of Berkeley. Later they served as members of the Oakland Assembly.

In 1938 J. V. and Berdette set forth in a travel trailer and for a time traveled the length of California as Bahá'í teachers. They then settled in Santa Barbara, where they remained until the community was well established. While in Santa Barbara, although he was well past the age of retire-

J. V. MATTESON

ment, J. V. built five unusual rustic homes, doing all the work himself, except for plumbing and wiring, and decorating the fireplace mantel in each home with the emblem of the Greatest Name carved in wood. The *Santa Barbara Press* published several illustrated newspaper articles describing his work. In 1954 they returned to the Bay Area and helped form the first Spiritual Assembly of the Bahá'ís of Eden Township, now called the San Leandro–Hayward Judicial District.

J. V. passed away in 1958 after a short illness. Berdette carried on alone until 1971. Their lives spanned the old world and the new world both materially and spiritually, and they found their greatest happiness in making some contribution to the establishment of the new World Order.

7

Postscript

My survey of the early days of the Bahá'í Faith in Berkeley from 1898 to 1925 ends here. Some of the events of the following half century I have recorded in an unpublished manuscript about my husband. As time goes on others, no doubt, will add to the Berkeley story.

In 1923 I left Berkeley and the University of California to enter Stanford University as a senior. It was the fulfillment of my childhood dream—to study at Stanford, where eleven years before 'Abdu'l-Bahá had been received with great interest and respect and where He had delivered an address that He Himself considered highly significant. The Stanford story, which starts with 'Abdu'l-Bahá's appearance there, is one of special historical importance. My own experience at Stanford, like the one just closing at Berkeley, would enrich my life immeasurably. The inspiring love for the Master, the faith, and the courage I found among the Berkeley Bahá'ís has never left me. I carried their legacy with me then as I do now, for I have always felt to be true what René Dubos, eminent microbiologist and Pulitzer Prize winner, has written:

I believe that I participate in a great collective undertaking which began long before me and will continue long after me

108 YOUTH IN THE VANGUARD

and of which the goal is not so much to go back to the Lost Paradise as to create the New Jerusalem. We are not only caretakers of the past; we are also responsible for the construction of tomorrow.[1]

Part Two

Early Days of the Bahá'í Faith
at Stanford University

8

'Abdu'l-Bahá's Visit to Stanford University and Palo Alto, 8–9 October 1912

"'Abdu'l-Bahá leaned on the rostrum, looked out and smiled at all those eager young faces. Eighteen hundred students responded with such instant applause that it rocked the building. It was an ovation."[1] Thus Ella Cooper later described the scene in Assembly Hall at Leland Stanford Junior University on the morning of 8 October 1912.[2]

Although He was elderly, broken in health, unschooled in books and the ways of the West, and until 1908 a prisoner, 'Abdu'l-Bahá had just given a brilliant address to students and faculty, administrators, and townspeople, in a famed institution of learning. There had been no barriers of age or country or scholastic background—only a warm empathy and mutual respect. 'Abdu'l-Bahá had been in complete command and had spoken calmly and with great ease. His subject was the intrinsic oneness of all phenomena.

'Abdu'l-Bahá had arrived in San Francisco five days before.[3] During His first day there Dr. David Starr Jordan, president of Stanford University, had called to invite Him to speak to a special meeting of the student body. On the morning of 8 October Dr. Jordan met Him at the Southern Pacific station in Palo Alto and escorted Him to the campus. "The Assembly Hall was packed to the ceiling" with an enthusiastic audience when the speaker arrived at 10:15 a.m.[4] There was football excitement in the air, as a rally to greet the world-famous Australian rugby team was scheduled to follow 'Abdu'l-Bahá's talk.

The *Palo Altan* commented on the extraordinary occasion: "It seemed to be a notable day when Abdul Baha from the far country of the Orient, met Dr. David Starr Jordan of the far western shore, both carrying the standard of international peace and universal brotherhood."[5] Dr. Jordan, one of the trustees of the Carnegie Peace Endowment and renowned for his own peace plan, introduced 'Abdu'l-Bahá to the audience:

> It is our portion to have with us, through the courtesy of our Persian friends, one of the great religious teachers of the world, one of the natural successors of the old Hebrew prophets.
> He is said sometimes to be the founder of a new religion. He has upward of three millions of people following along the lines in which he leads. It is not exactly a new religion, however. The religion of brotherhood, of good will, of friendship between men and nations—that is as old as good thinking and good living may be. It may be said in some sense to be the oldest of religions. . . .
> I have now the great pleasure, and the great honor also, of presenting to you Abdul Baha.[6]

'Abdu'l-Bahá captured the attention and respect of both students and faculty with His opening words:

> The greatest attainment in the world of humanity has ever been scientific in nature. It is the discovery of the realities of things. Inasmuch as I find myself in the home of science—for this is one of the great universities of the country and well known abroad—I feel a keen sense of joy.[7]

World War I was only two years away; the young men in this assembly were to be drafted to fight and die in it. Point

'ABDU'L-BAHÁ
in front of Memorial Church where He paused
during a tour of the Leland Stanford Junior University
campus on 8 October 1912 and read the inscription
on the stone plaque on the lower left corner of the facade
that reads ". . . erected by Jane Stanford
to the glory of God and in loving memory
of her husband Leland Stanford"

by point 'Abdu'l-Bahá showed the futility of war and built to
a poignant climax:

> Bahá'u'lláh especially emphasized international
> peace. . . . From every real standpoint there must and
> should be peace among all nations.
>   God created one earth and one mankind to people it. . . .
> but man himself has come forth and proclaimed imaginary
> boundary lines. . . .
>   . . . We live upon this earth for a few days and then rest
> beneath it forever. So it is our graveyard eternally. Shall man
> fight for . . . his eternal sepulcher? . . .
>   It is my hope that you who are students in this university
> may never be called upon to fight for the dust of earth . . .
> but that during the days of your life you may enjoy the most
> perfect companionship one with another, even as one
> family—as brothers, sisters, fathers, mothers—associating
> together in peace and true fellowship.[8]

The full text of this historic talk was published in the
Daily Palo Alto Times on 11–14 October 1912, the *Palo Altan* on
1 November 1912, and later in *Star of the West* and *The Promulgation of Universal Peace.*[9]

In closing the meeting Dr. Jordan said: ''We are all
under very great obligation to Abdul Baha for this illuminating expression of the brotherhood of man and the
value of international peace. I think we can best show our
appreciation by simply a rising vote of thanks.''[10]

There was thunderous applause followed by varsity
yells led by the cheerleaders. 'Abdu'l-Bahá was very much
amused by this demonstration and praised the students for
their lusty voices. He applauded with the rest when the
rugby team was presented and waited after the assembly to
congratulate the members on their record.[11]

That day the *Daily Palo Alto* gave a detailed account of
'Abdu'l-Bahá's appearance and the manner in which He
spoke.[12]

An aged man, with a long white beard and a benign and saintly face, stood on the platform of the Assembly hall this morning and demonstrated the utter uselessness of war and its waste. . . .

In a simple and dignified manner, with no more evidence of embarrassment than if he were addressing an assemblage of his native Persians, Abd-ul-Baha, or Abbas Effendi, brought the arguments of science, nature and philosophy together to show the universal brotherhood of man and the necessity for universal peace.

In the garb of his own country, a long brown toga which harmonized modestly with his dark complexion and the white turban, Sir Abbas presented a picturesque figure. Speaking quietly in Persian, his expressive features and gestures made the services of his interpreter seem at times almost superfluous.[13]

Assembly Hall, Leland Stanford Junior University, where 'Abdu'l-Bahá lectured on 8 October 1912. The building later housed the Business School and now is the home of the Sociology Department.

After the talk Dr. Jordan drove 'Abdu'l-Bahá around the campus to see the buildings, especially the beautiful Memorial Church with a plaque at the entrance, bearing, according to Ella Cooper's notes, an "all-inclusive inscription."[14]

'Abdu'l-Bahá, two of His secretaries, and Dr. Ray Lyman Wilbur, then dean of the Stanford Medical School, were photographed on campus. The Assembly Hall in which He had spoken is in the upper left hand corner of the picture.[15]

The Master was the guest of the Jordans at Xasmin House, their Stanford residence since 1896. Mrs. Jordan had prepared an upstairs bedroom where 'Abdu'l-Bahá might

'ABDU'L-BAHÁ
after His address in Assembly Hall (building on left)
at Stanford University, 8 October 1912.
Left to right: two secretaries of 'Abdu'l-Bahá,
Dr. Ray Lyman Wilbur, 'Abdu'l-Bahá

rest after luncheon. Instead of entering the room intended, He walked right past it and went into the children's room where He lay down and napped. This incident still impressed Mrs. Jordan when she was interviewed almost four decades later.[16]

(In 1924, Xasmin House became Manzanita, which served as a hall for women for some time but has since been demolished. I lived for a year upstairs in the hall that had been blessed by the presence of the Master. Possibly by chance my room was the very one in which He rested.)

During the afternoon of 8 October 'Abdu'l-Bahá left the university and was driven by Dr. Jordan into Palo Alto, where other important engagements still awaited Him.

Mrs. Isabella C. Merriman, a humanitarian, well-thought-of in the community, had the honor of entertaining 'Abdu'l-Bahá in her daughter's home at 925 Waverly Street, Palo Alto, for tea at 4:30 p.m., late dinner, overnight, and 7:30 a.m. breakfast.[17]

'Abdu'l-Bahá had an evening speaking engagement in Palo Alto. During the day He had been photographed walking under the trees on campus with Reverend Clarence Reed, minister of the First Unitarian Church of Palo Alto.[18] Reverend Reed was a very pleasant, broadminded man, and progressive in his thinking. His attitude toward 'Abdu'l-Bahá was most respectful. Shortly before 8:00 p.m., he conducted his guest to the church where a large assemblage had gathered.[19] The entire congregation arose spontaneously to honor the Master as He entered.

'Abdu'l-Bahá's message to the Christians was loving and gentle. Bahá'u'lláh had come to unite religions and nations.

> God is most kind. Consider what His Holiness Christ said: "Verily, the sun shines upon the just and the unjust alike." What a blessed statement this is! Even the sinner is not deprived of the mercy of God. What a sweet utterance! . . .
> His Holiness Baha'o'llah addresses humanity, saying, "Ye

are all the leaves of one tree and the drops of one sea." . . .
. . . All must live in the utmost . . . fellowship, and must
pass their days pleasantly, for this will win the bounties of
God and the bestowals shall surround them, and the King-
dom of God will become personified in the human kingdom.
And this is our wish in its entirety.[20]

Reverend Reed brought the evening to an impressive
close by asking the audience to pray silently for the coming
of the universal religion.

I feel that a man of God has spoken to us tonight. There is
no way I know to close the service than with a prayer—not a
prayer in spoken words, but a prayer in silence. Let each person pray in his own way for the coming of the universal
religion—the religion of love, the religion of peace, a religion
of the fullness of life.
(Silence.)
You are dismissed.[21]

The dinner that followed the talk was a festive affair.
Mrs. Merriman had spared no effort to serve a delicious repast with beautiful appointments. Undeterred by the fact
that there were twenty-nine persons in 'Abdu'l-Bahá's
party, she also invited Reverend Reed, Mr. H. W. Simkins of
the Palo Altan, and several members of the university faculty,
including Dr. H. D. Gray and Professor Samuel Swayze
Seward, Jr.

'Abdu'l-Bahá was very relaxed and witty; His sparkling
repartee delighted the company. Professor Seward, seated
next to 'Abdu'l-Bahá at the table, wanted to know which na-
tionality of people was most responsive to His message. The
Master replied, "The Persians." The professor questioned
which was the most difficult to teach. 'Abdu'l-Bahá answered, "The Turks." Seward then asked, "What about the
Americans?" Everyone burst out laughing when the Master
responded, "The Americans never like to stay on the same

car very long. They always want to transfer!'' Then He added, ''But when they come to the Bahá'í Faith they are firm and strong.''[22]

Professor Seward later recorded his impressions in a letter to Mrs. Ella Cooper. Eleven years after the event I was to hear Seward and Gray, my English professors, describe 'Abdu'l-Bahá and relate the stories told by Him that night. They were still enthralled by His charm and humor.

Mr. Simkins stayed on that evening after the others had gone and talked with 'Abdu'l-Bahá for a long time. As a result he published an edition of his newspaper on 1 November entirely devoted to the Stanford–Palo Alto visit.

XASMIN HOUSE
the residence of President and Mrs. David Starr Jordan,
where 'Abdu'l-Bahá was a guest at luncheon on 8 October 1912.
The author lived here, in the wake of the Master,
from 1924 to 1925, after the house became
a graduate dormitory called Manzanita.

The next morning before 'Abdu'l-Bahá left for engagements in San Francisco, Oakland, and Berkeley, a number of people gathered around Him as He spoke on several subjects. The one recorded in Mahmúd's Diary dealt with different beliefs about the station of Christ held by various denominations:

> "Some called Christ the God, the Word of God, or the Prophet of God . . . and thus created differences and contentions among themselves. Spirituality was drowned in hatred; and amity became replaced by enmity. His Holiness Bahá'u'lláh has closed all inlets to such differences. By appointing the Interpreter of the Book and by establishing the House of Justice. . . ."[23]

'Abdu'l-Bahá was happy and well pleased with His visit at Stanford and in Palo Alto. A significant chapter in the annals of the Bahá'í Faith had been written. Although He spoke in many colleges, churches, and clubs in America and Europe, the exceptional warmth of His reception at Stanford, as well as His own evident pleasure in the occasion, make 8 October 1912 stand out as one of the high points of His western tour.

There are many indications that both Dr. Jordan and 'Abdu'l-Bahá found the day memorable. Dr. Jordan, in his autobiography under the heading "The Bahai," wrote:

> Another visitor of the same year was the Bahai, Abdul Bahas, son of Baha O'llah, the famous Persian devotee, founder and head of a widespread religious sect holding as its chief tenet the Brotherhood of Man, with all that this implies of personal friendliness and international peace. Through an interpreter the kindly apostle expressed with convincing force a message accepted, in name at least, by good men and women all through the ages. He asked for some of my own essays to be translated into Persian and cordially invited me to his abode of peace in the hills of Damascus.[24]

What a genius in human relations was the Master! Years later Jordan remembered His courtesy. When I was a student at Stanford from 1923 through 1925, Jordan, as chancellor of Stanford, went out of his way to make it possible for me to hold weekly Bahá'í meetings on campus. Then in his seventies, he himself spoke on the teachings of the Bahá'í Faith on two occasions. At one point he wrote a letter to President Wilbur to put in a good word for the Faith.

DAVID STARR JORDAN, 1915,
was president emeritus of Stanford University
when Marion Carpenter sought him out to record his memories
of 'Abdu'l-Bahá's visit to Stanford.

Again in 1925 he wrote to the director of lectures on behalf of Jináb-i-Fáḍil. Later that year he served as the gracious honorary chairman for a three-day conference for world unity sponsored by the Bahá'ís where he spoke at the opening session on the essentials of his peace plan. Further evidence that Jordan was affected by the teachings of 'Abdu'l-Bahá is his statement on 6 March 1929, two and a half years before his death: "'after many occasional breaks into mysticism I have grown very sympathetic with the work of the Bahá'í people and their point of view. . . .'"[25] He also recommended that an article about 'Abdu'l-Bahá be written for a series of biographical sketches that included one of himself.

'Abdu'l-Bahá on His part showed appreciation of the Stanford experience, not only by His sincere and disarming kindness in asking Dr. Jordan for some of his writings and inviting him to His home in Haifa, but in other ways. He wrote a special Tablet to H. W. Simkins, one of the editors of the Palo Altan, expressing pleasure in the visit Simkins had paid Him, thanking him for publishing His address, saying that He would never forget his cordiality as long as He lived, and promising that He would pray for him. He offered the editor a copy of the talk He had given at Temple Emmanu-El in San Francisco, if he should wish to publish it.

Three full-length addresses accordingly appeared in the Palo Altan of 1 November 1912: "To the World of Science," "Message to the Church," and "Message to the Jews." The Tablet to Simkins in Persian and in English was included as well as articles by the editor and the reprint of an article from the London Chronicle, which contains the now familiar tribute to 'Abdu'l-Bahá: "Abbas Effendi leads his followers over what is elsewhere called the Mystic Way; but wherever they march, they tread with practical feet."[26]

'Abdu'l-Bahá made many references to His day at Stanford later in His travels and referred Dr. Auguste Forel to the Stanford address when He sent the Swiss Bahá'í scientist the

Tablet entitled "Proofs of God's Existence."[27] In London on His way back to Palestine, when asked by newsmen what His impressions of America were, 'Abdu'l-Bahá replied that "material civilisation had advanced greatly, and he hoped that divine civilisation would be likewise established." He further noted that "American universities were carrying on a most profitable and encouraging work" and praised Dr. Jordan as "'a very wise and erudite man, whose mind is full of thoughts of peace.'"[28]

Finally, there is one last indication that 'Abdu'l-Bahá felt His Father's Cause had been well served at Stanford. In 1914 He wrote from Mt. Carmel to the believers of East and West, commenting on the variety of places where He had spoken in His travels.

> In the universities of Europe and America, such as the University of Oxford, England, and the Leland Stanford University in San Francisco, California, which are considered in the vanguard of educational institutions of the world, eloquent addresses were delivered. In the last mentioned university there were present 175 professors and 1800 students. . . .
>
> Undoubtedly you have read the contents of the American and European newspapers. . . . For example, amongst them might be mentioned the Palo Altan . . . Christian Commonwealth . . . etc. The philosophers, professors and literary men have expressed their opinions concerning this Cause in these periodicals. . . . This was again through the Mercy and Providence of the Blessed Perfection. . . .
>
> In short, although 'Abdu'l-Bahá considers Himself as a drop, yet this drop is connected with the Most Great Sea. . . . As it is said: "The originator of all these voices is the King himself" or in other words: "It is through his assistance."[29]

Shoghi Effendi also singled out the day at Stanford for special notice. In God Passes By he referred to "the enthusiastic reception accorded Him ['Abdu'l-Bahá] at Leland Stanford University when . . . He discoursed on some of the noblest truths underlying His message to the West. . . ."[30]

Shoghi Effendi included it as one of a number of "scenes revolving around that majestic and patriarchal Figure" that can never be "effaced from memory," and one of the "highlights of the unforgettable Mission He ['Abdu'l-Bahá] undertook in the service of His Father's Cause."[31]

Young Shoghi Effendi was attracted to Stanford as a possible university for his graduate studies; as a youth he sent for the prospectus of courses and kept it on his desk.[32] His letter to me in 1925, as well as one written on his behalf by Dr. J. E. Esslemont (quoted in the following chapter), show the marked interest he had in the Bahá'í work at Stanford.

The reverberations of 'Abdu'l-Bahá's visit can never all be recorded. In addition to the recollections of Professors Seward and Gray found in Chapters 9 and 10, those of a few others should be noted.

In 1950 Mrs. David Starr Jordan, in an interview on 26 September, remarked, "I did meet 'Abdu'l-Bahá. I was repeatedly surprised by the modernity of the Bahá'í religion and its aptness for our problems for this day. The twelve principles are universal and have eternal value."[33]

In October 1950, after a commemoration in Palo Alto, a genteel lady, Mrs. Percy Martin, widow of Professor Martin of the History Department, came to the front. "I was present at the Unitarian Church that night; I heard 'Abdu'l-Bahá speak," she said. When I asked what He was like, she replied, "He was the most venerable man I ever remember hearing."[34]

In 1958 Arthur L. Dahl, Jr., interviewed two Stanford professors, Albert Leon Guérard and Harry Rathbun, who had heard 'Abdu'l-Bahá speak at the assembly, one as a professor, the other as a student. Guérard, associate professor of French in 1912, and later professor of general literature, paid tribute to the Bahá'í Faith in the last book he published. He corresponded with Horace Holley for many years and in 1959 wrote, "I have known Bahaism and individual Bahaists for nearly half a century. I have the greatest respect and sympathy for their ideals."[35] A month later he wrote Holley, "Mr. Arthur L. Dahl writes me that you would like to reprint my recent letter in the *Baha'i World* and in *Appreciations of the Baha'i Faith*. I would consider it an honor."[36] Also in 1959 he wrote his former student, Arthur L. Dahl, Jr., saying, "Among the documents you sent me a while ago, there was a ten-point statement of Baha'i policy . . . including world government and an international language. I happen to be in full agreement with that statement, and I know of no church, group or party with which I am in such complete accord."[37]

Professor Harry Rathbun of the School of Law and the Graduate School of Business described himself as a student and "a green, immature kid" at the time he heard 'Abdu'l-Bahá. He remembered that the occasion was unusual, that the hall was packed, and that Jordan made the introduction. Despite his youth Rathbun was apparently impressed by the Master's personality.

Clearly, the day was a memorable one for all involved. During my years as a Stanford student in 1923–25, I would come to see through my contacts with faculty and students that the reverberations of 'Abdu'l-Bahá's visit were still being felt. The magic of His presence and the impact of His teaching lingered on.

9

In the Wake of the Master— Experiences of the First Stanford Bahá'í Student

In the fall of 1923 I motored up from Santa Paula to enter Stanford University as a senior. I clearly remember the excitement and anticipation that swept over me as I turned into Palm Drive and saw ahead the university buildings with their terra-cotta tiled roofs and the blue mountains in the distance. This was where 'Abdu'l-Bahá had addressed a special assembly of faculty and students exactly eleven years before. If only I could have been there then!

I thought back to a day in my childhood in October 1912. My family was sitting on the front porch of our home in Los Angeles—my parents reading sections of the Sunday newspaper, and my brother the comics; I was playing with my family of twelve dolls. We all stopped and listened when my mother declared: "It says that a saintly man named 'Abdu'l-Bahá, the Son of a Prophet of God, spoke here and in San Francisco about a world religion. . . . Now he has left California."

Son of a Prophet of God? Come and gone? Could this be true? Impossible. Or was it? We were strangely stirred by the account. Had we missed an event of many lifetimes?

Two years went by before we again heard of 'Abdu'l-

Bahá. A woman named Leslie O'Keefe [Long] came to our door selling a product; she also told us about 'Abdu'l-Bahá and the Bahá'í Faith. From that day on she gave us more and more of the Message, as information about the Faith was called. When we moved to Santa Paula, she moved soon after and lived in one of our apartments on "Sunny Slope." My mother, brother, and I became Bahá'ís; much later my father joined the Faith.

Now, approaching the Quad, I recalled another experience. I was a ninth grade student; my English teacher had just graduated from Stanford. She came often to our house. One day my mother and I showed her copies of the Palo Alto papers with the articles about the Master's visit. We pointed to the headline in the 11–14 October 1912 *Daily Palo Alto Times:* "Abdul Baha Speaks at Stanford University." I was crushed and disappointed when, without looking at those spectacular accounts, she turned to an ad on the back for "The Ideal Ladies Tailoring Company" and laughed at the picture of a woman in an out-of-date long coat and a big bowl-shaped hat.

Those newspapers (before me now, brown and falling apart) were my cherished girlhood possessions. In high school I had made up my mind that when the time came for college, I would go to Stanford. 'Abdu'l-Bahá had spoken there. His spirit would linger on.

However, by some Laylí-and-Majnún, ironic twist, it was the University of California I entered in 1920.[1] My unexpected good fortune took me for three years to Berkeley, there to meet and fall in love with Ali Yazdi, and then to Stanford in 1923.

Now as I approached Roble Hall at Stanford, I had certain objectives in mind: to get a B.A., an M.A., and a teaching credential; to seek out President Emeritus David Starr Jordan and professors who had welcomed 'Abdu'l-Bahá; and, above all, as the first Stanford Bahá'í student, so far as I

knew, to spread the teachings of the Bahá'í Faith in the wake
of the beloved Master. I knew I had a responsibility, and I
welcomed it.

Soon my Bahá'í books were unpacked and put on my
desk—*Bahá'í Scriptures, Some Answered Questions, Tablets of
Abdul Baha, The Book of Ighan, The Bahai Proofs, The Oriental
Rose, Abbas Effendi: His Life and Teachings,* and *The Promulgation of Universal Peace, Vol. I.* [2] (The books in those days were
few in number, tended to be bound in black or navy, and
looked rather forbidding. There were none of the colorful
and attractive bindings we have today, but it didn't matter;
we loved the Writings.) My pictures were hung—the one of
'Abdu'l-Bahá taken in Haifa with my camera three years before, the picture of the Master taken when He was in Paris,
and the "To Live the Life" poster that had been hand lettered,
decorated, and framed. I had scarcely finished arranging my
Bahá'í effects when a troop of girls came bursting in; we had
been told by aunts and friends to look up each other. My
newfound friends glanced around the room excitedly and
shouted, "What's going on here?" I was overjoyed as they
besieged me with questions about the Bahá'í Faith and took
all my little "blue books" and leaflets. These eager girls—
Bobs; Henrietta; Ethel; my roommate, Mary; and (the next
year) Gretchen; Ruth; and Grace—became the nucleus of
the weekly meetings. For me classes and finals were inciden-
tal; weekly meetings were the important thing.

The oneness of mankind, a universal religion, the
equality of men and women were considered extreme,
visionary teachings in the 1920s. Racial equality shocked
many people, who would say, "That's too idealistic; do you
really believe it could happen?" To walk down the street
with a person of a different race, or even of a different na-
tionality, was considered rather bizarre behavior. Despite
the general conservatism, I found at Stanford quite a number
of students who were markedly responsive to the Faith.

The girls wanted to help, but where could we have

meetings? The study in my room was fine, but the general feeling was that we must have "men," which was impossible in our rooms at Roble Hall. (The idea of coed dorms was still a half century away.) When I inquired, I was told that religious groups could not meet at the Women's Clubhouse on campus, though I noted that the Christian Scientists did. It was a matter for prayer, and I repeated over and over, "God will assist all those who arise to serve Him."[3]

While I was investigating places to meet, a letter came from Kathryn Frankland saying that years before she had told a woman chiropodist in Palo Alto named Dr. Gibson about the Bahá'í Faith. When I called on the doctor, she was delighted to see a Bahá'í. As I reported in a letter to Mariam Haney, she was "'very lovely and eager for Bahai companionship and news of the activities.'"[4] The second time I visited she suggested I use her office-home for my weekly meetings. I was grateful, though a bit unnerved by the metal and leather "throne" that stood ominously in the room. Oh well! If the room were full, would it show?

My first Bahá'í "public" meeting in Palo Alto was held at Dr. Gibson's on 8 November 1923. Though I was a shy young person, I was fearless where the Faith was concerned. I boldly invited Dr. David Starr Jordan, my professors H. D. Gray and S. S. Seward, and other notables to the series that began that night. Dr. Jordan wrote to say he regretted not being able to attend the meetings because of the Thursday evening conferences in his home, but he sent "wishes for the success of your movement."[5]

The following account of the first meeting I sent to Mariam Haney. She published it as part of an article on Bahá'í activities at Stanford in the 17 December 1923 *National Baha'i Bulletin* with the comment that this record "will be one of the sweet stories connected with Baha'i history."[6]

In spite of mid-term examinations, we had a number of students present, among them a Chinese student; an officer

Marion Carpenter (left), Mary Bateman,
Barbara Probasco (sitting)

Roble Hall, Stanford University

Left to right: Barbara Probasco (in white),
Mary Bateman, (?), Marion Carpenter,
Margery Carpenter

Ruth Fowler, Gretchen Wulfing
(a niece of Kathryn Frankland)

Ethel McGough

Marion Carpenter

Left to right: Howard Carpenter, Marion Carpenter,
Ali Yazdi, Ethel McGough

of the Cosmopolitan Club; a young woman who is going to China as a missionary, and another very remarkable girl who is doing post graduate work. Mr. and Mrs. [Leroy] Ioas also came down from Burlingame to lend their loving cooperation. Mrs. [Ella] Cooper's talk was of course perfectly glorious. She herself is a heavenly soul—brilliant and severed. She spoke with such charm and magnetism, that every one simply loved her and loved what she said. . . . I could scarcely keep my eyes from her radiant face. She gave a splendid illustration of the religious situation: The Christian, Mohammedan, Buddhist, Zoroastrian and Jew, all ascending a high mountain, each one following a different path and each one expecting to find His Prophet at the top, but when they arrive they find the very same Spirit to receive them. That Spirit we recognize as Baha'u'llah. . . . So the meeting was successful and I pray it will have far reaching results. . . .

. . . Stanford *must* become illumined for the Beloved Master sent out the Cry of Universal Peace here eleven years ago.[7]

As the article stated, the next day I received many encouraging letters that made me very happy; among them was one (which may have been from the secretary of the university YMCA) that said:

I have always been much interested and impressed with the Teachings. . . . and I hope I may be able to attend occasionally. . . . If it should ever seem desirable to your group to have a more public meeting place than a private residence, I should like to suggest the —— Hall. It is our policy to make our institution as much of a community center as we can, and I am especially glad to establish contacts with such groups as yours.[8]

Further contact with residents of Palo Alto came when Mrs. Cooper introduced me to Mr. and Mrs. John Noble Blair, who lived on Cowper Street. I was invited to tea parties a number of times and had a standing invitation for tea at

4:45 p.m. to talk with them about the Faith. Together Mrs. Blair and I planned an elegant Bahá'í tea for her friends from town and mine from school; we asked Ella Cooper to speak on the Faith.[9] Again I wrote invitations to my professors and their wives. It turned out to be a lovely party and gave prestige to the weekly meetings.

The Blairs would have welcomed us each week for our meetings, but their home was far from campus. At this point the other girls and I thought it best to save the time we spent on the trip into town and hold the events in my study room at the dorm—without men.

As it became clear that we needed a broader base for our teaching of the Faith, I hoped that Dr. Jordan might help us secure the use of a room at the Women's Clubhouse, the center of student organizations. I was also anxious to talk with him about 'Abdu'l-Bahá and the Faith.

Jordan had retired in 1913 after twenty-two years as the president of Stanford. Now he was seventy-three years old and the beloved chancellor. A great, vital man with enthusiasm for life and a wealth of knowledge, he challenged the students, broadened their horizons, and helped them to understand and respect other people. His Thursday night conferences were an important part of campus life. As the students sat around the fireplace in his home, he might start off the evening's discussion by asking, "What shall we talk about tonight?" Sometimes he would answer his own question. For example, once the topic was "Idiots!" He began with superpatriots and launched into bigotry.

I felt that the time had come to interview Dr. Jordan. I requested an appointment to see him and arrived, considerably awed, at his office.

I found him to be an imposing yet gentle man. He received me kindly and immediately responded when I told him I was a Bahá'í student who had come to ask his impressions of 'Abdu'l-Bahá on His visit in 1912. He told me that he had taken pleasure in presenting the Apostle of Peace to the faculty and students, that He had spoken with convincing force on the brotherhood of man, and that the message had been enthusiastically received. I clearly remember that Dr. Jordan showed genuine appreciation of the Master's graciousness and was truly sorry that when he had been in Europe Palestine had seemed far away and his time was too short to visit Him.

We talked together about the principles and the progress of the Faith. I told him of the interest of the students and the need for a general meeting place on the Quad. He said that if I would send him a letter requesting use of the Clubhouse, he would mail it to President Wilbur himself. Not long after, I received a letter from Dr. Jordan and one from President Ray Lyman Wilbur granting permission to use the Clubhouse. (Unfortunately, these two letters have been lost.)

The Women's Clubhouse was perfect for our purpose. From then on we met there every week as long as I was at Stanford, except once—the night of the Pajamarino Rally. On the advice of the girls, and to please them, we cancelled the meeting. I still feel acute remorse when I remember what happened that Thursday night. Hundreds of boisterous, laughing pajama-clad students jostled their way in serpentine. As I rushed with the others past the Clubhouse, I heard one student at the door ask another, "Isn't there any Bahá'í meeting tonight?" An inquirer, and I wasn't there!

I received another letter of historic interest from Chancellor Jordan dated 24 April 1924. This time I had written to ask if he would speak on the Bahá'í Faith at one of his Thursday night conferences. He replied that he felt the Bahá'í Movement would be a topic of special interest but that he did not feel adequately acquainted with it to make it the subject of a conference; however, he would keep it in mind.[10]

He did, indeed, do just that, for at two subsequent conferences he spoke wisely and sympathetically on the Bahá'í

Faith. I did not have the opportunity to hear him because of my Thursday Bahá'í meetings, but many students did and told me about his comprehensive talks.

Dr. Jordan was a true friend of the Faith. Among his generous and encouraging acts, there is yet another I must record: early in 1924 he offered us the use of his own office in the quadrangle for Bahá'í meetings. We were most grateful but continued to meet at the Clubhouse.

Bahá'í events were announced weekly in the two dining rooms at Roble Hall. They also were written up each week, often both before and after the meeting, in the Dippy—*The Stanford Daily*. We had a friend on the staff, and the articles were excellent, often attracting new people to our meetings.

I began holding Bahá'í "Feasts" with my friends in February 1924. (In those early days we had no idea that the Nineteen Day Feast was for Bahá'ís only, as Shoghi Effendi later made clear.)[11] For these occasions I bought a blue tea set and a Chinese serving plate. Like manna from heaven, frequent packages of luscious candied figs and orange peel, salted nuts, cookies, and tangerines arrived from my parents at "Sunny Slope." I selected the devotional readings with care. These Feasts at Roble were popular, especially the one at which my mother, visiting me from Santa Paula, spoke in her dear, winning way. I continued to hold them, as well as the weekly meetings, throughout my time as a student at Stanford.

My roommate, Mary, and I faithfully observed the Fast in 1924; we enjoyed the early prayers together; breakfast was an odd repast—two quarts of milk procured from the Roble kitchen each night. The Fast in 1925 at Manzanita came during hectic days: the English literature examination covering the Anglo-Saxon period through modern times was at hand, and I was making big plans for Jináb-i-Fáḍil's visit. Grace and I rose very early for prayers and for breakfast prepared on my hot plate and waffle iron. At dawn we went to our desks until class time.

In the spring of 1924 my friends and I invited our much-loved dean of women, Mary Yost, to a Feast. It was one of the high points in my Stanford experience. An account of the occasion, based on my letter to Mariam Haney, was published in the 15 September 1924 *National Baha'i Bulletin:*

> I know you would like to hear about our last big meeting. I invited Dean ———— of whom we are all so proud. The meeting was in my room—an informal Feast. The Dean asked us to tell her about the Movement, for she knew little more about it than the Name. This all of us combined to do and evidently made an impression, for the next day she told one of the Professors that she had been to a Baha'i meeting with the girls and that "we certainly had vision."[12]

After the Feast we all trooped up sorority row in an overflowing exuberance of spirit to take her home. As we said good night, Miss Yost cordially invited us to have a Bahá'í meeting at her home at the beginning of the fall quarter in 1924. Of course, we accepted her invitation. The meeting was memorable—the setting beautiful, both Dean Yost and Ella Cooper lending grace to the occasion, and Aunt Ella giving the Message that night with a special glow. Subsequently, Mary Yost served as one of the patronesses for the March 1925 Conference for World Unity in San Francisco.

One of my professors whom I invited to our meetings was Samuel Swayze Seward, Jr. Referred to as "Sammy" by his adoring students, he was the favorite of the English Department. A scholarly man with a little goatee and a great sense of humor, he had received a degree at Columbia University and had studied at Oxford. In addition, he had been decorated several times for bravery under fire in relief and ambulance service during the First World War. He was a Swedenborgean and a man of peace.

As a teacher he brought out the best in his students; we slaved over our themes and cherished his comments. His wisdom went beyond the rules in the book. For example, in his course called Teacher's English we were learning how to correct high school compositions. My brother had sent me a clever paper he had written, which I edited with such a heavy hand that it would have discouraged the most earnest of budding authors. Seward taught me how to look at the good, bring out the best, and confine the corrections to only a few points at a time.

In 1912 Seward had been greatly attracted to 'Abdu'l-Bahá when he heard Him speak at the student assembly, and again when he was seated next to Him at dinner. He glimpsed the spirit of the Master, but it must be said that he was more completely convinced by His wit during the lively exchange at dinner.

One day after class Seward asked if I had time to come into his office. For an hour and a half he regaled me with his recollections of that day in October 1912. I especially wanted to know how the students had reacted to such a holy man. "With great respect and interest," he said. "'Abdu'l-Bahá won them!" Seward recalled that one of the dinner guests had asked how He liked California, and the reply had been that He liked it very much; its climate and vegetation reminded Him of Palestine. Seward related several stories illustrating 'Abdu'l-Bahá's spontaneous humor and repartee and describing the night at 925 Waverly Street in Palo Alto.[13] Some of this I shared with my parents in my letters home.[14]

During my two years at Stanford there were other enjoyable talks in Seward's office and at his home, where I met his wife and daughters. At the end of my stay at Stanford, I ran into Sammy downtown, and we walked for a bit. He asked, "Are you going to get married now?" I replied that I was thinking about it. He took from his wallet a picture of his little daughters, Margot and Jean, and said, "This is a good reason!"

The morning after Ali and I arrived at the La Playa in Carmel on our honeymoon, we went down to breakfast. We entered the dining room as inconspicuously as possible, yet who should be there but Sammy. He came toward us with arms outstretched and gave us congratulations and a blessing we could never forget! Four years later after the Big Game in Berkeley (the traditional football game between the rivals Stanford and Berkeley) he came to see us at our home. We were very sad to read of his passing in the August 1932 *Stanford Illustrated Review.*[15]

Another of my English professors who had heard 'Abdu'l-Bahá at the student assembly and at dinner was Dr. H. D. Gray.[16] He was truly interested in the Bahá'í Faith and did a great deal to help me on campus. After he received an invitation to the first meeting, he replied that I had sent him the wrong date! It could be; I had a lot of things on my mind. Later he attended a lecture at the Clubhouse by Mr. Mason Remey, then a member of the National Spiritual Assembly. At one point as a surprise, Gray himself gave a fascinating and comprehensive lecture on the Bahá'í Faith in an English class I was taking. Afterward, he was obviously delighted at the splendid and convincing job he had done, as I shared the news with my parents in a letter home.[17] Many years later his neighbor, Mrs. Percy Martin, told me that Gray continued to be intensely interested in the Bahá'í Faith.

The coed who helped me most in spreading Bahá'í principles was Barbara (Bobs) Probasco (Bach). I met Bobs in 1923 on my first day at Roble, and she became my ally and lifelong friend. She was an intelligent, vivacious girl who enlivened every situation; she had a way of giving people nicknames that stuck, like mine—Noggs. She spoke of the Faith with courage and zest to friends, professors, and family. Excerpts from some of her letters written during vacations show her enthusiasm.[18]

1 July 1924

Speaking of Aunt Emma reminds me we recently had a talk in which she told me that of course now I didn't accept Christ—belonging to some "Hindu cult." We became ever so much more amiable when I gently changed her mind, and she even said she'd read one of the little pamphlets. She lost her antagonism and said that she had read the prayer of 'Abdu'l-Bahá that I have on my bureau every day. But Noggs, I have only one pamphlet left. Have you any more you could send me? I like to keep them with me, for so often they seem to be needed.

11 July 1924

. . . I'm glad we promised to write once a week for I feel as if I simply have to hear from you. . . . I had an old high school friend (doesn't that sound ancient) over to lunch last week and grasped the opportunity to tell her of the movement. She had heard the name from a friend of hers. . . . I gave her some of the material you sent me, and thanks a lot for sending it. She seemed very much interested and said that from what she read it seemed "water tight." Wasn't that lovely? Ruth . . . goes to Cal, is very clever and a darling kid, said she'd phone Mrs. Frankland whom I told her about and find out more about the Movement. Mother read some of the pamphlets you sent but made no comment. Still she didn't say anything derogatory either which is a favorable sign. Don't you think so? I shall just have to go to the Teaching Convention with you and your mother. I think it will be heaps of fun and terribly interesting. I love my "Little Ben," and it fits my purse just beautifully. . . .[19]

25 July 1924

I saw Helen . . . and told her of the Cause. She is a Christian Scientist . . . and seems terribly interested in the Movement. She said she and Esther decided to dedicate their lives to the cause of Universal Peace, and I think she may find her solution in the Bahá'í Cause . . . Doesn't it seem wonderful that there really are people we can work with next quarter? . . .

2 September 1924

It is so wonderful to be with the people who have given one the Message and so doubly nice when those people are Noggs and Noggs' mother.

How was the meeting Friday night? . . . Mrs. [Cordelia] Cline has meetings Monday afternoons in Burlingame . . . I saw Mr. and Mrs. [Leroy] Ioas Monday up at the tennis courts. They both seem robust and hearty and wished to be remembered to you.

We have a high school teacher with us. She's very nice and seems very interested in the "Oriental Rose" which we are reading together. I'm sure you'll like to talk to her of the Movement. . . .

In September 1924 I met Gretchen Wulfing, a niece of Kathryn Frankland. We got acquainted while standing in line for mailboxes at the little Stanford "P.O." She became a lifelong friend of my family and the Faith. Gretchen was a very real part of my Bahá'í work at Stanford; her kindness and warmth were a constant support. She was always there serving, as she has been ever since. I admired her intellectual ability and her understanding, calm way with people—gifts that later made her an outstanding director of elementary education for the Oakland Public Schools. (My grandchildren have a shelf of the textbooks Gretchen wrote for Ginn and Co. and the California Schools.) She gave her Aunt Kathryn loving help during her last years. I know of few persons who have served more people in extremity than has Gretchen.

In the early 1920s Bahá'í youth in America were few and far between. Bahá'í college students, so numerous today, were very rare in 1923—a scattering of one or two at the University of Toronto, Cornell, Howard, University of Illinois, University of Michigan, and, of course, Leland Stanford. It is small wonder that the youth were cherished and praised, and received much encouragement from older Bahá'ís.

In October 1923 Mr. William H. Randall, president and treasurer of the National Spiritual Assembly, wrote my mother, acknowledging a small contribution I had made to the National Fund on my birthday, and encouraging my service to the Faith: "It is truly blessed that this young girl entering womanhood knows the Manifestation of God, and is able to dedicate her love and her offering on her 21st birthday to this glorious Cause. May 'Abdu'l-Bahá bless her in her splendid service to the Kingdom. . . ."[20] A month later he wrote: "Particularly do I think of Marion and realize how beautiful it is not only for the Cause that she has become illumined, but how beautiful it is for her to follow the pathway of Life with the Lamp of the Bahá'í Light."[21]

While at Stanford I corresponded with Mariam Haney in Washington, D.C. She often included excerpts of my letters in her editorials in the *National Baha'i Bulletins*. Her letters poured forth such a profusion of praise that to quote from them with even the barest semblance of modesty requires a number of ellipses; I quote one in part to bring back the sweetness of a devoted early believer:

> Strange! I was just wondering when o when! some dear friend would be in that University holding aloft the Standards of Divine Truth! It was a very remarkable experience to open your letter and proceed to read of the lovely services you are rendering. . . . I love you so very much. I love the . . . qualities which you manifest, I LOVE your ALIVE spirit which I feel even in Washington! . . . wherever you are, you seem to SHINE for the Bahá'í Cause. . . .
> . . . I was thrilled when I read . . . how you persevered and determined to start the work there, and that Mrs. Cooper decided to come down for the first meeting. This is just per-

fectly thrilling news, for I know how Mrs. Cooper can attract. . . . our Divine Master has promised the most great confirmations upon the head of the person who strives to spread the Message. . . . And our Beloved Guardian will be so pleased to hear about this effort at that great University. . . . I can't help think[ing] how much I had Leland Stanford on my mind, and now our beloved Marion is there and we know . . . there will be a LIFE there that the students will wonder about, even if they do not understand.

Years ago I expected every one to believe the Message the moment they heard it, for it has always been so absolutely REAL to me, more true and more real than this existence of ours,—and I used to almost want to shake people and make them wake up. Now, however, I have come to realize that we can lead people gently along the path. . . . I think now it is marvellous to watch "the growth of the soul" on its journey toward GOD. . . .

. . . I pray the dear Master to send you successive confirmations. If I can do anything to serve you at any time, just please let me know. I am ready joyfully to do anything within my power.

Under separate cover I am sending you a little contribution of literature with my love because the lovely work you have attempted has greatly touched my heart. . . .

P.S. Please keep me advised as to how you progress with the work there.[22]

Several articles in the *National Baha'i Bulletin* shared accounts of my Feasts, meetings, contacts with students, faculty and residents of Palo Alto, as well as the support given me by other Stanford students, including my brother.

From January to September 1925 my brother Howard was a freshman at Stanford, and I was a graduate student. It was an exciting time that I remember with nostalgia.

Howard was special in our family, and we loved him dearly. When he was an infant and later as a young child, he had barely survived pneumonia; we marveled at his courage and strength of character. An obstacle to him was simply something to be overcome. He finished high school early, then undertook to build a strong physique by a strenuous regimen of gymnastics, tennis, and diet. He learned to play the coronet for his health and for pleasure. Having succeeded in helping himself, he organized the boys in the neighborhood in a program of calisthenics and proper food, and no candy bars, to the amazement of their mothers.

HOWARD LUXMOORE CARPENTER
Marion Carpenter's brother, and the
second Bahá'í to attend Stanford University

My brother grew up in the Faith; he became a confirmed Bahá'í as a teenager through conversations with Howard MacNutt. The MacNutts and Mrs. Julia Grundy came to our home in Santa Paula as a teaching team in November 1924—the MacNutts to speak and Julia to sing. Ministers and neighbors gathered to hear them. My mother wrote me at the time:

Howard is a dear and is taking a keen interest in the coming of the MacNutts. . . . I have rented . . . the Glen City Theater for a 3 o'clock lecture, and we are doing all in our power to advertise it. Howard has written forty-eight letters of invitation today and is sending them at his own expense. He also wrote up the notice for the paper, and the best thing of all, he went over to Mr. Humbert today and asked him if he would tell his class in P[hysical]. S[cience]. to go to the lecture and take notes and give them extra credit. All his own idea.[23]

A second letter reported further on the effect of the Mac-Nutts' visit:

The MacNutt party with Howard added to it left about 11 o'clock for Hollywood. We really had a heavenly time, and I think our family received the most good out of it. Your father

HOWARD MACNUTT AND FRIENDS
Seated, left to right: Howard Carpenter, Fred Barbour (Babo)
Middle row, third from right: Howard MacNutt; *sixth from right,* Shahnaz Waite

was all attention, and Howard dear was simply carried away. He thought we should both go to the City [Los Angeles] and attend the meetings, said it was a chance of a lifetime. . . . Mr. MacNutt asked him to join the party, which he did with such a shining face.[24]

In a third letter Mother added:

It has been worth more to Howard than a year's college work to be with Mr. MacNutt. He is really a wonderful man with a spiritual vision.[25]

Five weeks later Howard was registered at Encina Hall, Stanford. He created something of a stir by requesting a Japanese roommate. Asked why, he replied, "Because I am a Bahá'í." Yoshio was a fine friend; he and other of Howard's classmates attended our meetings.

Howard was a brilliant, witty student who saw half-truths and prejudices for what they were. On the one hand, he was outspoken and satirical; on the other, he was exceedingly kind and gentle. He had a rare balance of humor and reverence, of intelligence and faith. It was fun having him on campus—we saw each other every day—and we worked together for the Faith. He was so full of joie de vivre, so full of promise, how could anyone have known he would die at the age of twenty-nine.

Not long ago I was upstairs in the old Stanford library and recalled a moment of decision. My brother and I had been studying together when he turned and asked me seriously what career I thought he should follow; he wanted to be of service as a Bahá'í. I immediately answered, "Study medicine. Be a doctor."

Of course he had considered this before, but from then on his path was clear. He graduated from Stanford in 1928 and entered the Stanford Medical School in San Francisco, where he received his M.D. in 1932. Married in 1929, he and his wife Marzieh Nabil were much involved in Bahá'í activities in the San Francisco area, then in Eastern Europe, and later in Persia until shortly before Howard's untimely death in 1935.

At Christmas in 1924 my father gave me an Overland coupe, which I called "Peter Pan." We used it to attend Bahá'í events and plays in the City. Early in 1925 Howard, Bobs, and I were speakers on a panel at the Western Bahá'í Conference in San Francisco. Our talks were published in *The Bahá'í Magazine: Star of the West,* March 1925, under the heading "The Larger Vision: How Three University Students See the Needs."[26] And Ali was there! A group picture shows the four of us in a row. Sheikh-Ali is holding a little girl—Farrukh Ioas.

Marion and Peter Pan

The big drive of the spring quarter in 1925 was planning a schedule for Jináb-i-Fáḍil's lectures. I interviewed the heads of several organizations, explained our purpose, and invited them to join us in sponsoring this Bahá'í speaker. In addition, I wrote to Dr. Jordan, asking if he could perhaps help me in securing a platform for him; he used his good offices and wrote to the director of programs.

It was a busy time, as there was much planning to do, the M.A. comprehensive exam was at hand, term papers were due, and it was the Fast. I lost a few pounds, but we put together an exciting series of talks, many of which I described in my letters home.[27]

The 5 March lecture was held at the Little Theater under the auspices of the Bahá'ís, the Education Club, and Women's Education Club, the YWCA, and the Chinese Students Club. There were other meetings, too, including one in the lobby of Roble Hall for Sunday vespers—for both men and women—where Jináb-i-Fáḍil spoke on proofs of the exis-

Bahá'í youth of Northern California at Western Bahá'í Conference
in San Francisco, 1925
Front row, left to right: Kazuo Kaibe, Masao Yamamoto,
Michiaki Yamamoto, (?), Fumiko Yamamoto, (?), Margaret Rutledge
Middle row: Ali Yazdi holding Farrukh Ioas, (?), Howard Carpenter,
Marion Carpenter, Barbara Probasco, (?), (?), (?), (?),
Marion Holley, (?), (?) Ioas, Emma Lou Weaver, Nadeen Cooper
Back row: Lorne Matteson, Hiroshi Yamamoto, Shinji Yamamoto

tence of divinity. I was very excited over the response to the Faith, and wrote to tell Shoghi Effendi. I also offered to serve in Haifa or Persia.

In response, Shoghi Effendi through Dr. J. E. Esslemont, his secretary, wrote a long letter full of excellent suggestions for college teaching. It was followed by an inspiring section written by the Guardian himself.

> c/o Shoghi Effendi,
> Persian Colony, Haifa,
> Palestine, 3rd May, 1925

To Miss Marion Carpenter
1209 Stanford University
California

Alláh-u-abhá!

Dear Bahá'í Sister,

Shoghi Effendi was greatly interested and pleased by your letter of March 31st—so much so that he had it translated into Persian and read at a meeting of the friends. We are delighted to hear that you have managed to establish a regular weekly Bahá'í meeting in the Club House in the campus and we pray that it may become permanent and grow in numbers and influence, and that soon you may have a Local Spiritual Assembly in the University.

I was greatly interested lately in reading a book called "The Life Changers", by Harold Bigbie, describing a movement among University Students for a consecrated Christian life, initiated by a man called Frank Buckmann [Buchman], which has already become international and seems to have achieved really remarkable results in many cases. Mr. Buckmann [sic] and a party of his friends called on Shoghi Effendi a few months ago. I hope this start you have made at Leland Stanford University may be the beginning of a work among University undergraduates that will spread to other Universities and become something much bigger even than that of Mr. Buckmann [sic] and his group of "Life-changers." If, as we believe, Bahá'u'lláh is the prophet of the new age in which we live, then in the light of His teachings and in the strength of the new spiritual outpouring through Him, we ought to achieve even greater things than are possible to those who walk in the light of the "old dispensation" and have not yet become fully aware of the value of the New Revelation.

We hope that soon you may find opportunities of carrying the message to the undergraduates of other universities, or of linking up with Bahá'í students at other Universities and encouraging them to start Bahá'í meetings also. Then inter-university meetings of Bahá'í groups could be arranged, exchange of speakers and so on, and from this germ you have started an organization might grow that would have very powerful and far-reaching effects. A "summer school" or Bahá'í Camp for undergraduates in Vacation time might prove very valuable.

We are very glad to hear that the lectures given by Mr. Remy [Remey], Mrs. Cooper, Jináb-i-Fádil and others were so successful and that your friend . . . has already become a devoted and active Bahá'í.

Entire and selfless devotion is what is most needful. The brighter our torch burns, the more light will it give and the more readily will it impart its blaze to others. It is fine too that you have the cooperation of your brother Howard, and of friends on the staff of the college paper.

The blessings of Bahá'u'lláh and the Beloved Master will assuredly be with you in this work and Shoghi Effendi and the friends here will offer heartfelt prayers that you may be richly confirmed in your service to the Kingdom.

Shoghi Effendi does not think it necessary for you to come to Haifa at present. His correspondence and other duties leave him very little time for translation work, and the Girls School on Mt. Carmel cannot be started until there is a good deal more money in hand for it. Conditions in Persia are at present too unsettled to make it advisable for you to go there. So it seems as if, for the near future, it would be better for you to work in America, where there is certainly ample opportunity. We pray that you will be clearly guided to whatever God would have you do, and we hope you will keep us informed of your activities, from time to time, so that we may keep in as close touch as possible with you and your group of co-workers.

Shoghi Effendi was very pleased to see the articles by your brother, Barbara Probasco and yourself in the March Star and hopes that you will all three be enabled to do great service to the Cause both by tongue and pen.

With kindest regards and best wishes in which Shoghi Effendi and all the friends here join,

Your brother in the service of the Beloved,

J. E. Esslemont

My precious fellow-worker:

Your letter with its refreshing news rejoiced my heart. Surely the seeds which our Beloved has so abundantly sown in the fertile soil of that great University are germinating under your loving care and I trust great results will be speedily achieved. I would be delighted to learn of the formation of a regular, elected, Spiritual Assembly in the heart of that far-famed seat of learning and assure you of my keen desire to help it grow in power and influence in any way I can. As to your future career, I feel that for the present, until the conditions in Persia are stabilized you should concentrate your energies and efforts on publicity work, through the spoken as well as the written word. I will not fail to pray for you from the bottom of my heart and assure you of my deep appreciation of your much-valued efforts.

Shoghi[28]

I was greatly buoyed up by these letters. I could see clearly the direction I should take during, and after, one more quarter at Stanford.

The halcyon years that Ali and I had spent serving the Cause at the University of California had ended in June 1923. Stanford abounded in men, and coeds were few and very popular because of the "quota" system. But among the "roughs" with their dirty cords and droopy socks, no one came near measuring up to Sheikh-Ali. How I missed him! Meanwhile, he was far away in the High Sierras on his first civil engineering job for the Southern Pacific Railroad and terribly lonely.

One day chief engineer D. J. Russell, a very kind man, who was then in the mountains (and who later became president of the company), looked at Ali and asked him if he were homesick. When Ali answered, "You might call it that," Mr. Russell wired headquarters for a railroad pass and gave him time off with pay to come and see me.

Another time Ali was sent down to the Southern Pacific Hospital in San Francisco because he was ill. As soon as he could get out of bed, he left the hospital without notice and headed for Palo Alto to call for me at Manzanita Hall. I was so overcome with excitement that I had to ask my roommate, Grace, to entertain him while I tried to recover my equilibrium. We had a few hours together before he went back to the hospital to be scolded by the nurses, get well, and return to the mountains.

It was a time of separation, but there were letters back and forth. Boxes of long-stemmed roses were sometimes at my door when I came in from classes, and I sent books to the Sierras. It was also a time of anxiety: consent from our parents to marry, as is required by Bahá'í law, seemed unobtainable.[29] I was vacillating because our future together was unclear, but Ali always had faith. With both of us praying, he was transferred to San Francisco.

A sampling from Ali's letters written during these difficult years shows the spirit of a totally dedicated young believer—his worship of the Manifestation, his gratitude, his wonder at the beauty of the world, his manifold interests, his eternal optimism, his abiding faith, and his love— qualities he never lost. The excerpts also show how he encouraged me, whether from the mountains or by my side, praising without stint any small service I performed for the Cause.[30]

CISCO
21 October 1924

You want to know where I am located "anyway." I am in the High Sierras, 6,300 feet above sea level, 186 miles from San Francisco, 9 hours by train. Is that specific? . . .

Yesterday I took a walk up the track and visited the bridges

on which work has been started. It was about 5 o'clock and
Marion! You should have been here! The mountains were at
their best, the climate was mild, and the sun just setting. Rave
on! But I enjoyed it immensely and in my enthusiasm recited
my prayers aloud. I do that quite often. . . .
    . . . I nearly died laughing over the newspaper clippings
you sent me. Can you imagine? Before ending let me congratulate you on the Bahá'í work you're doing—simply
wonderful, but I am not surprised.

TRUCKEE
5 November 1924

Last Sunday I took the train to Cisco, which is the nearest
post-office, and asked the lady at the desk if I had any mail.
"Let me see," she said, "I th-ink you have a letter; I am not
sure tho." And she took a big bundle of letters and started
reading the names off. But mine didn't seem to be in the list
until the very last envelope. This she held up and with a smile
on her face slowly uttered the verdict: "And *this* is the one we
have all been waiting for!" I forgave her on the spot, for I recognized the handwriting.
    Well, there was good news in it and lots of it. The
entertainment in your room, the good time you're having,
your father's visit, the new Corona [typewriter], the Paris
dresses and the prospect of a new car . . . *and* you're going
with me to the Big Game [between Stanford and Berkeley]! . . .
    I was awfully glad to hear of the good time you had with
your father, but I had to laugh at your "He must be fond of
me." How could he help it?!! It's a good thing that you became such a splendid driver, now that you are going to have a
machine all your own. . . .
    A word about the newspaper clippings. The simple reason
I found them *funny* is that I didn't realize the fact that Aḥmad
[Sohráb] was a prince.[31] You remember of course that the announcements of the Bahá'í Meeting was in a whole *Daily Palo
Alto,* not a clipping. And that is the thing that made me laud
your activities in the Cause. Is it all clear now?
    And now about the Big Game. I am not going to say how

happy I was to learn that you could come with me; I'll leave this to your own judgment. I'll also leave it to you to arrange the time after the game. A few suggestions might be helpful, therefore—How would you like to have dinner at the "States," then go to a good show (you'll make the choice), then end with a dance at some hotel in the city.

CISCO
6 February 1925

I expect to be in Berkeley Saturday afternoon, Feb. the 14th and stay until Sunday evening. . . . I don't know a thing about the program arranged for Jináb-i, but will soon be informed. . . . I am so glad you can stay in Berkeley where we can be together and still be close to San Francisco. And I want you to go with me to a symphony concert . . . if there is any given by the San Francisco Symphony Orchestra. . . . And I haven't danced with you for ages, but I don't dare suggest that, *this time.*

Marion, I am seriously thinking of resigning my position up here; no use of wasting my time in the woods. I have a little plan in mind, but I won't consider it before I hear what you think of it. It's rather daring, but it's time I woke up. . . .

Thanks very much for the reading suggestions. Think I'll start with "Portrait of a Lady."

CISCO
9:00 p.m.
25 February 1925

There are a thousand ways I could start this letter, but none would come even near showing you how happy I am. Shall I tell you the cause of all this? Well, I had a birthday gift today; a book [*An American Idyll*] and a little card in it! I was so elated, that it was a full half hour before I realized I hadn't thanked 'Abdu'l-Bahá for them, and I was ashamed of myself. Then I went out and looking at the beautiful snowclad mountains, bathed in sunshine, I thanked the Manifestation, and thanked and praised and thanked!

I expect to start on the book tomorrow, but while cutting the sheets today (they were stuck together) I couldn't avoid seeing a few words throughout the book, and I gather from them, that the U.C., Persia and a university in Germany figure in it; that gives it a familiar background. Then on the cover, it says: "a life story of Love and Achievement," etc., etc. I can hardly wait to read it.

CISCO
10 March 1925

Last Sunday, I received a few college papers from #1209, whoever *that* is; but today, I had a letter from one Marion Carpenter #1209 etc., . . . and everything is rosy again.

I am awfully glad to hear that Jináb-i's talks were well received; glad for the Cause and for you. It is remarkable how you could place notices for these talks in such conspicuous places in the Daily Palo Alto. In one copy, they were announced in three different places; you are a great little girl, Marion!

Hope you will do as well in Anglo-Saxon. Just imagine you like the horrid thing, and it will be easier. Aren't I rich in advices! Would I were an Anglo-Saxon knight of old; then I would put on my best armor and come down to help you. As it is all I have to offer are my prayers, but *they* are heartfelt. Here's for your success!

Have I read "An American Idyll" yet? Rather! And Marion, I had such a happy time reading it! But it isn't too good to be true. Their love was great, but I know of a greater love than theirs. And I know of a great treasure they did not possess, so I believe their "record can be broken" athletically speaking. That did not detract from my enjoying the book. The walks they had together in utter happiness, the special whistle, the affected limping, meaning that he had peanuts in his pockets, the babies falling into the Italian fountain, while they were visiting some German prof., the way the bones of their Sunday chicken would be cleaned of all traces of meat, *and* their subsisting on food samples!!! Naive and therefore, enjoyable. We should have read this book together. . . .

I am trying to get a job in San Francisco. Please pray that I
succeed, Marion. . . . Had a letter from my father; he says
they were all very happy to hear that I had such a good time at
your home last Christmas, and they send you their Love.

By summer quarter I was writing to Ali in San Francisco!

MARION to ALI

28 July 1925

Would you like to come down to the meeting next Wednesday . . . ? It begins at 7:00. Sometime I'd be awfully glad if
you'd take charge of a meeting on "what is a Bahá'í?" . . .
I have to go and call on some Bahá'í prospects that live on
the campus, a mother with a daughter in school, whom they
wrote me about from the City. I hope to have luck with them.
Tomorrow afternoon I'm being taken to a fashionable tea
by Mrs. John Noble Blair at the home of Mrs. Colonel Jones.
Thirty-five "interesting . . . [ladies]" are to be there. I shall
wear gloves and refrain from saying anything intelligent. I
hope you didn't ruin my hat so that I can't wear it.

ALI to MARION

SAN FRANCISCO
6 a.m.

31 July 1925

I would love to come . . . to your meeting next Wednesday
and unless something unforeseen and uncontrollable hap-
pens, I shall arrive on the S. P. train at 6:30.
CAN'T you come with me to Geyserville? I'd take [you] in
the train or bus and bring you back Sunday evening early. I
think the trip would do you good. Will call you up this afternoon at 5:15 and ask you about it.

That quarter Ali came often to the Farm, as the Stanford
campus was known.[32] When he spoke on "What is a Bahá'í?"
at the Clubhouse, my friends were immensely impressed.

Time at Stanford was running out for me, but there were still some very special occasions. My life has been filled with golden Bahá'í days without number, and John Bosch's seventieth birthday party at Geyserville is surely one of them. How clear are the recollections of that beautiful day: the going, the coming, the people, the emotions.

Sunday morning, 2 August 1925, I arose early and was dressed by 5:40 a.m. Roble Hall was absolutely quiet; all the girls were sleeping. I raised the curtain and looked down from the third floor window; a certain dear, romantic young man was there in the courtyard looking up, and I waved. Ali had come down from the City by train to get me. We and all the believers from miles around were going to Geyserville to wish John Bosch a happy seventieth birthday. A white fog closed around us like a veil as we walked briskly into Palo Alto, chattering excitedly.

It was an adventure, not an easy trip, to the Bosches', for Geyserville is located some 130 miles from Stanford. There was only one train out of San Francisco, with many connections, and we had to catch it. My letter home shared our excitement and the details of the day.[33] About a hundred Bahá'ís from the Bay Area were there, gathered under the big Douglas fir. The tables were laden with grapes, plums, and peaches, and there was a huge birthday cake.

John Bosch came out, looking very distinguished in a white serge suit, white linen vest, and Panama hat. He was handsome with his white hair, moustache, and beard. As he greeted us, he looked lovingly at each one with his clear, twinkling eyes. Louise Bosch, fair and beautiful, was fifteen years younger than John. In a sheer white summer dress and a big picture hat over her curly hair, with her blue eyes shining and smiling, there was an aura about her. They were an ideal couple; we all adored them.

There were talks that day by Leroy Ioas, Orcella Rexford, and Sheikh-Ali Yazdi. I recall that Ali spoke about the Bahá'í Summer School he had attended in Esslingen, Ger-

JOHN D. BOSCH

with handsome white beard, seated right of center, with his wife Louise to his left, on the occasion of his seventieth birthday, 2 August 1925, Geyserville, California. Marion Carpenter and Ali Yazdi (standing directly back of the Bosches) left Stanford at dawn to catch two trains, a taxi, and a ferry to Geyserville, returning to the dormitory after Marion's lock out (curfew) time but finding the door still open by a happy coincidence.

many. He made us feel that the love of the Bahá'í friends was the same anywhere in the world. I was an impromptu speaker.

Late in the afternoon we started the relay trip back to the university that ended in a mad dash up Palm Drive just in time to avoid a lock out, or curfew, at the dorm. Ali's letter to me a few days later showed he, too, had enjoyed that historic second day of August.

ALI to MARION

SAN FRANCISCO
6:30 a.m.

4 August 1925

I started to write you last night, but I still was a "little" tired, and I didn't want my letter to reflect the mood. Anyway, I love to write in the early morning, when I am rested and fresh, when everything is asleep, and the air is cleanest. . . . Then I remember the many early morns, scattered all over the Earth, when I went out to face Nature, alone; came in touch with the intangible, and had flying glimpses of what real happiness could be! Some day, Marion, I'll take you out in the early morn, where Nature is beautiful, and tell you more about it.

But again I am waxing poetic (in spirit only, not in expression!)

So you did make Roble before the door was locked, *after all!* . . . I was proud of you, all day. You may not see it, but you were a *great* help in making all those train and boat connections. . . . You don't know how I enjoyed this bit of cooperation, how I enjoyed that walk at 10 p.m., and every minute we had together. But I must stop this raving, or you'll "bawl me out"![34]

Right up until the time I left Stanford there were weekly meetings and opportunities to teach as recorded in my letters to Ali and his to me.[35]

MARION to ALI

11 August 1925

This afternoon I went to tea at Mrs. Blair's in Palo Alto. I met some lovely older people, some that I knew before, and a nice girl who is an assistant in the Chemistry Department. We sat out on a patio overlooking a beautiful garden. . . .

You didn't mention coming down Wednesday; so evidently Mr. [Howard] Hurlbut can't come. Perhaps you will pray for me a little at 7 o'clock.

ALI to MARION

14 August 1925

6:30 a.m.

In the first place, I want to ask you if you would like to go to a matinee of "No, No, Nanette," Sat. the 22nd. . . . I'll get all the dope about the dinner dance at the Palace or St. Francis tomorrow sometime. . . .

What sort of meeting did you have last Wednesday? I hate to confess it, but I forgot all about Hurlbut.[36] Will you forgive me? It must be hard to take the responsibility of the meetings in an intellectual center like Stanford for two years as you did. I am most, most proud of you, and I not only admire you, but hope that someday in the *not* distant future, I'll be able to stand by you, and work with you; even take charge of the meetings, as often as you'd want me to and a lot more.

MARION to ALI

17 August 1925

Of course the "speaker of the evening" will be met at the train. . . . Howard [Carpenter] will be there, so don't go running away. I am looking forward to this meeting. You have no idea what a relief it is to me.

At my last weekly Bahá'í meeting on the Farm, I explained to my college friends that it was the wish of Shoghi

Effendi that a Spiritual Assembly be established at Stanford. Hardly anyone was twenty-one years old, but there *were* nine attracted students who agreed to carry on. They elected officers for the following year for a Bahá'í college club—the name had not yet been coined, but that is what it was.

To have been at Stanford in the wake of the Master had been a blessed experience. Now it was time to leave academe; I must try my mettle.[37] Shoghi Effendi's words were fresh in my mind: "I will not fail to pray for you from the bottom of my heart. . . ."[38]

Ali had come down the night before I left with a bon voyage gift from Goldberg Bowen, a fancy grocery store in San Francisco, but we could not say good-bye. One consideration was uppermost between us: we must see what continued prayer, patience, love, and respect for our parents might yet achieve. Sure enough, by the following May (1926) the Guardian was writing me to congratulate us on our engagement:

> My dear fellow-worker:
> May this projected union prove happy, enduring and fruitful. I will supplicate on your behalf at the holy Shrines that your heart's desire may erelong be fulfilled, that your life in future may stand as a living testimony to the harmony and fellowship which the Faith of Bahá'u'lláh has established between the East and the West.[39]

On 31 August 1926, exactly one year and a day after my departure from Stanford, Ali's and my hearts' desire was fulfilled: we were married!

10

Letters Home, 1923–1925

My mother was not above reading my letters to friends before her Friday night meetings—and she kept them. It is strange to come on them now after these many years. A selection tells firsthand what it was like in those exciting early days on the Quad at Stanford. [1]

November 1923

Last Wednesday I went to Mrs. [John Noble] Blair's for tea, wore my brown velvet dress, rajah hat, etc. Mrs. Blair was very nice, and we had a lovely time together. Her apt. is most attractive—decorated with things she has collected on her travels, I imagine. I enjoyed the way she exercised the gentle art of conversation—determining the other person's interest and starting from that line-up. After we had talked for awhile, she asked me what I was most interested in, and I told her Religion. You can imagine how time flew after that. She told me how they met the Dreyfus-Barneys on their way to India . . . a year and a half ago . . . and from them first heard about the Bahá'í Movement. Then later in Pasadena they were guests of friends of Mrs. [Amelia] Collins and entertained with them in Mrs. Collins' flat. They were tremen-

161

dously impressed with a wonderful painting they saw there and asked . . . about it. Thus they heard about 'Abdu'l-Bahá. When they went to S[an] F[rancisco], they attended the meetings and met Mrs. Cooper who called on them, etc. Although Mrs. Blair claimed to know very little about the Movement, she asked lots of intelligent questions. Mr. Blair came in later, and he also is much interested—is going to give a talk on the Bahá'í Religion to a group of men who have a club in Palo Alto. When they heard that Mrs. Cooper was coming to speak soon, they offered their apartment and began counting the chairs and planning for more. It will make a very nice setting for a meeting. . . .

Mr. [Leroy] Ioas is coming to speak this Tuesday night, and I will have the meeting at Dr. Gibson's.[2] I have just sent out . . . announcements.

The Blairs live at Cowper Court, but it is way down in Paly [Palo Alto], so it doesn't relieve the situation for weekly meetings. . . . Mrs. Blair said to come any afternoon for tea, for she always has it at 4:45.

November 1923

I wrote to Mrs. [Shahnaz] Waite about this Dr. Curry, who held the Bible discussion groups here last week, and who was so glad to hear about the Bahá'í Movement in the hour and a half talk we had together, and asked her to get in touch with him at the U.S.C. Y.M.C.A. . . . this weekend.

In regard to your meetings—no one knows as well as I do just how you feel. . . . I think the Greatest Name repeated quietly and calmly and confidently within our hearts is the antidote 'Abdu'l-Bahá intended we should use. . . . I am afraid we are not yet arrived at the "Valley of Contentment" "after crossing the ascents of this lofty, exalted journey."[3] I wish we could both learn to be *content* with the opportunities God has given us to serve His Cause.

Last Tuesday night our meeting was so nice, but absolutely uncalculated. I had the reading picked out on the International Tribunal as a timely subject, now that everyone is discussing the Bok Peace Plan, and expected quite a bunch. But after dinner one by one the girls told me they had to study for an ex[am] or *wash their hair*. . . . I decided I didn't "give a darn" (to put it crudely) if *nobody* came, because I was crazy to read the last *Star [of the West]*. Then at 7:30 Mary came in and asked if anyone was coming. I said I didn't know but would wait a half hour, and if no one came, and she wanted to come in and crawl up on my bed, we could read or talk together. She said O.K. and went to study for half an hour. Then pretty soon Ethel came in and wanted to know who was coming. . . . Ethel wanted to know why we always had the meeting so formal and serious that they were scared to breathe. I thought that was a good criticism, and so, when Mary came, we abandoned all ceremony and had a *marvelous* spiritual meeting on subjects they suggested—just talking *chummily*. On a number of points I was able to turn immediately to the "Words" [the Bahá'í writings] and read.

If you get this Tuesday, think of us lots at 8 o'clock for Mr. Ioas is to speak.

17 January 1924

Thanks for the *Star* and the clean waist. . . .

I had a nice letter from Dr. Gardner, the University Chaplain, in answer to some leaflets I sent him. He said, "Be sure I sympathize with you in your effort to spread the good news of the Bahá'í Movement. Anything which will remove prejudice, exalt spirituality, and lift our minds to the great universal ideas must do good. I hope you found a home for your meetings. With all good wishes, I am yours sincerely, D. Martin Gardner." Wasn't that nice?

I get through [finals] Mar. 21 at noon—Naw-Rúz.

Won't it be nice if we can go to the Feast in the City? The Fast will come just before and during final exams, but it will give me time to study. I know I shall wish you were here to help me keep it.

. . . so many many thanks for my darling pajamas that look so Chinesey.

5 February 1924

Had hoped to tell you before this how my first Feast went off. There were seven of us present (in the study), and one more came quite late. Two of the girls were new, one quite new, and the rest my faithfuls. It really went off very well due to the fact, I suppose, that I had everything (both reading and food) prepared and thought out beforehand. In the May 1923 *Star* on p. 60, there are some excellent qualifications given by 'Abdu'l-Bahá for the spiritual teacher.[4] One of them is that the teacher's thoughts must be at peace . . . "Otherwise there will be no result whatever."[5] It surely does help.

I tried to make the meeting very easy and informal and happy. Before I read the prayer for the Feast, I told the girls about the Nineteen Day Feasts and how they are held in all the Bahá'í Assemblies for the purpose of creating love.[6] . . . (When I heard Jináb-i-Fáḍil speak to a meeting of friends in S.F. he said that in the book of Aqdas it is decreed that the friends should come together once a month [every 19 days] for a Feast. "God has desired to establish love in your hearts by all the earthly and heavenly means." . . .) After we had the prayer, I gave a little explanation of the Movement. . . . Then the different girls read the selections . . . which I had given them to read over to themselves previous to the meeting. Bobs takes public speaking and reads wonderfully well. I gave her the notes from Miss Thompson's diary, "Abdul-Baha's First Days in America" (found in *Star*, Vol. VIII, p. 32) which are so glorious.[7]

Mary read excerpts on "Prayer" from one of the *Stars*, Ethel the parables . . . of Ios, and Henrietta . . . "Heavenly Artists," an account of the meeting of an artist, an actress, and a musician with 'Abdu'l-Bahá. . . . We each read from the Tablet of Bahá'u'lláh which came with the last letter of Shoghi Effendi . . . closed with the other Feast prayer, and proceeded to indulge in the material feast.

I had hot chocolate with lots of marshmallows on top, buttered nut bread, candied figs (the girls love 'em, and so do I), mints, and tangerines. I also had "spiritual candies," which took very well. (Ethel did the typing for me, and I tied the verses around little chocolate sticks.)

Monday I went to Mr. and Mrs. Blair's for tea, and we made plans for Mrs. Cooper's coming next Tuesday.

Yesterday the University held a memorial service for [Woodrow] Wilson in the chapel. It was filled with students, and the service was quite impressive.

Last night I went to a Bible study class. They were taking up Mark. Dr. Morgan of the Y.M.C.A. is in charge. The most interesting idea I carried away was the correspondence between the Revelation of Christ and John the Baptist, and that of Bahá'u'lláh and the Báb. I have sometimes wondered why Bahá'u'lláh should have been a *follower* of the Báb before His declaration. The question was brought up in connection with Christ, why was He baptized by John. Dr. Morgan said it was to set the example and also in this way to graft Himself onto John's great movement, which was a good idea, I thought. There are so many conditions and events in this Day which correspond to those in the time of Christ. But it almost crushes me to listen to the "blind leaders of the blind." What do you think about this class? There is very little opportunity to give the "light" there, I'm afraid.

14 February 1924

Have been wanting to write you about the results of Mr. Remey['s] coming here. Mr. L—— a senior . . . was greatly interested. The next day he stopped me on Quad and asked where he could get books and more information. I told him at the library and that I had some I would be glad to lend him. So that night he came over. . . . One *fruit*. Wish I had time to write you about lots of things. . . . However, I am enclosing some sheets from my notebook telling about the unexpected talk I had with my favorite professor. It was a unique experience. . . .

Friday I went to see the University Librarian and prevailed upon him to request some Bahá'í books from the Library Committee. . . .

The fast will not be hard to keep because . . . I brought down Margery's el stovo which I can use in my room for [breakfast before dawn]. . . . Fortunately, dinner comes . . . late enough. . . . If only we didn't have to gobble so fast at dinner. My tongue gets all mixed up trying to masticate with such violent velocity. Why they [the girls] consume an entire meal while you would put away a cracker! I thought I was a speedy eater, but no! . . .

It might be well to send our Tablets to the Archives, but it seems a pity not to have them available. Let's talk it over during vacation.

Enclosure of 14 February 1924

Just had a real experience. If every day were as full of delightful surprises as this and yesterday and the day before, I should have to keep a diary to keep from dying of pure joy and exultation.

Sammy, that is Prof. Seward, just called forth the most enjoyable little spinal column ripples—just when I was least expecting a thrill. An hour and a half's discussion of poetic structure is stupifying, and who would have suspected that after it all Sammy was going to stop . . . and ask me into his office for a chat—if I wasn't in a hurry. Who would have been in a hurry . . . 'specially after having sent an invitation to him and his wife to attend the meeting at Mrs. Blair's last Tuesday.

Yes, that was what he wanted to speak about. His wife had received the invitation but had not known whom it was from. Afterwards a Miss —— whom Mrs. Blair invited, told Mrs. Seward of the lecture and that a Miss Carpenter was in charge. This got around to Prof. Seward and hence and wherefore.

He told me about his personal contact with . . . 'Abdu'l-Bahá. He not only heard 'Abdu'l-Bahá speak at the assembly of students but also was invited to be with Him at dinner at Mrs. Merriman's daughter's home where the Master stayed. He sat next to Him at dinner. What struck Seward especially was 'Abdu'l-Bahá's "perfectly delightful wit and humor." The Persian retinue was so . . . awed . . . that the devil in Sammy prompted him to ask some questions to which he said he got (through the interpreter) the cleverest quick retorts. He asked 'Abdu'l-Bahá if He found America to be a good field for His teachings. 'Abdu'l-Bahá very quickly replied (and Seward said he didn't like to have Him get the best of him that way), "No, the people are too self-satisfied." Our beloved 'Abdu'l-Bahá—always ready to meet people half way—and more!! Sammy's appreciation was surely not of the great spirit, but he did enjoy to the fullest the loving, laughing 'Abdu'l-Bahá.

Seward told me about this Mrs. Merriman—how she put the members of the party in every conceivable part of the house, made beds on top of tables, put a mattress on the bath tub and finally had everyone stowed away except herself. Then she found a lean-back chair which she put in the clothes closet, closed the door, and went to "bed." Mrs. Merriman told Seward about it afterwards, and I imagine time and Sammy's rhetoric added to his perfectly killing description. I asked him about Mrs. Merriman and where she lived now. He said in heaven—that he was sure she was in heaven. He described her as "a very high-strung, nervous, imaginative person who bungled a good deal. She was in charge of the Humane Society and was always having to investigate horses hitched out in the cold, and children without enough to eat. . . ."

Seward asked me if 'Abdu'l-Bahá was still living and

925 Waverly Street, Palo Alto, California,
where 'Abdu'l-Bahá and His party were overnight guests
of the humanitarian Mrs. Isabel C. Merriman at the home
of her daughter Mrs. Fredrica Marriott. After making beds
for the entire party, Mrs. Merriman found a lean-back chair for herself
and spent the night in a clothes closet.

then wanted to know who was in charge. I told him about Shoghi Effendi, and he said he was glad to know that such a fine, splendid line was enduring. He also asked about the teachings and the organization.

A Mr. Weaver came into the office and Prof. Seward introduced us. Mr. Weaver listened to our talk, and then he said he was glad to hear us talking along this line and could he have my address, etc. I also got his so I can send him notices. . . . Professor S. said, "Mr. Weaver, look here, you can be a Bahaist too, and so can everybody!"

Isn't life a glorious surprise? We never know when a Seward is going to bring out these reminiscences or a Mrs. Blair is going to . . . open her apt. because she met the Dreyfus-Barneys in India, Mrs. Collins in Pasadena and was tremendously impressed by her portrait of 'Abdu'l-Bahá, and then met Mrs. Cooper.

These contacts will go on forever. Nothing is lost in the spiritual universe any more than in the physical universe. Why not then talk when we can talk, mention the name Bahá'í whenever there's a chance, and think the Greatest Name when we can't do anything else. It all helps! I *know* it does. Alláh-u-Abhá.

Mary and Bobs are proving to be . . . [very helpful]. Mary told a Mr. Garrison that she danced with the other night that she thought she was going to be a Bahá'í. He not knowing what a Bahá'í was, she told him a little, and he said he would like to know more. So I sent him an announcement of the meeting, and he came.

Then Mary told Mr. L—— something about the Movement . . . and that same night, without knowing . . . I asked him to the meeting, and he came. . . . So we have glorious team work.

I was much touched by little Bobs' effort. With all enthusiasm she went to Miss F—— of the Citizenship Dept. and told her she was sorry she hadn't come to the Bahá'í meeting last Tuesday. (Upon Bobs' suggestion I had sent her an invitation.) She said, "Oh you are responsible for the notice I had." Bobs told her yes, that she thought she would be interested. Miss F—— said, "Well to be very frank, I'm not at all interested in religion or anything that I can't take into the laboratory and prove." I hope these familiar discouragements will not down Bobs' ardent enthusiasm. This is the 2nd time a teacher has cut her.

L—— has awakened to what it is all about. There is hope for *everyone*!

22 February 1924

I was . . . astonishingly asked as a great favor to be the speaker at the Unitarian Young People's society this Sunday night . . . on the Bahá'í Movement. Isn't that great? I hope I can do it well. . . .

At the meeting last Tuesday we had one new person present, and after the hour was over, we continued for two hours more on some very lively discussions. But since we tried to settle the economic problem, religion and science, prophecy, and a dozen other things all at once we didn't get very far even in that length of time. So we decided to go more particularly [into a topic] after this rather than raise all these questions at once. . . . The girls are very eager to know and willing to be convinced.

26 February 1924

. . . I went with Marion T——, the girl who asked me to speak at the young people's meeting of the Unitarian Church, and Mary, to the supper they had at the church. It was a crazy meal—boiled potatoes, brussels sprouts, fried fish, bread, ice cream, and sweet chocolate. . . . At eight o'clock the meeting began. . . . I talked for about three quarters of an hour and tried to give a general survey of the Cause—purpose, scope, history, principles, etc. . . . but I don't feel that I did justice to my subject. Before I had hardly started one older man went to sleep—which was amusing but scarcely flattering. The rest of them kept awake and seemed interested. . . . When I got through, they beseiged me with trick questions. I wish I had been up to snuff and perhaps I could have done better.

But I must tell you the *glad* news about today in Professor Gray's class. Gray is taking Professor Brigg's class . . . on Elizabethan Literature. . . . Gray is the one I wrote you about who told me he heard 'Abdu'l-Bahá.

Well, he was lecturing . . . on Hooker who wrote "The Ecclesiastical Polity," . . . in the 16th century, on religious problems of the day. He [Gray] told about Hooker's idea of the continuity of Divine Revelation. He then began to talk about what I immediately recognized as the Bahá'í Movement. He told about the great Bahá'í principle of belief in all the Prophets, about Bahá'u'lláh and 'Abdu'l-Bahá and spoke most highly of Bahaism in general. He told of 'Abdu'l-Bahá's speaking here at Stanford and of the impression He made upon him. In fact, he devoted the rest of his lecture to the subject, and you can imagine how thrilled I was!!

Then he asked if we had any questions and asked me if I approved of what he had said of Bahaism and if he had been fair. . . . I corrected one error and told him I thought he had been very fair and that he had inspired me to read Hooker, whereas otherwise I might have little interest in "The Ecclesiastical Polity." He said that I would surely be sore at him after reading Hooker. (I see I shall have to get busy on this ponderous volume.) Well, it was quite glorious.

After class I was approached by a girl I had a feeling might be interested. She said she was "awfully dumb" and wanted to know all about it [the Faith]. Grand chance, of course, and due to Prof. Gray. So the ball rolls and bounces along. . . .

Tuesday night most of my regular crowd had gone up to Oakland for the last Cal-Stanford basketball game. They had asked me to postpone the meeting, but, as another girl spoke to me in the morning about coming, I decided to have it anyway. So there were four of us—Henrietta, a reformed Jewess; Lydia, daughter of an Episcopal minister; Mary, Mormon extraction; and lil' me, a "heathen." For the reading I had 'Abdu'l-Bahá on "The New Day," Marjory Morten on "Segments of the Circle" (*Star*, Sept. 1, 1922), and 'Abdu'l-Bahá's "Address to the Jews" at Temple Emmanu-El in S.F. . . .[8]

Can I persuade you from keeping the "symbolic" side of the Fast this year? Remember that you should not do it if the Doctor says it would be injurious. Try to be a bit scientific . . . and not misuse your little self!

. . . I am going to a dance with Mr. L——. He is . . . not at all interesting—the "100% American" type as Prof. Seward calls them, but in spite of these defects I have agreed to trip the light fantastic with him. . . . I hope to work up some enthusiasm . . . within the next week.

4 March 1924

This is such a glory of a day—sun streaming into my room in great gobs, birds singing like mad outside, and all the world good and beautiful! I must shortly hie me to the library, but here's a note to lessen the space between here and there.

Mary had breakfast and prayers with me, and we both enjoyed it very much. . . .

Yesterday I had to go out to the hospital for a . . . treatment, and for exercise I walked clear back to the Hall . . . three miles, but I surely enjoyed it. . . . On the way I stopped at Mrs. Blair's . . . and had a nice half hour with her—refusing tea, however. She is really a lovely person to know. She told me how she met Professor Gray again a couple of weeks ago at Mrs. Jordan's tea and had a good little talk with him on the Movement in which he said he was much interested.

We are having loads of fun with the ukelele. I can tune it now and play "Miss Jane Petulia," "O Mr. Moon," "I'll Take a Box of Whitman's Chocolates," and lots of other noble airs.

10 January 1925

Last Wednesday night we had one of the most successful meetings of the year with ten present, four of them new.[9] Howard brought one of his roommates, and I brought mine. The assistant secretary of the Stanford Y.M.C.A. came and showed *great* interest. . . . Today I received a letter from him which said, "I wish to let you know that I enjoyed attending the Bahá'í meeting led by you Wednesday night. Although I do not fully understand its "raison d'être" I appreciate the worthiness of its aims. I can but wish you success in getting students to think along lines of interreligious, international, interracial friendship and harmony." Pretty good, eh?

Tomorrow night Bobs is going to take charge.

I am on the trail of "number 45." My assignment for Advanced Eighteenth Century Literature (5 in the class) is no more illuminating than that. It's a course in library research. . . . Well I've researched for two hours now and haven't the remotest idea what or who it is. Am consumed with curiosity. . . .

It is *glorious, glorious* to have Howard here! We see each other every single day, sometimes once, usually twice, and often more times each day. . . . He seems to be getting a great joy out of college life and is quite acclimated. It "shocks" me that he wears no garters and that he regularly enters his room by the window, but otherwise he seems to be unharmed. . . .

Of all the joys of this material world which I have ever experienced, Peter Pan (the ultimate name of my automobile) is the most joyous. It simply thrills me to death to have it to "get there" in. I have developed an overpowering love of driving and am constantly amazed at my utter skill. How can I ever be grateful enough? . . .

This afternoon Ruth (my roommate), another girl, and I are hostesses at the Graduate Women's Tea. . . .

Saturday night I went to a Women's Club House dance with Mr. L——. . . . Of all the . . . boys. . . . Well, anyway I wore my Paris green and black dress. . . . I forgot my house key, and L. had to crawl in the front hall window to unlock the door.

25 January 1925

Jináb-i-[Fáḍil] and his family come to S.F. the 10th of February. . . . Howard and I are planning to go up the weekend of Feb. 14 and take in as many of the talks as we can.

Mrs. Cooper and Mr. Ioas called on me twice Wednesday afternoon here at the house and also tried to find me at the library, but I was studying behind the stacks, and they didn't find me. I was most grieved not to see them, for it was the night of our meeting.

Wednesday night I thought we were going to have a very small meeting, but besides four steadies there were three new persons, one of them a Phi Beta Kappa, and all of them highly intellectual older girls who seemed intensely interested and want to come more.

I had a nice letter from Dr. Jordan this week. I wrote him asking for any help he could give me in getting Jináb-i before the student body. He said he was placing my letter in the hands of Professor Robinson, who has charge of such exercises.

8 February 1925

I had Howard and his friend W—— for lunch today. . . . This afternoon I went to the train to meet Dora Mallory. (You remember the missionary girl) who has come

back to finish up her work. . . . I like her very much.
Howard is such a comfort to me and such a help with
the Cause.

10 February 1925

H[oward] and I went to the Cosmopolitan Club last
night. I secured an opening for Jináb-i [there] March 10.
You sent so many cookies that I am going to have a
Feast at the meeting tomorrow night.

February 1925

Fritz Leiber was so good . . . in "Hamlet" . . . last
Saturday that we want to go again tomorrow night to see
him in "The Three Musketeers." . . .
You can't imagine how overjoyed I was with all the
grand *food*. . . . There is only one of the cookies left, which
isn't very strange . . . because they were the best I ever
ate. . . . I am being very choice with the candied orange peel
which I am retaining as a special treat. . . .
Last night . . . after dinner, Margery, Ruth, and I went
to hear Oxford debate against Stanford on the Prohibition
question—Oxford against it. . . . It was very amusing . . .
to see the different styles of debating of England and
America. . . .
We had a good meeting again last Wednesday with
eight present. Howard brought both of his roommates who
seem like very nice boys, look very young, and like the right
kind. The rest were our regular attendants, except for one
new girl. Katholine H—— had me over to dinner at Roble before the meeting. She and Gretchen are big helps. Gretchen
has promised me that she will lead as soon as she feels she
knows enough, but that the more she attends the meetings,
the more she realizes how much there is to know. She is a
lovely girl. Our subject for last time was "The Coming of the
Great Master." I gave an informal talk followed by readings

from *Divine Philosophy* on "The Revelator," and ended by inviting constructive criticism of the subject, additions and questions. . . .[10]

I feel very much pleased about the Y.W.C.A. openings I got today for Jináb-i. . . . I was talking to Miss Capps, General Secretary of the Y.W. work here, about the Persian who was coming to S.F. to speak under the auspices of the Bahá'í Assembly, and that I was hoping to have him speak before the Student Assembly, but hadn't had a very hopeful report from the Chairman. . . . She said, "Do you think the Y.W.C.A. backing would help?" I told her I was sure of it. Then she asked if the Y.W. couldn't have him for three meetings! She said this speaker would be just the thing, and she was greatly interested in the list of topics—said she would like to hear him speak on all of them. So she is planning a mid-week Y.W. meeting at Roble, a Sunday Vesper service . . . and a Y.W.C.A. Cabinet meeting . . . on Thursday. She says she is sure he will "take" well. . . . I am tickled pink over her response, because I hadn't even thought of going to Miss Capps about openings; hadn't even talked to her until this morning. The Y.W. and Y.M. are surely our friends here. Miss C. wants the Cabinet meeting to be just for the . . . twelve officers and heads of . . . committees. They have a dinner. . . . Since it is a very select group of girls, I think it is one of the best openings imaginable. . . .

I tried to get the University Chapel, but Dr. Gardner replied that the pulpit was taken for every Sunday this academic year, and that he would hope to hear the distinguished visitor elsewhere. I have yet to hear from Dr. Jordan to whom I have written for backing.

14 February 1925

The enclosed picture is a "lovely" thing which I ask you to look at and tear into shreds, or park in a bureau drawer, but show to *no* one. The eyes are so glassy that I'm sure they

will break, and the cheeks look as if they were full of soap
suds. It is one of my teacher's application pictures. Do you
think I could ever get a job on it?

Yesterday for three hours and a half I waited in line to
see a principal from Paso Robles who had come to hire
teachers. Only $1,600 a year. It seems odd to be thinking of
making my living. . . .

Last night I went to the Rams Head Show and afterwards Howard took me to the Cast Dance. We had the most

MARION CARPENTER
Teacher's application picture, February 1925.
"The eyes are so glassy that I am sure they will break,
and the cheeks look as if they were full of soapsuds. . . .
Do you think I could ever get a job on it?"

fun together. I danced with both of his roommates who were roughing the dance [that is, attending without a date].

This noon I entertained Bobs and her mother and two Tri Delt girls who came to the last meeting. It was a real success. . . .

I turned down two invitations today from men I don't care much for.

20 February 1925

We are keeping the prayer for the nineteen days as requested. Howard and I are sending $—— together for the disaster in Persia.[11]

Did I tell you Lydia and I were invited to Professor Seward's for Sunday supper? We had a jolly time, and his wife and two children are darlings.

Howard took charge of the meeting Wednesday night, and it was just splendid. He took for his subject, "The Bahá'í Movement Is the Fulfillment of Prophecy." There was much competition with lectures, . . . but we had six present.

After the meeting Howard and I went for a brief ride and finished up with a fruit salad at Wilson's. That finished me, and I haven't been the same since. I went to bed yesterday under Gretchen's solicitous care and felt much better this morning. I want to feel . . . very husky by tomorrow morning at 9:00 when we gambol up to the City. . . . Gretchen, Howard, and I are going, and we expect to have a fine time. . . . At 12:30 we meet Margery for lunch. The meeting where we will hear Jináb-i is at the Bahá'í Home at 2:30. . . . Ali is taking Marg, Howard, Gretchen, and me to a play of Bernard Shaw's at the Playhouse in Berkeley. Sunday afternoon Betty Clark has invited "the Carpenters and their friends" to tea. She little knows what she is in for.

February 1925

R—— is doing the best publicity work for us in the *Dippy*. A notice of the meeting goes in before, and an account of it the day after. As a result new people drop in all the time. Last Wednesday a Mr. Jenkins, a member of the Cosmopolitan Club, came, and Ruth's sister from San Jose came with her.

26 February 1925

Jináb-i talked on the "Proofs of the Existence of God." He is just as winning as ever. His vocabulary is remarkably large, and his grammar quite surprising. . . . We were sorry not to hear him more than the once, but it rained very hard all day Sunday, and Monday I had to . . . work at the Cal library on a young thesis [long term paper] I am writing. But I am looking forward to his being down here. This Sunday . . . he speaks at the Vesper Service at Roble Hall, [and] a Y.W.C.A. meeting. The same night he speaks at the Humanist Club at the Unitarian Church. Then Thursday . . . there is to be a mass meeting in which seven clubs are joining in presenting Jináb-i. . . . I think it is very decent of them to help in sponsoring this lecture. They agreed on the subject: "Modern Education in Persia." I do hope this will go across big.

Saturday night [in Berkeley] we . . . went to see . . . "The Devil's Disciple" . . . with Ali. It was excellent. Sunday morning I had the six Japanese children [Hiroshi, Masao, Shinji, Michiaki, Fumiko, and Wataru Yamamoto] including the little sister who is the darlingest child I ever saw, for their meeting [Bahá'í Junior class]. . . . There was a little American girl present, Howard, Ali, Gretchen, and I. . . .

Monday noon Ali took us to lunch at Ennors, and then he left for the mts. at 2 o'clock. Gretchen and I went to the libe and studied until 5. . . . After supper we started back and got here about 9 o'clock after an awfully good time. Margery was surely marvelous to all of us. . . .

Yesterday noon I was asked to speak to the Student Forum, at their luncheon, on the Bahá'í Cause. Of course I did it. We were in a particularly noisy room, and I had some difficulty . . . bellowing above the sound of coffee cups, etc. Howard went with me. Then I had the Y.W. discussion group to go to yesterday, and the Bahá'í meeting last night. It was a full day.

Our meeting was on the Oneness of Mankind. There were two new people, the nephew of President Wilbur whom Howard brought, and a girl friend of mine, besides two who have been a few times before. I have a "conference" tomorrow afternoon with one of these boys who has some questions to ask. Oh, we are doing a thing or two!

Five people gave to the Bahá'í Flood Relief Fund, . . . and I didn't . . . ask a soul. Bobs gave $5; Howard, $5; R——, $1; I, $5; and Gretchen sent a check. Wasn't that perfectly great?

3 March 1925

The Rabbs and Ioases brought him [Jináb-i] down. The Vesper Service at Roble was well attended, though there were more older people than students, about sixty present. He [Jináb-i] talked half an hour and was well received.

The talk at night was the great occasion. There was a large attendance at the church, and a more sympathetic, interested audience I have seldom seen. Jináb-i's talk on "Cooperation of Eastern and Western Ideals" was simply marvelous. They *wished* him to talk on the Bahá'í Movement, and he did with a great deal of wisdom and charm. . . . I am as fond of hearing him as ever. After his talk many people asked questions, excellent questions. If Bahá'ís in the audience had been instructed to ask them, they could not have brought out better points. Well, I was most pleased. The Unitarian minister, Mr. Robinson, is certainly very generous to the Bahá'ís. He received Jináb-i most kindly. . . .

I wish it were possible to have Jináb-i in Santa Paula

while Howard and I are home for spring vacation. . . . He
finishes in San Francisco March 23, and I believe could stop
in Santa Paula on his way to L.A. It seems too great an undertaking for one person. Here I have had the cooperation of
dozens of people in making posters, in writing newspaper
articles for the Palo Alto and campus papers, in sending out
notices to sororities, in helping me write letters to special
people, etc. I am sure the meeting in the Little Theater is
going to be a success as a result.

The Fast is going off fine. . . . Ruth is lovely about it;
goes to bed early and gets up early when I do.

15 March 1925

We had our meeting last night just the same, although
we are making our big plans for Jináb-i tonight. Two new
women came in and were much impressed and pleased, also
surprised, for they had expected to see a bunch with towels
wrapped round their heads. When they saw a comparatively
intelligent group of college students, it must have been quite
a shock!

18 March 1925

The meeting for Jináb-i Thursday night went off very
well, only I had expected more present. There were probably
about one hundred there. Miss Capps, the secretary of the
Y.W., introduced Jináb-i in a very lovely way. I was greatly
pleased over that. There were a number of professors present, and some of them asked questions afterwards.

The party drove down before dinner. Mrs. Cooper
couldn't come, but Henry brought them down. Mrs. Cline
came and brought Mrs. Probasco. . . .

A couple of fellows from the *Quad* office came over and
asked to take the "Sheik's" picture for the . . . Stanford annual. I do hope it turns out well. . . . They took a flashlight of

Jináb-i in the living room of Manzanita.

We had dinner at the Union. At the last minute I realized that there might be a number who would like to have dinner with Jináb-i and told one or two. . . . When we got together there were thirteen . . . ! We had a big table shut off at one end of the dining room. Jináb-i didn't get much to eat because they kept him busy answering questions.

Yesterday we left at 9:00 a.m. for the City . . . in the afternoon Howard and I went out to the House to hear Jináb-i talk on "Bahá'u'lláh, His Life and Teachings." It was excellent. I learned that the *Seven Valleys* and many of the prayers were written while Bahá'u'lláh was living in the Cave in Kurdistán. . . . New people are becoming interested in S.F. . . .

Margery took Beth and her friend and "us children" to Camille's French Restaurant for dinner. We not only looked every one of the seven courses in the face, but ate discreet portions of each. I was afraid it might prove fatal after the simple life, but I find myself quite all right. . . .

We plan to leave here Saturday morning, Naw-Rúz, and get home that night. We could probably get in by 8 o'clock to have the Feast with you. Wouldn't that be great?

I'm terribly worried over . . . Anglo-Saxon. . . . It is the most loathesome thing I ever got in for, and I have the most awful inhibitions about studying it. And the worst of it is that I *have* to have it.

2 May 1925

We had our Riḍván Feast, and it was the best meeting of the quarter I think. There were eight of us present, and all had been before, so they were interested. We had a splendid discussion. In spite of its being a busy night they all stayed and talked for a long time about it.

This week I have been reading Tolstoy's *Anna Karenina* for the novel course. It is over one thousand pages long, and

I had to stay up rather later to get it done on time. Yesterday, after writing a report on it all afternoon and evening, I was completely exhausted, so tired I could hardly sleep.

May 1925

Last Sunday Ali called up from Berkeley and wanted to come down to Stanford. . . . He arrived just a little before four. . . . We had a brief time until seven when his train left. We drove around . . . and had supper at Wilson's. . . .

Howard had a letter from Father today in which he said that he hoped you would consent to sell the Santa Paula property and move nearer us children. . . . It's hard to tell what the best time is to break away but . . . the sooner, the better, am I not right? I believe you would like it in the north. We youngsters like it heaps. And bless your dear untiring heart, you surely need a new field to work in! If the ground is not fertile, it is better to go where the fresh plants are . . . longing for cultivation. . . . I can't keep from crying as I write this because I know more than anyone else how you have struggled in Santa Paula. I'm not the only one who knows either, because 'Abdu'l-Bahá said that your efforts are "well-known to the friends," and it is very true. . . . you are indeed an angel.

6 August 1925

I wish I could write every day. Things to write do pile up so! We had two new people at the meeting last night—a Buddhist Japanese boy Howard . . . brought and a girl I brought. The others were repeaters. It was a very good meeting on the Temple. The Filipino boy bought one of the pictures of the Temple.

Yesterday afternoon I went out to Prof. A——'s house to derive help in my French. I saw the literal significance of his remark, that he always had a baby a year old, when I set foot within the house. There were five little A——s—

swarming all over everything; the oldest one five and the youngest one mo. Really though I have never seen so many darling, unusual children tout ensemble. They were so sweet and just smiled all the time and tumbled over one another like little puppies. They were so pretty and did such cunning things without being intrusive or aggravating. I just loved them. A—— is never going to send them to school to be ruined, and he is not going to teach them himself until they have a need or show a desire to learn something. At present they are mightily interested in the moon, and he is teaching them astronomy.

He is not going to teach them to read for quite a while because it ruins their eyes. And he ought to know . . . he is only about thirty-five and has read himself so near-sighted that it is sad to see him making out the letters through his big silver-rimmed glasses. His house is full of books all tumbled together.

The children have all decided what they want to be, except the "babiest." It was simply darling to hear them lisping in a very matter-of-fact way about their future vocations. One boy is going to be a nicky-nicky—that is an engineer . . . interpreted. The girl is going to be a nurth (nurse) and the two younger boys are going to thee (sea). A—— gives them sharp-edged tools to play with as soon as they are old enough to grasp hold of anything and encourages them to do things for themselves. . . . They were so gentle and well-behaved, and yet A—— never scolded them sharply. I asked if the children all clamored for food at dinner, but they have a better system. When they arrive at the table, they fold their hands as quickly as they can and are served in the order in which they do it. . . . I am quite enthusiastic over some of this.

Mrs. A—— was out and didn't get back until just before I left. A—— said she was not intellectual, but quite the only wife for him. . . . The house was a wreck—not a curtain anyplace and only the most rudimentary furniture.

After I had been there a couple of hours, A—— had me read a page of French and declared unhesitatingly that I had a reading knowledge of French. Hence that requirement is worked off. Now I have absolutely nothing to do but my thesis.

Yesterday morning I received my reply from George Bernard Shaw!! He didn't write a letter but filled in his remarks between the lines of mine. I haven't ceased laughing yet, it was so good, but hardly the thing I can put in my thesis. . . . In the first place he declares, "I am not a satirist. I am a socialist. If you think I am a satirist, you are probably a fool—in the Scriptural, not the abusive, sense."

He didn't answer my question if he had been in America, but avoided it thus: "I do not pick on the Americans. I chaff them for their good just as I chaff the English or any other nation."

But the best of all was his answer to what I asked him about his *Life-Force*: "Oh really, this is too much. Decidedly you ARE a fool, Marion. Write your thesis on Teddy Bears, and keep in your depth." . . .

Isn't it lovely? It is so flattering to be satirized by the great satirist himself.

I had the best time Sunday. It was a long day and quite a trip, but I'm glad I went. Ali collected me at 5:40 [a.m.], and we walked down to Paly (no street cars running so early) in the most exhilarating, beautiful fog. We took the 6:30 train to S.F. Eight minutes in a taxi got us to the Ferry Bldg. in time to catch the Sausalito Ferry, in time to get the only train to Geyserville. The occasion was Mr. Bosch's birthday. There were about a hundred Bahá'ís there from ten different assemblies.[12] It was all outdoors under an enormous . . . fir. The tables were loaded with fruits of all kinds, and the friends brought sandwiches, cakes, salads, etc. . . . It was all very lovely except that they called on me for a speech, and I had to up and do it. . . .

I met lots of lovely people for the first time and some

darling Bahá'í girls [Marion Holley (Hofman) and Emma Lou
Weaver]. I met Juanita Storch, and I think she is very nice.
Her little girl was there too. Ali brought me back to Stanford
that night and out to Roble. [We ran the last stretch because it
was after the 10:30 p.m. lock out, or curfew. By luck there
was a substitute housemother, and the door was still open.]

The finale of my Stanford days was described in a letter,
not to my parents, but to Sheikh-Ali on 31 August 1925, the
morning of my arrival home in Santa Paula:

> I managed to get packed somehow, and by 2:20 Howard
> had all the mirrors and rugs and suitcases and boxes of books
> tied decoratively around Peter, and we sped forth. . . . One
> tire refused to bear up under its burden, and we had to stop
> and have it vulcanized. It was then that we made our first at-
> tack on the gorgeous basket [which you gave me]. It was
> really the most wonderful thing to have along and saved us a
> great deal of time. At dinner we just rushed into a place and
> got soup and then ate fruit and candy while driving along.
> Thus we arrived unscathed at 1:40 a.m. The folks were de-
> lighted to see us even at that unholy hour.
>
> Father was tremendously interested in the basket of fruit.
> And at two o'clock in the morning he must needs sample the
> various kinds and discover what was in the depths. In fact the
> whole family has enjoyed it with me. . . . I wish you could
> have seen it straight through. . . . There wasn't any sawdust
> after all, but instead all the fruit was carefully wrapped. It had
> all these different things in it: plums, peaches, figs, pears,
> oranges, nectarines, grapes, pecans, almonds, chocolate[s],
> and a can of candy in the cutest shapes. Everything was very
> choice and perfectly delicious. I wish you could know how
> much I appreciate your doing this for me. . . . By the way,
> Mother thinks you terribly extravagant. . . .
>
> We hear the most encouraging news about the subscrip-
> tions to the Temple. Mrs. Waite wrote that in Los Angeles
> they have pledged themselves as individuals to give over
> $6,000 in five years. Some have pledged to pay before that

MARION CARPENTER
a teacher at last, August 1925, had accomplished her
goals of obtaining a bachelor's degree (her M.A. was awarded in 1928)
and a teaching credential, of interviewing Dr. David Starr Jordan, who
had welcomed 'Abdu'l-Bahá, and of spreading the teachings
of the Bahá'í Faith in the wake of the Master.

time. And in Chicago they have raised $10,000. I think this is so exciting. Undoubtedly we shall soon have the $400,000 necessary to begin the next story. This is a wonderful business to be shareholders in, isn't it?[13]

Yes, college days were over. Being the first Bahá'í at Stanford University, not long after 'Abdu'l-Bahá's epic visit there, had been one of the most exhilarating experiences of my life. I left Stanford with complete assurance that other youth would carry forward the good news of the Bahá'í Faith. The "real" world awaited. I was ready to face the future—in Ali's company, God willing—with a tremendous sense of eagerness and joy.

11

Down the Years

Howard and Marzieh Carpenter

Many students have performed service at Stanford in the years since 1925, including, of course, Howard Carpenter and Marzieh Nabil (Carpenter, Gail). Marzieh, a beautiful and fascinating young lady, the daughter of Dr. and Mrs. Ali-Kuli Khan, registered at Stanford in 1927 as Marzia Nabil Khan and was called "our Persian princess" by the girls at Roble. She was taking a bath one day when a woman reporter from the *Daily* came to get information. The reporter went ahead with her interview anyway. She shouted her first question over the transom: "Be you royalty, or be you not?"

Marzieh and Howard organized small weekly discussion groups downstairs in Roble Hall. Marion Holley (Hofman) came quite regularly, as well as a few contacts. Joyce Lyon (Dahl) first heard of the Faith when Marzieh spoke at one of these meetings; after the meeting Marzieh and Joyce went to the medical lab to meet Howard, who had not been able to attend the meeting.

In June 1929 Marzieh and Howard were married. She was elected Phi Beta Kappa and earned her bachelor's degree with great distinction. In 1932 she received her M.A. from the University of California as Howard received his M.D. from the Stanford Medical School. The two maintained an active Bahá'í life, speaking and writing while pursuing their studies. Howard, undaunted by a serious illness, served as chairman of the Spiritual Assembly of San Francisco and on a number of Bahá'í committees. A talk he prepared at this time was published years later as an article in *World Order*.[1]

At the first session of Geyserville Bahá'í School in 1927 Howard and I spoke on "The Bahá'í House of Worship." According to Grace Holley, at 10 a.m. on 9 August

> Our beloved chairman, Shahnaz [Waite], again read the prayer and the beautiful Temple Song . . . and then turned the meeting over to Marion Carpenter Yazdi. The subject was "The Temple." Mrs. Yazdi sketched briefly the significance of the Temple in the religions of the past, and then in a deeply reverent manner showed what the Mashriqu'l-Adhkár will mean to the world of the future. Howard Carpenter gave us a description of the Temple at Chicago as it now appears, a tragic picture.[2]

Soon after that opening session, Howard and a Bahá'í carpenter from near Geyserville built a little cabin, high on the hill—the first building to be put on the property after it was given to the school by John and Louise Bosch. In the fall of 1932 as Howard and Marzieh were leaving for Vienna, Louise Bosch wrote Howard that Julia Culver was interested in buying the little cabin:

> I wish I cd send you every cent that you have spent for it. In the meantime it has served the Summer School as a "show-place," many friends went up to see it each year, and they all admired the situation and view that you had chosen. . . .
>
> You are going to a land of greater beauty. And you will bring beauty there thru and by your knowledge acquired by so many years of effort.[3]

The couple sailed from San Pedro, California, 9 September 1932 on an Italian freighter; Dr. Carpenter was the ship's physician. After receiving his certificate in advanced ophthalmology from the University of Vienna, the two, at Shoghi Effendi's request, had the opportunity to travel with Martha Root, "that archetype of Bahá'í itinerant teachers and the foremost Hand raised by Bahá'u'lláh since 'Abdu'l-Bahá's passing. . . ."[4] Marzieh writes of Martha and the three weeks in 1933 when she and Howard traveled and taught with her in Central Europe and the Balkans:

> I helped as Martha's "advance man" in Vienna. On 31 January 1933 she lunched in Vienna with Queen Marie and

DR. HOWARD CARPENTER and MARZIEH CARPENTER
aboard the S.S. *Fella,* leaving San Pedro, California,
for Vienna, Haifa, and Ṭihrán

Arch-Duchess Anton—they sent for her. Then Howard and I left with Martha for Budapest and Belgrade. On 18 February she had tea in Belgrade with Prince Paul and Princess Olga. Martha was a top P.R. person—it's really incredible how she would take on a city, all by herself—and soon ambassadors and professors and editors would be serving the Cause through her.

Noting dates in Maḥmúd's Diary I later realized Martha was actually doing a follow-up on the Master's Budapest pioneer journey! Looking for people who saw Him etc.—groups to . . . which He spoke. Martha more than once made me share her platform, and I wish I could find the Budapest news picture showing Martha listening to my talk! On 10 February Howard dined at the Budapest Rotary Club. I think he was introduced and spoke a few sentences. Howard . . . visited some hospitals on our Balkan teaching journey.

. . . February 23 at the Belgrade railroad station (the Esperantists, to honor Martha, having brought a green flag on a cane, to wave goodbye) was the last time I saw Martha. Next day we left for Sofia.

. . . We were five weeks in Bulgaria helping Marion Jack from February 24 to March 31. Then we went to Saloniki, Greece, and taught. Flew to Tirana [Albania] April 4 (my first flight) and taught, saw individuals, left April 12. The Guardian wrote us—to Vienna—to go to Tirana (en route to Haifa). . . . When we read the Guardian's letter, we had never knowingly heard of Tirana, but of course looked it up and went.[5]

Martha Root wrote to Ella G. Cooper on 28 November 1935, expressing "great love and admiration" for Howard and Marzieh and saying, "I pray for them both, and always I am so grateful for all they did in Europe. It meant a great deal to the Cause in Europe, their glorious work."[6]

In Haifa Marzieh and Howard spent three weeks receiving instructions from the beloved Guardian. He wanted them to live in Ṭihrán and be very tactful; their work would be preliminary to future international cooperation; they must stress that East and West are one; and they must not become discouraged. The Master would guide and sustain them.

Their letters from Haifa were optimistic, but the news we received from Persia was sad and disturbing. Howard became very ill with Malta fever and recovered slowly. It seemed impossible to get a doctor's license, though eye disease was rampant. Keith Ransom-Kehler was dying of black smallpox—and finally a stroke—in Iṣfahán.[7]

Shoghi Effendi hoped they would carry on, and they helped where they could. On 26 April 1934 in Ṭihrán Howard performed a cataract operation on a Mrs. Rúḥání of Qazvín without a nurse or assistant. Marzieh has written that: "The strain was horrible, especially as there was a glaucoma involvement. [It was] in an ordinary room—me off in a

MARZIEH CARPENTER
at Geyserville Bahá'í School in California

corner."[8] Relatives watched until it was over—successfully.
Before he could get a license, Howard worked in the hospital
of Dr. Bakhtiar, who was not a Bahá'í.

Finally the license was approved. But just as the future
began to look bright, the active, eager, brilliant Howard was
stricken with poliomyelitis and was paralyzed from the waist
down and could only lie prone. At the worst of his illness,
when pneumonia had set in, the treasurer of the National
Spiritual Assembly came to the hospital with a gift of money
from the Guardian. According to Marzieh, "It was very
moving to feel his loving care."[9]

For a while Marzieh worked on a newspaper and slept
on a cot in Howard's room. There were months of suffering.
One day Raḥmat 'Alá'í, a Persian Bahá'í, came to visit Howard in the hospital. When he saw that Howard was not receiving proper treatment, he arranged to have him brought
to his home. There he and Najmíyyih, his wife, a registered
nurse, cared for him with skill and devotion, just as they had
for Keith when she was dying. Adelaide Sharp, an American Bahá'í in charge of the Tarbíyat School, and her mother
brought American delicacies.[10]

The doctors advised a return to the United States as the
only hope for improvement. So the arduous long trip back to
San Francisco began. Marzieh remembers:

> Leaving Persia in a touring car, Raḥmat, a large man, sat un-
> comfortably, riding backward for days on a small seat, so he
> could steady Howard's stretcher that was slanted across the
> back section of the car.
> The Baghdád believers were very kind, and sat with us at
> the hotel. We flew Baghdád-Damascus, over the desert. I've
> never appreciated British reserve more than I did that morn-
> ing we left Baghdád. The flight was considerably delayed, so
> seats could be removed from the plane, as Howard had to lie
> on the floor. After we were finally settled, the British
> passengers filed into the plane, and not one of them looked at

us. . . . I remember holding up a mirror for Howard so he could occasionally see a little from the window.

We motored Damascus-Haifa. The Guardian received me and Najmíyyih 'Alá'í May 8/35, spoke Persian to us—I still have the Persian sentences. He was wonderful to Howard and me—said we mustn't think we had failed. He arranged for an ambulance and insisted Howard be carried to all the Shrines including Bahjí. . . . One day at table he said, "Trials and sorrows are the oil that feeds the lamp; we must have the patience of Job." He said Bahá'ís mustn't run away from difficulties—"if we persevere, something extraordinary takes place, and the problem is solved." He did everything possible for the two of us, although he was carrying the whole Bahá'í world. He had the friends in Beirut meet our boat.[11]

They had spent nine days with the Guardian, and each of those days he came to see and talk with Howard.

After a forty-day boat trip they were met in Boston by Marzieh's parents, Ali-Kuli Khan and Florence. In New York the concerned members of the National Spiritual Assembly, friends, and relatives greeted them on 13 June 1935. Madame Khan wrote to Howard's mother on 14 June 1935:

Howard and Marzieh sailed safe and well-pleased last evening at 7 p.m. [for Los Angeles and San Francisco].

The entire N.S.A. came, in a body, to the steamer to call upon them. Mr. Mountford Mills (Ch'rman of the N.S.A. and also Ch'rman of the N.Y. Local Assembly), Mrs. Stewart [Stuart] French, Roy Wilhelm, Alfred Lunt, Mr. McDaniels [McDaniel], Carl Scheffler, (Bertha Herklotz, Sec'ty of the N.Y. Assembly) etc. Roy called three times. He brought lovely flowers, a box of nuts, Bahá'í literature they wanted, and a car containing a wheeled-chair to carry them to his home (which last they could not avail themselves of!). . . . The N.S.A. were very touching in their deep sympathy and kindly spirit—and all left apparently much cheered. . . .

Howard is showing very great spirit and courage, and he will win with such high resolve. . . . He calmly directs everything and everybody, just like a wise and trained physician. He has ripened and sweetened and matured thru his great suffering. Both have been thru enough for one life-time. . . . Mrs. Carrie Kinney . . . came also to see Howard and Marzieh . . . and Mr. Curtis Kelsey . . .—a few other people called. All praise Howard and Marzieh with great and heartfelt praise. . . . The Guardian cabled Roy to do everything to make their landing (or arrival) at New York comfortable. . . . They really needed us in both cities.

We did not know the Guardian had cabled Roy; and this was another evidence of his tender love, care, and great regard for them. . . .

Both truly look very blooming and serene.[12]

Marzieh's recollection of this time continues: "We had to go through the Canal then, some three more weeks of torment, because planes in those days wouldn't take you if you couldn't walk on—a tragic contrast with 1932 departure! Father and Mother Carpenter met our boat in Southern California. . . ."[13]

The journey ended on 2 July; they were met in San Francisco by Howard's sister Margery and Berkeley Chief of Police Greening and taken by ambulance to the University of California Hospital. Marzieh's diary says, "So he'll have the care he needs, at last."[14] There were headlines and smiling pictures in the *San Francisco Call Bulletin*: "Stanford Man in Gamble with Death Wins," "S. F. Doctor Fights Back from Paralysis: Borne Thousands of Miles over the World on Litter."[15] Howard was quoted: "You never know how the scenery looks until you see it horizontally."[16] He added: "And you don't know how kind people are, of all nationalities, until you undertake to do your traveling on a stretcher, absolutely motionless."[17]

Howard struggled with all his courage, but he could not survive. He died in Berkeley on 24 November 1935 and was buried in Sunset View Cemetery. Leroy Ioas conducted the service. Of Howard he said:

> in the land of the birth of the Bahá'í Faith, in pursuit of exemplary services to establish the unity of the East and the West, he contracted an illness from which he was never to recover. During this illness in Persia, notwithstanding the hopelessness of it, and the intense suffering, his life showed forth patience, fortitude and spiritual happiness, possible only through the great love of Bahá'u'lláh. In this affliction his spirit mellowed and he became a radiant example of true Bahá'í life. Even after the arduousness of the return to America, he was a source of reassurance and inspiration to all the friends.
>
> Thus his services to the Cause of God became more glorious in his life of radiant acquiescence. In his death, his deeds attained even greater glory. Indeed, only when the spirit of Bahá'u'lláh has brought humanity to its goal, and the people have achieved a universal consciousness, and only then, will the worth of Howard's services to the Cause of God become apparent. Then it will be realized that in the short span of his sojourn in this phenomenal realm, he became a strong link in the bond of unity gradually enveloping the world, and a permanent pillar in the tabernacle of universal peace.[18]

Leroy wrote me this moving note on 10 January 1936:

> Of all the young Bahá'ís that I know, I was more attached to him [Howard] than to any. I expected to see him attain great heights in his services to the Cause, but I did not expect those heights to be reached in the manner they were. We know so little of the ways of God. We need more confidence in the Will of God and appreciation of His gifts, even though outwardly they may be burning fire.[19]

Lines from the memorial article by Marzieh in *The Bahá'í World* describe her husband well: "His brilliance, his almost surgical frankness, his hatred of sentimentalism, his intellectual approach to the Cause of Bahá'u'lláh, his utter devotion to the furtherance of Bahá'í institutions, were a light and guide to those who accompanied him through his brief life."[20]

Beloved Shoghi Effendi expressed his grief and the sorrow of all of us in a number of cables and letters; they still carry comfort. In a letter dated 18 December 1935 written on his behalf and addressed to my mother, Shoghi Effendi said:

> Not only the American friends, but also all the believers in the East who had the pleasure of knowing the doctor, mourn this heavy loss, and fully share your afflictions and sorrows. For they had found in him not only a valuable co-worker, but also a dear friend from whose association they could derive continued inspiration and encouragement.
>
> What, indeed, contributed most to endear him to the friends were the remarkable qualities of his heart. He was to them a living example of utter selflessness, devotion and love. He was so gentle, so kind, so lovable, that everyone who met him could not but feel deeply attracted to him.
>
> His attachment to the Cause was even more remarkable. His great, nay supreme consideration was to be of some service to the Faith, in whatever capacity, and no matter in which place or country. The friends in Persia can never forget the services he was able to render them during his stay in that land. Next to the late Mrs. Ransom-Kehler he may, indeed, be well considered as the foremost American believer who has, in the last few years, been assisted in rendering invaluable help to the Persian believers in their efforts for the establishment of the Administration in their country. . . .[21]

In his own handwriting Shoghi Effendi added:

> With a heart overflowing with love, tenderness, and sympathy I share your afflicting sorrows and am overwhelmed by the sense of loss and grief which earthly separation from so beloved a son must necessarily produce. To him I am attached by such ties that death can never sever. I had a profound admiration for the noble qualities which distinguished his Bahá'í life. I will pray for him with the ut-

most fervor. Feel not disconsolate, for the state in which he is now is such as none can describe. [2]

Since Howard's death Marzieh has continued to serve the Faith with distinction. Today she is widely known as an historian, translator of Bahá'í sacred texts, essayist, and biographer. She is highly regarded for her colorful books on the Middle Ages, the Renaissance, and the Victorian era.

Marion Holley (Hofman)

Marion Holley (Hofman) is another of the early Stanford Bahá'ís. She was the oldest child of Harry and Grace Holley, also Stanford graduates who later became Bahá'ís in Visalia, California.

For this book Marion wrote an autobiographical sketch including a description of her metamorphosis from a teenage agnostic to a devout believer at the age of twenty-two and of her first meeting with David Hofman, who was to be her future husband.

When I went to Stanford, I was an active and convinced Bahá'í. As I recall, I had spoken in 1924 [1926] at the National Convention in San Francisco, and in Visalia I shared in the Bahá'í life and activity. [23]

I was only sixteen when I entered Stanford in 1926; had I been older, probably I should not have been so impressionable. I think the only Bahá'ís there were Marzieh, Howard and I, and they organized a weekly discussion group. . . . The only public meeting I remember was in a fair-sized hall or lecture room in 1927, for Rúhí Effendi, who was then travel teaching in the U.S. By that time, the agnostic, behavioristic nature of my studies (I was a Social Science major) had affected me, for I had quite a long talk with Rúhí Effendi, and later, from the East coast, he wrote me a long . . . letter trying to convince me that one shouldn't stay agnostic, but seek and try to find the truth of the Faith.

I do not recall any attempt to teach the Faith to others, on my part. I think I was shy about it, unsure of my own position, and also very taken up with life at Stanford—debating society, athletics (I was all-star in hockey, basketball, and track events), by then the sorority I joined chiefly to be with Joyce [Lyon (Dahl)], and, of course, studies. My degree was "with great distinction"; I think only one man was higher academically in my class. Also in 1928 I won a place as high jumper on the American Olympic team, and went to Amsterdam, and after, to Paris and Brussels—all very exciting at eighteen years. At the end of my third year, I craved to specialize, and transferred to the University of California at Berkeley, where I took only courses in anthropology, sufficient for a degree, had I not wished, for sentimental reasons, to take my degree at Stanford, which I did in the succeeding summer term. (My uncle was in Stanford's first

MARION HOLLEY (HOFMAN)
in New York in 1928 on her way to
Amsterdam as a member of the
American Olympic team

graduating class, my father graduated in 1901, and mother in 1904.)

I forgot to mention that I was studying singing, piano and organ in my first year, as I had wavered between Stanford and a music school. It was too much, and I had to drop the music—but the first year was a *very* busy one.

Joyce had graduated by the time I moved to Berkeley, but came to share an apartment with me. Certainly I never made any attempt to tell her about the Faith. . . . It was my mother's interest in Joyce, and her introduction to Mme. Dreyfus-Barney, when Joyce went to Paris for a year, that opened the door for her.

Of course, we did not sign declaration cards then. At no time did I "withdraw." I just didn't believe in God for a few years, and tried to explain the Manifestations by some theory of great men, in accordance with my studies. Fortunately for me, I was unemployed and living at home in Visalia, the year after graduation (summer 1930). Mother was an active Bahá'í, and many visitors came, including Martha Root and Keith Ransom-Kehler. I drove Martha and Mother to her meetings.

MARION HOLLEY (HOFMAN)
A graduate of Stanford University,
she later proved to be a dynamic Bahá'í speaker.

Keith was with us about a month, and, due to heart trouble, would rest in bed all morning. I used to sit with her, and found her conversation fascinating. But it was *never* about the Faith; she had the wisdom not to try to persuade me, as everyone else did. Consequently, I sat in the back row of the second room, for each of the three talks a week she gave in our home, and took notes. Keith knew, although I didn't, that she had "pulled me up by my bootstraps," for she said something of the sort to Marzieh, in Ṭihrán. [Marzieh: "Keith told me she revived Marion Holley with a pulmotor."[24]] Despite my unbelief in 1931, I served on the Visalia Assembly, as they were one down! But after thinking over all that Keith had said, in 1932 I declared my faith in Pasadena, was appointed to give a study course for youth (this after being asked to represent the Assembly at the World Council of Youth . . . held at the California Institute of Technology in Pasadena).[25]

All during those years, 1926–1932, I think I attended everything at Geyserville, with my family, including the Unity Feast the year before under the Big Tree on August 2, 1925.
. . . Keith convinced me intellectually. But when I met May [Maxwell] in 1934—she spent some weeks in southern California—a spiritual confirmation was added.

David [Hofman] toured the U.S. with Lorol Schopflocher, driving her car and running the projector. May introduced us on the 'phone when he rang her hotel on arrival. (She was his spiritual mother; he lived ten years in Canada as a young man.) That night we met at a banquet which the Los Angeles Assembly gave for Lorol, and were at once attracted. When he could, he returned to L.A., hoping to become a successful film actor, and we both served on the LSA there and were active in teaching. He returned to England in 1936, and before long wrote to suggest that we marry. It was not possible (a long story) until 1945, but the beloved Guardian approved it in 1936, when I wrote to him.[26]

It was a pleasure to know Marion Holley during the several years she lived in Berkeley and San Francisco. She was an outstanding champion of the Faith, a truly dynamic and moving public speaker who was always in demand. Our small children, great fans of hers, were delighted whenever she spoke. After one of her forceful talks to a packed room at the Yazdi studio, we overheard our son Robert say, "She picks you up like a pillow and shakes you out. It's scary sitting on the front row." His younger sister Barbara, not to be outdone, added, "She scares the rabbit out of me."

Charlotte and Gladyce Linfoot, in Piedmont, California, gave the bridal shower just before Marion left us to live abroad. Though we were poignantly aware of the separation involved, I recall how happy we were for her.

After Marion and David Hofman were married in Northampton, England, in 1945, she helped considerably with his publishing house of George Ronald. When he was elected to The Universal House of Justice in 1963, she took over the management of the firm for twelve years and is still actively engaged as editor and advisor. She and her husband live in Haifa, Israel.

Joyce Lyon (Dahl)

Joyce Lyon was not a Bahá'í during her years as a Stanford student. It seems important, however, to include her story since she first heard of the Faith at Stanford and has gone on to become an active and deeply committed believer. It was from Marzieh Nabil, when she spoke to a small group at Roble Hall, that Joyce first heard of the Faith. She was a close friend of Marion Holley. Marion's mother, Grace, arranged for Joyce to meet Mme. Dreyfus-Barney in Paris, during a year abroad. On shipboard returning to the United States, Joyce picked up the February 1931 *Baha'i News*, which had been given her by a friend, and, while reading Bahá'u'lláh's Victory Tablet, realized that she was a Bahá'í.[27] From 1936 to 1940 she was an isolated believer in Palo Alto and, after her marriage, served on the Assembly there for many years.

Joyce and Arthur Dahl's home in Pebble Beach with its magnificent view of Carmel Bay was the setting for many notable Bahá'í events. It was special for us when Ali was invited to speak or conduct a wedding, and we stayed overnight. I recall a morning after breakfast when he was asked to talk just to the four Dahl boys on the Central Figures of the Faith and his own experiences with 'Abdu'l-Bahá and with Shoghi Effendi. Now young men, the Dahl sons serve the Faith in many parts of the world.

The hospitable Dahl home was also the setting for the marriage of our daughter Barbara to James Markert on 8 November 1958. Charles Wolcott and Arthur Dahl, both members of the National Spiritual Assembly at the time, conducted the service. The rehearsal dinner dance at the country club the night before, the wedding cake, the potted chrysanthemums that lined the deck, the music—how expressive of Bahá'í love were the arrangements made by the Dahls that day! Letters from guests poured in; all said "perfect." "If you had started the day Barbara was born to plan

JOYCE LYON (DAHL), 1928

the perfect setting and the perfect service, this would have been it."

I am greatly indebted to Joyce for some of the valuable material used in this account. She is always generous with her time and very helpful. A member of the Auxiliary Board for protection, Joyce now travels through Nevada and parts of California. One of her assistants is Barbara Markert. The lifetime of service Joyce has given to the Faith can be thought of as another episode in the continuing story of the Bahá'í Faith at Stanford.

A Brief Mention of Others

Many other Bahá'í students have taught the Bahá'í Faith at Stanford. Among those of a younger generation, all well known to me, are Farru<u>kh</u> Ioas;[28] Anita Ioas (Chapman); Isobel Locke (Sabri), who became a Bahá'í at Stanford;

JOYCE LYON (DAHL), 1933

Firuz Kazemzadeh; Nosratollah Rassekh; Amin Banani; Dwight and Kenton Allen; our own daughter, Barbara Yazdi (Markert); John McHenry; Marsha Wolcott (Gilpatrick); Karen Hogberg (Leonard); Judy Phillips (Sill); Keith and Arthur Lyon Dahl; Robert Phillips; and many others. Recent graduates from Stanford include Shirin Javid (Abtahi), Behrooz Rezvani, Kamal Zein, Andy Allen, and Dr. Vida Bertrand. Saba Mahanian, Ata'u'llah Arjomand, Monireh Kazemzadeh, William Cocke, Paul Akhtar Khavari, Ron Lillejord, and Faramarz Yazdani were members of the 1981 Bahá'í Club at Stanford. Afsaneh, the wife of Faramarz, wrote at the time: "We enjoy every minute of living in this beautiful and blessed University."[29]

So it is that for six decades a succession of devoted Bahá'í students has followed with zest in the footsteps of 'Abdu'l-Bahá.

12

Triumph

A miscellany of memories concludes the story of the early days of the Bahá'í Faith at Stanford.

It is of special historical interest that in 1911 Lua Getsinger, while on a teaching trip through California with Dr. Amínulláh Faríd, spoke at a large meeting in Palo Alto, thus opening the way for the coming of 'Abdu'l-Bahá the following year. Many students and members of the Stanford faculty attended this gathering.[1]

In 1927 Rúḥí Effendi, a cousin of Shoghi Effendi, was a guest in our Berkeley home on his arrival in California. As a member of the Inter-Bay Planning Committee, I went back to the campus and arranged for a lecture by Rúḥí under the auspices of the Stanford Fellowship and the Cosmopolitan Club. On 30 November at 7:30 p.m. he spoke on "The Bahá'í Movement" in the Little Theater.[2]

In the early 1930s Martha Root reported in an article that she gave a lecture at Stanford under the joint auspices of the YMCA, the YWCA, the International Relations Group, and the Japanese Club.[3]

Even before there were Bahá'ís living in Palo Alto, the San Francisco Spiritual Assembly held, in the Community Center, at least one anniversary observance of 'Abdu'l-

Bahá's visit. The Twenty-Fifth Anniversary on 10 October 1937 at 2:30 p.m. in the same Community Center was addressed by Mrs. Loulie Mathews and Leroy Ioas. Around 1948 Leroy Ioas spoke in the classroom opening into the Chapel at a small but impressive event. Arthur L. Dahl believes that the famous psychologist B. F. Skinner was also a speaker that day.

In 1950 and 1951 Ali and I spoke at well-attended observances. We also went to Stanford for meetings when our daughter Barbara was a student. Ali talked for the newly formed Bahá'í Club on 21 May 1952. Barbara was a freshman reporter; an article and her father's picture appeared on the front page of the *Daily*.

The celebration of the Fiftieth Anniversary of the Mas-

STANFORD BAHA'I CLUB, 1954
Front row, left to right: Valerie Rassekh, Kenton Allen,
Karen Hogberg (Leonard), Barbara Yazdi (Markert), John McHenry
Back row, left to right: (?), Roderick Ward, Marsha Wolcott (Gilpatrick),
(?), Nasratollah Rassekh

ter's visit, held in October 1962, was outstanding. The believers of the Peninsula combined their efforts; and the newspapers of both the Peninsula and the Bay Area did their part. Ali spoke on 'Abdu'l-Bahá and his memories of Him in Egypt and in Haifa. The audience was warm and responsive. One person commented, "Your wonderful talk brought 'Abdu'l-Bahá very close that night—everyone felt it."[4]

Dr. Daniel C. Jordan lectured to a group of professors on campus recently. Firesides with speakers, music, and slides are currently being held in the dorms. Large numbers hear of Bahá'u'lláh when ready-made audiences gather outside Tresider Union on Student Activities Day. The Bahá'í clubs of Stanford and Cal hold joint activities. The Stanford Club sponsored a successful weekend for Bahá'í college clubs at Bosch Bahá'í School, 22–24 January 1982.

The Santa Clara West Spiritual Assembly, which included Stanford, has been functioning for some time. The policy of the National Spiritual Assembly has been for a nearby Assembly to sponsor a Bahá'í college club. Yet the haunting, eager words of Shoghi Effendi in his letter to me in 1925 still echo down the years: "I would be delighted to learn of the formation of a regular, elected, Spiritual Assembly in the heart of that far-famed seat of learning. . . ."[5] An Assembly in the heart of Stanford! What a triumph that would be! It is incredible that at the exact moment of concluding my story I should receive the following climactic news:

STANFORD UNIVERSITY

4/2/81

Dear Mrs. Yazdi:

. . . Thanks to you and your recommendation the National Spiritual Assembly last week called us and said it's all right to change the name of our assembly to Stanford. I thought you [would] like to know and it [would] make you happy.

With Love,

Faramarz [Yazdani][6]

The recognition of the Spiritual Assembly of the Bahá'ís of Stanford University is an historic first. At present Stanford is the only university in the world with the honor of having formed its own Spiritual Assembly. Grateful tears of joy well up in celebration. I praise 'Abdu'l-Bahá and Shoghi Effendi for this consummation; and into my grateful thoughts drift memories of those early believers and the warm encouragement and direction they gave to me as the first Stanford Bahá'í. Especially do I remember the words of Mariam

FIRST SPIRITUAL ASSEMBLY OF THE BAHÁ'ÍS
OF STANFORD UNIVERSITY, 7 JUNE 1981
Front row, left to right: Ata'u'lláh Arjomand; Saba Mahanian; Althea Miller
Back row: Faramarz Yazdani; Afsaneh Yazdani; Don Miller; Pamela Carr; Bill Cocke; (not pictured, Dr. Vida Bertrand, Stanford lecturer in French literature)

Haney published in the *National Baha'i Bulletin* of 17 December 1923:

> . . . with her very commendable and amazing enthusiasm, she longed to start a group which would one fine day develop into an Assembly, through the Divine Bestowals.[7]

The dream has now come true.

Notes

Notes

Foreword by Ali M. Yazdi

1. Nabíl-i-A'ẓam [Muḥammad-i-Zarandí], *The Dawn-Breakers: Nabíl's Narrative of the Early Days of the Bahá'í Revelation*, trans. and ed. Shoghi Effendi (Wilmette, Ill.: Bahá'í Publishing Trust, 1932); Shoghi Effendi, *God Passes By*, rev. ed. (Wilmette, Ill.: Bahá'í Publishing Trust, 1974), pp. 3–320.—ED.

2. Shoghi Effendi has indicated that the history of the Bahá'í Faith will be comprised of three ages: the Heroic, the Transitional (or Formative), and the Golden. The Heroic Age covered the period from the declaration of the Báb in 1844 to the ascension of 'Abdu'l-Bahá in 1921. The Transitional Age began in 1921 and will be "the Age in which the institutions, local, national and international, of the Faith of Bahá'u'lláh . . . take shape, develop and become fully consolidated, in anticipation of the third, the last, the Golden Age destined to witness the emergence of a world-embracing Order . . . the establishment of a world civilization and the formal inauguration of the Kingdom of the Father upon earth as promised by Jesus Christ Himself." Shoghi Effendi, *God Passes By*, rev. ed. (Wilmette, Ill.: Bahá'í Publishing Trust, 1974), p. 324. See also ibid., pp. xiii–xvi.—ED.

3. The term "Center of the Covenant" refers to 'Abdu'l-Bahá's position as appointed successor of Bahá'u'lláh, Head of His Faith, and sole authorized Interpreter of His teachings. In a

215

special document He called "The Book of the Covenant" (Kitáb-i-'Ahd) Bahá'u'lláh instructed His kindred and the entire body of believers, upon His passing, to "turn, one and all, their faces towards the Most Mighty Branch ['Abdu'l-Bahá]" (Bahá'u'lláh, *Tablets of Bahá'u'lláh Revealed after the Kitáb-i-Aqdas*, comp. Research Department of the Universal House of Justice, trans. Habib Taherzadeh et al. [Haifa: Bahá'í World Centre, 1978], p. 221). It is the existence of a central authority deriving its origin and power from explicit instructions in the Faith's sacred writings that has preserved Bahá'u'lláh's teachings from corruption and His Faith from schism.—ED.

4. The term "Manifestation of God" is used by Bahá'ís to refer to the Prophet-Founders of the world's major revealed religions (for example, Moses, Buddha, Christ, Muḥammad, the Báb, and Bahá'u'lláh). Bahá'u'lláh has written: "As a token of His [God's] mercy . . . He hath manifested unto men the Day Stars of His divine guidance . . . and hath ordained the knowledge of these sanctified Beings to be identical with the knowledge of His own Self. . . . They are the Manifestations of God amidst men, the evidences of His Truth, and the signs of His glory" (*Gleanings from the Writings of Bahá'u'lláh*, trans. Shoghi Effendi, 2d ed. [Wilmette, Ill.: Bahá'í Publishing Trust, 1976], pp. 49–50).—ED.

Preface

1. The Master (Áqá): A title by which Bahá'ís refer to 'Abdu'l-Bahá. The title was originally given Him by Bahá'u'lláh. Of this Shoghi Effendi writes: "He ['Abdu'l-Bahá] alone had been accorded the privilege of being called '*the Master,*' an honor from which His Father [Bahá'u'lláh] had strictly excluded all His other sons." (*God Passes By*, rev. ed. [Wilmette, Ill.: Bahá'í Publishing Trust, 1974], p. 242.) Guardian: This term refers to Shoghi Effendi Rabbani, 'Abdu'l-Bahá's eldest grandson appointed by Him in His Will and Testament as "Guardian of the Cause of God (Valíyy-i-Amru'lláh)"—world leader of the Bahá'í Faith and authorized interpreter of its teachings. Shoghi Effendi served in this capacity from 'Abdu'l-Bahá's passing in 1921 to his own death in 1957.—ED.

Part One
Early Days of the Bahá'í Faith in Berkeley, 1898–1925

Chapter 1: The Beginning, 1898–1912

1. Jináb-i-Fáḍil-i-Mázindarání [Mírzá Asadu'lláh] was a
learned and energetic Bahá'í teacher from Írán. In 1920 he was
directed by 'Abdu'l-Bahá to travel to America in order to stimu-
late and assist Bahá'í communities throughout the continent.
(See H. M. Balyuzi, *'Abdu'l-Bahá: The Centre of the Covenant of
Bahá'u'lláh* [London: George Ronald, 1971], p. 443.) In 1923, at the
invitation of American Bahá'ís, he made another extensive teaching trip through North America, for which he won Shoghi Effendi's praise. (See Shoghi Effendi, *Bahá'í Administration: Selected
Messages 1922–1932*, 7th rev. ed. [Wilmette, Ill.: Bahá'í Publishing
Trust, 1974], pp. 31–32, 49, 54.) For details on his visit to Berkeley
and San Francisco in 1921 and 1924 see Chapter 4, pp. 55, 56, 57–
58, 59, 60, and 62, and Chapter 10, p. 164. For details on his visit to
San Francisco and Stanford University in 1925 see pp. 146–48 and
Chapter 10, pp. 174, 175, 176, 178, 179, 180, and 181–82.—Ed.

2. 'Abdu'l-Bahá, in *Bahá'u'lláh and 'Abdu'l-Bahá, Bahá'í
World Faith: Selected Writings of Bahá'u'lláh and 'Abdu'l-Bahá*, rev.
ed. (Wilmette, Ill.: Bahá'í Publishing Trust, 1976), p. 365.

3. Ella Cooper, "Early Days of the Cause in the West,"
Geyserville Bahá'í School, Geyserville, Calif., 7 July 1942.

4. Accounts of what prompted this visit vary slightly. According to Willard P. Hatch ("Edward Christopher Getsinger," in
*The Bahá'í World: A Biennial International Record, Volume VI, 1934–
1936*, comp. National Spiritual Assembly of the Bahá'ís of the
United States and Canada [New York: Bahá'í Publishing Committee, 1937], p. 495): "quoting Dr. Getsinger: 'Mrs. (Phoebe)
Hearst read of me in the newspapers in 1897, and called me to her
Hacienda. She was regent of the University of California . . . gave
her the Message.' (Of the Bahá'í Faith.) In response to this call Dr.
and Lua Getsinger went to California together, and not many
months elapsed before Mrs. Hearst expressed the wish to visit
'Abdu'l-Bahá. . . ." According to Ella Goodall Cooper ("Henrietta Emogene Martin Hoagg, 1869-1945," in *The Bahá'í World: A*

Biennial International Record, Volume X, 1944–1946, comp. National Spiritual Assembly of the Bahá'ís of the United States and Canada [Wilmette, Ill.: Bahá'í Publishing Committee, 1949], p. 520: "Dr. and Mrs. Edward Christopher Getsinger had come from Chicago hoping to interest Mrs. Hearst in the new Revelation." According to O. Z. Whitehead *(Some Early Bahá'ís of the West* [Oxford: George Ronald, 1976], p. 15): "Some time before 1898, Lua Getsinger . . . visited San Francisco. During this trip she called on Mrs. Hearst and spoke to her about the Bahá'í Faith."—ED.

5. Mrs. Hoagg lived in Berkeley at some point soon after she became a Bahá'í in 1898 or 1899. Because of this she left her Bahá'í library to the Berkeley Local Spiritual Assembly in her will.

6. Cooper, "Early Days of the Cause in the West."

7. Helen Hillyer is mentioned in the papers of Ella Cooper in the National Bahá'í Archives and in a history of Helen Goodall ("A Pioneer at the Golden Gate," *Star of the West,* 13 [Nov. 1922], 203) as the person who first told the Goodalls of the Bahá'í Faith. Another account ("Ella Goodall Cooper," in *The Bahá'í World: A Biennial International Record, Volume XII, 1950–1954,* comp. National Spiritual Assembly of the Bahá'ís of the United States [Wilmette, Ill.: Bahá'í Publishing Trust, 1956], pp. 681–82) states that it was Ann Apperson herself who told them.—ED.

8. Cooper, "Early Days of the Cause in the West."

9. Ibid.

10. According to "A Pioneer at the Golden Gate" (p. 203), "a letter was received by Miss Hillyer from Mrs. Hearst requesting her to come at once to Cairo. She very graciously insisted that Mrs. Goodall's daughter Ella should accompany her; therefore a cablegram was despatched to Acca asking for permission." Further accounts of arrangements for this pilgrimage can be found in several places, including: Whitehead, *Some Early Bahá'ís,* pp. 15–16, 21–22; Ramona Allen Brown, *Memories of 'Abdu'l-Bahá: Recollections of the Early Days of the Bahá'í Faith in California* (Wilmette, Ill.: Bahá'í Publishing Trust, 1980), pp. 17–18; Hatch, "Edward Christopher Getsinger," p. 495; and Marion Holley, "May Ellis Maxwell," in *The Bahá'í World: A Biennial International Record, Volume VIII, 1938–1940,* comp. National Spiritual Assembly of the Bahá'ís of the United States and Canada (Wilmette, Ill.: Bahá'í Publishing Committee, 1942), p. 633.—ED.

11. The Persian Consul in Port-Said, Egypt, who arranged all the early passports was Aḥmad Yazdí, Ali Yazdi's uncle. In July 1928 he entertained Ali and me in Port-Said. In July 1981, while on pilgrimage to the Bahá'í World Center, my daughter, grandchildren, and I, with Aziz and Soraya Yazdí, 'Alí Nakhjavání, and Mrs. Músá Banání, visited his grave in the old cemetery in 'Akká.

Ella Cooper was a guest of the Yazdí family in Ramleh, Egypt, on her return from 'Akká in the spring of 1899. She held the newborn baby —Ali—in her arms; a group photograph was taken.

Helen Hillyer married Dr. Philip King Brown, a prominent San Francisco physician. Some years later she invited Ali Yazdi to dinner and to speak on the Faith to her whole family, which she had gathered together for the occasion.

12. The house has since been torn down. The three original palms identify the location.

13. Ramona Allen Brown to Marion [Carpenter] Yazdi, 23 March 1962, author's personal papers. (We have used house style for punctuation and the transliteration of Persian and Arabic words. Ramona Allen Brown describes the occasion more fully in her *Memories of 'Abdu'l-Bahá,* pp. 4–6.—ED.)

14. Other descriptions of "The Peach Tree" can be found in Brown, *Memories of 'Abdu'l-Bahá,* and in "Ella Goodall Cooper," p. 682.—ED.

15. See Marion Holley, "Joseph G. Bray," in *The Bahá'í World: A Biennial International Record, Volume VIII, 1938–1940,* comp. National Spiritual Assembly of the Bahá'ís of the United States and Canada (Wilmette, Ill.: Bahá'í Publishing Committee, 1942), pp. 672–73.

16. The designation "Knight of Bahá'u'lláh" was given to certain Bahá'ís who, during the Ten Year World Crusade launched in 1953 by Shoghi Effendi (Guardian of the Bahá'í Cause), left their homes to resettle in specific areas of the globe in which no Bahá'ís had previously resided.—ED.

17. Mrs. Winterburn and her husband were among the ear-

liest Western Bahá'ís. According to Ella Cooper ("Early Days of the Cause in the West"), they studied art in Paris, made a pilgrimage to 'Akká in 1904, and then returned to California in 1905.
18. A sketch of Ella Bailey's life based on information she gave me is included in Chapter 6.
19. Mariam Haney, "Mrs. Helen S. Goodall," ed. Ella Cooper and Bijou Straun, TS, p. 2, Ella G. Cooper Papers, National Bahá'í Archives, Wilmette, Ill.
20. 'Abdu'l-Bahá to Goodall, in Haney, "Mrs. Helen S. Goodall," p. 14. (An approved translation of this Tablet does not yet exist; consequently, this translation cannot be considered authentic.—ED.)
21. J. V. Matteson, Naw-Rúz talk, Oakland, Calif., 1928.
22. The term "Feast" refers to an institution of Bahá'í community life known as the Nineteen Day Feast. This gathering, established by the Báb and later confirmed by Bahá'u'lláh, is held in Bahá'í communities once every nineteen days (the Bahá'í calendar consists of nineteen months of nineteen days each, with the addition of four or five "intercalary days" to complete the solar year). The Nineteen Day Feast fulfills an important administrative purpose since it affords Bahá'í communities a regular occasion to consult on matters of importance to them, as well as to hear reports from and make recommendations to their local and national administrative bodies. The Feast also has spiritual and social aspects.

In earlier stages in the evolution of the American Bahá'í community, when the Bahá'í administrative system was still largely undeveloped, Feasts served primarily as occasions for talks or readings from the Bahá'í writings and fellowship. The author's use of the term includes gatherings of this nature.—ED.
23. Haney, "Mrs. Helen S. Goodall," p. 7.
24. Shoghi Effendi, *God Passes By*, rev. ed. (Wilmette, Ill.: Bahá'í Publishing Trust, 1974), pp. 257, 386.
25. For accounts of this trip see Amine DeMille, "Lua Getsinger—Herald of the Covenant," *Bahá'í News*, no. 489 (Dec. 1971), p. 3, and Ella Goodall Cooper, "'Preparing the Way' in California," *Star of the West*, 2, no. 16 (31 Dec. 1911), 12–13.—ED.

26. Getsinger to Agnes Parsons, 17 April 1911, Agnes S. Parsons Papers, National Bahá'í Archives, Wilmette, Ill.

27. Getsinger to Parsons, 1 September 1911, Parsons Papers.

Chapter 2: 'Abdu'l-Bahá's Visit to Berkeley, 9 October 1912

1. See Allan L. Ward, 239 Days: 'Abdu'l-Bahá's Journey in America (Wilmette, Ill.: Bahá'í Publishing Trust, 1979), pp. 147–64.

2. "Notes from Diary of Juanita Storch," TS, pp. 4–5, author's personal papers. (We have used house style for spelling, punctuation, capitalization, and the transliteration of Persian and Arabic words.—ED.)

3. Dr. [Frederick] D'Evelyn, "The Coming of Abdu'l Baha to California," Herald of the South, no. 3 (Aug.–Sept. 1926), p. 5. Ella Cooper, another member of the party who greeted 'Abdu'l-Bahá, also gives 3 October as the date 'Abdu'l-Bahá arrived in San Francisco by ferry in her list "Addresses by 'Abdu'l Baha in California" (TS, p. 1, Ella G. Cooper Papers, National Bahá'í Archives, Wilmette, Ill.). The list begins: "Oct. 3—1.30 AM Arrival of Abdul Baha and Party, S. F."

'Abdu'l-Bahá's arrival in San Francisco on 3 October is confirmed in several other sources: Frances Orr Allen, "Abdul-Baha in San Francisco, California," Star of the West, 3, no. 12 (16 Oct. 1912), 9; Ramona Allen Brown, Memories of 'Abdu'l-Bahá: Recollections of the Early Days of the Bahá'í Faith in California (Wilmette, Ill.: Bahá'í Publishing Trust, 1980), p. 34; Mariam Haney, "Mrs. Helen S. Goodall," ed. Ella Cooper and Bijou Straun, TS, p. 9, Cooper Papers.

However, according to H. M. Balyuzi ('Abdu'l-Bahá: The Centre of the Covenant of Bahá'u'lláh [London: George Ronald, 1971], p. 286) and Allan L. Ward (239 Days, p. 165), 'Abdu'l-Bahá arrived in San Francisco by train on 1 October.—ED.

4. See "Interview between Abdul-Baha and a San Francisco Newspaper Reporter," Star of the West, 4 (16 Oct. 1913), 206–07, and "Abdul-Baha's 'Welcome' to California: Address Deliv-

ered at the Home of Mrs. Helen S. Goodall, Oakland, California, October 3, 1912," *Star of the West,* 4 (27 Sept. 1913), 190–91, 194.

5. See note 3.—ED.

6. The *Sun and Letter* was mistaken about the date of 'Abdu'l-Bahá's talk at Berkeley High School, which took place on 9 October 1912.

7. Diary of Mírzá Maḥmúd-i-Zarqání, 25 March 1912 to 5 December 1912, TS, pp. 354–55, entry for 5 October 1912, National Bahá'í Archives, Wilmette, Ill.

8. 'Abdu'l-Bahá "went to see the Greek Theatre at the University of California . . . and praised the structure." Ibid., p. 404, entry for 22 October 1912.

9. Bishop Parsons was asked if he would like to have an interview with 'Abdu'l-Bahá in San Francisco. He welcomed the opportunity and was greatly moved by the experience. Ella Bailey said his voice shook when he spoke of it afterward.

10. 'Abdu'l-Bahá spoke in the old auditorium on the corner of Allston Way and Grove Street that was replaced in 1950 by the Berkeley Community Theater.

11. 'Abdu'l-Bahá's talk at the Berkeley High School is referred to as His "only public address . . . in Berkeley" by Frances Orr Allen in "Abdul-Baha in San Francisco, California," *Star of the West,* 3, no. 13 (4 Nov. 1912), 11. She makes no mention of His talk to the Berkeley Short Story Club. This latter occasion is discussed by Ramona Allen Brown in *Memories of 'Abdu'l-Bahá,* p. 40. —ED.

12. Diary of Mírzá Maḥmúd-i-Zarqání, p. 360, entry for 9 October 1912.

13. "Address by Abdul Baha: High School Auditorium, Berkeley, 8 P. M., October 9, 1912; Introductory Remarks by Mr. Herman I. Stern of the Board of Education," TS, pp. 1–2, Cooper Papers. (We have used house style for spelling, punctuation, and the transliteration of Persian and Arabic words.—ED.)

14. Even as late as 1944 virtually none of the published accounts of 'Abdu'l-Bahá's California visit (including "Cities of North America Visited by 'Abdu'l-Bahá in 1912," in *The Bahá'í Centenary: 1844–1944,* comp. National Spiritual Assembly of the Bahá'ís of the United States and Canada [Wilmette, Ill.: Bahá'í Publishing Committee, 1944], p. 90) mentioned His talk in Berkeley, and private papers were not available to the public. On 20 July 1937 Leroy Ioas wrote to Ali Yazdi, chairman of the Berkeley Local Spiritual Assembly, to find out if and when 'Abdu'l-Bahá visited Berkeley. At that time I started to research the matter and interviewed Frances Allen and Ella Bailey and learned all I could; Miss Bailey had been ill in the hospital the night of 'Abdu'l-Bahá's talk, but she was able to provide information. I also talked to Kathryn Frankland as I reported in a letter to my parents in 1944: "I am gathering material for a history of the Faith in Berkeley. Hope to have Mrs. Frankland for lunch next week and take down all the material I can get." Kathryn lived in Southern California in 1912, but, of course, she came with her daughter Helen to be near 'Abdu'l-Bahá. Years later I discovered an entry for 9 October 1912 in Emogene Hoagg's faded diary in the Berkeley Bahá'í archives.

Ella Cooper and Bijou Straun worked for many years on a projected "California Book"; yet even after Mrs. Cooper's death in 1951 the notes were not available. When Bijou went to a rest home in 1956, Ali, Florence Haake, and I were asked to sort out her Bahá'í effects, including the Cooper-Straun notes. Florence, as secretary of the San Francisco Local Spiritual Assembly, was given these notes, which she classified and sent to the National Spiritual Assembly. I first procured a copy of 'Abdu'l-Bahá's talk from Florence in 1974.

15. "Address by Abdul Baha: High School Auditorium, Berkeley," author's personal papers. (We have used house style for capitalization, spelling, and the transliteration of Persian and Arabic words. An approved translation of this address does not yet exist; consequently, this translation cannot be considered authentic.—ED.)

16. The tokens of His love 'Abdu'l-Bahá bestowed on Georgia Ralston that night and on other occasions during His stay in San Francisco gave her a center of strength that stayed with her the rest of her difficult life. 'Abdu'l-Bahá presented to Georgie, as she was affectionately known to her friends, a beautiful Persian rug that went with her always, even brightening the bleak little room in Oakland where she lived in the thirties—and was at last her only possession. The changes and chances of the world—the loss of her husband and of her family's great wealth, her friends, her social position—never affected her abiding devotion to 'Abdu'l-Bahá. In the time of the single room I was often with her and drove her to Feasts. I listened enchanted to her stories of the blessed days in San Francisco in 1912 when she drove the Master to Golden Gate Park in the afternoons (the beauty and the peace refreshed Him); the little battery-driven car always had a part in her reminiscenses.

'Abdu'l-Bahá, too, remembered Georgia Ralston. In a Tablet written in 1917 (but delayed because of World War I) 'Abdu'l-Bahá wrote: "From the time of our separation up to this hour thou wert and art ever in my mind. I have not forgotten thee even for one day. . . ." In a letter accompanying 'Abdu'l-Bahá's Tablet Aḥmad Sohráb wrote: "This afternoon I spent . . . in the presence of Abdul-Baha. . . . He mentioned your name and Mr. Ralston's, and brought to mind when you used to take him in your electric car to the Golden Gate Park." ("Letter and Tablet to Mrs. Georgie Ralston," *Star of the West*, 9 [4 Nov. 1918], 143, 142.)

Chapter 3: The Faith Gathers Momentum, 1912–1925

1. Mr. Ralston, the son and namesake of William C. Ralston, Sr., the well-known nineteenth-century tycoon of San Francisco, was, to my knowledge, the only member of the Committee who was not a Bahá'í. For the leaflet issued about the International Bahá'í Congress, the official program, and Tablets from 'Abdu'l-Bahá about it, see *Star of the West*, 5 (19 Jan. 1915), 258, 260–61, 264–66.

2. For a record of the Official Reception see *Star of the West*, 6 (17 May 1915), 25–34; ibid. (5 June 1915), 38–40.—ED.

3. See Mary Hanford Ford, "The Feast of Rizwan," *Star of the West*, 6 (5 June 1915), 35–37. Included is a picture of the many Bahá'ís who attended the Feast.—ED.

4. Ibid., p. 35.

5. A sketch of the life of Kathryn Frankland is included in Chapter 6. See also 'Alí and Marion Yazdí, "Kathryn Frankland, 1872–1963," in *The Bahá'í World: An International Record, Volume XIV, 1963–1968*, comp. The Universal House of Justice (Haifa: The Universal House of Justice, 1974), pp. 337–40.

6. Mrs. Frankland hoped to will this house to the Berkeley

Spiritual Assembly for a Bahá'í center. Julia Culver invested $2,000 toward the project, but Mrs. Frankland found it necessary to sell the house to pay for her pioneering projects.

7. A sketch of the life of Kanichi Yamamoto (Moto) is included in Chapter 6. See also Marion Yazdi, "Kanichi Yamamoto: 1879–1961," in *The Bahá'í World: An International Record, Volume XIII, 1954–1963,* comp. The Universal House of Justice (Haifa: The Universal House of Justice, 1970), pp. 931–33; Marion Yazdi, "Kanichi Yamamoto," *Bahá'í News,* no. 556 (July 1977), pp. 4–8.

8. For Shinji Yamamoto's account of life in the relocation camps see "Conversations with Americans," *World Order,* 10, no. 2 (Winter 1975–76), 53–58.—ED.

9. Sketches of their lives are included in Chapter 6.

10. 'Abdu'l-Bahá to Kathryn and Alec Frankland, 31 Ádhar 1919, Tablets of 'Abdu'l-Bahá, National Bahá'í Archives, Wilmette, Ill. (An approved translation of this Tablet does not yet exist; consequently, this translation cannot be considered authentic. The date on this Tablet is a curious amalgam of East and West, no doubt an oversight on the translator's part: Ádhar is one of the months of the Persian [but *not* Muslim] calendar; the year given is, of course, the Gregorian.—ED.)

11. "Report of Twelfth Annual Mashrekol-Azkar Convention: Held in New York City, April 26th–29th, 1920," *Star of the West,* 11 (27 Sept. 1920), 174.

12. Excerpts from these letters are found in Chapter 4.

13. "The world is full of women's eyes, / Defiant, filled with shy surprise, / Demure, a little overfree, / Or simply smiling roguishly; / It seems a gorgeous lily-bed, / Whichever way I turn my head."

14. A. Elizabeth Carpenter to Marion Carpenter, circa late 1920, author's personal papers. (We have used house style for punctuation and the transliteration of Persian and Arabic words. —ED.)

15. The Franklands had asked permission as early as 1907 to make the pilgrimage. To Kathryn Frankland 'Abdu'l-Bahá revealed a Tablet with the reply: "Postpone this matter until some other time." (See 'Abdu'l-Bahá, *Tablets of Abdul-Baha Abbas,* 3 vols. [New York: Bahai Publishing Society, 1909–1916], I, 235.)

16. Marion Carpenter to 'Abdu'l-Bahá, 29 August 1920,

author's personal papers. (We have used house style for transliteration of Persian and Arabic words.—ED.)

17. Frankland to Marion Carpenter, 2 December 1920, author's personal papers. (We have used house style for punctuation.—ED.)

18. 'Abdu'l-Bahá to Marion Carpenter, 20 November 1920, as reported in Frankland to Carpenter, 2 December 1920, author's personal papers. This was a message conveyed verbally and thus does not have the authenticity of a signed Tablet in an approved translation. (We have used house style for capitalization and punctuation.—ED.)

19. These included photographs of Mrs. Frankland arranging carnations; Mrs. Frankland reading to her daughter; Mrs. Frankland, Mrs. Ralston, and Mrs. Cooper at the Sphinx; the knighting of 'Abdu'l-Bahá; and the now well-known picture of 'Abdu'l-Bahá about to sign a Tablet.

20. 'Abdu'l-Bahá, in a Tablet dated 8 October 1920, wrote to William Randall: "Jináb-i-Shaykh 'Alí, the distinguished son of Ḥájí Áqá Muḥammad, is a sensible and cultured young man of good behaviour. He will be going to America to complete the courses of sciences and arts which he has been studying in Berlin. Probably he will remain about two years in America. Thou shouldst treat him with the utmost consideration and kindness." ('Abdu'l-Bahá to Randall, 8 October 1920, trans. The Universal House of Justice, 1 February 1982, author's personal papers.) The author was surprised to learn, while on pilgrimage in 1981, that 'Abdu'l-Bahá had also sent on 9 December 1920 a Tablet to Ruth Randall with instructions concerning Ali Yazdi. The author was given a copy of the Persian original, and has since received, on 1 February 1982, a translation of the Tablet verified by The Universal House of Justice. To Roy Wilhelm 'Abdu'l-Bahá wrote on 6 September 1920: "His honor Sheikh Ali is going to America. He is a youth of good manners and temperament and is of an accepted family at the Threshold of God. Therefore you will do your best to help him in managing his affairs." ('Abdu'l-Bahá to Wilhelm, trans. Azizullah S. Bahadour, 6 September 1920, author's personal papers. The Persian original of this Tablet has not been found; consequently, this translation cannot be considered authentic.) In a Tablet in His own handwriting, received by Sheikh-Ali shortly after his arrival in the United States, 'Abdu'l-Bahá wrote: "Render thanks unto God, that in this blessed age thou hast stepped forth into the world of existence, been nursed from the breast of the love of God and hast been reared in the bosom of divine guidance, and that now with the permission of 'Abdu'l-Bahá and by His leave thou art proceeding to America to study the sciences." ('Abdu'l-Bahá to Ali Yazdi, circa 1920–21, trans. The Universal House of Justice, 1 February 1982, author's personal papers.) The author is deeply grateful to The Universal House of Justice for providing translations for three of the four Tablets, which show 'Abdu'l-Bahá's tender concern for Sheikh-Ali.

21. "Reports—Berkeley: By the Secretary, Marion Carpenter," *The Magazine of the Children of the Kingdom,* 3 (Mar. 1922), 32.

22. Shahnaz Waite, "The Teaching Conference in the West," *The Magazine of the Children of the Kingdom,* 4 (Dec. 1922), 22.

23. Mirza Ahmad Sohrab, "The First Western Bahai Teaching Conference," *The Magazine of the Children of the Kingdom,* 4 (Mar. 1923), 30.

24. 'Abdu'l-Bahá, in Bahá'u'lláh and 'Abdu'l-Bahá, *Bahá'í World Faith: Selected Writings of Bahá'u'lláh and 'Abdu'l-Bahá,* rev. ed. (Wilmette, Ill.: Bahá'í Publishing Trust, 1976), p. 365.

25. Several years later in 1928, while visiting Ali's family in Egypt, we were invited to spend the evening with Mr. Kilany, one of our friends who had been president of the Cosmopolitan Club. There we enjoyed a delicious twelve-course dinner in his luxurious Cairo home. The ladies of the household were not visible, but we could hear rustling and soft voices nearby.

26. Martha L. Root, "The Bahá'í Movement and North American University Circles," in *The Bahá'í World: A Biennial International Record, Volume IV, 1930–1932,* comp. National Spiritual Assembly of the Bahá'ís of the United States and Canada (New York: Bahá'í Publishing Committee, 1933), p. 464.

27. William L. Chenery, "Mr. Zero: The Man Who Feeds the Hungry," *Survey,* 1 Oct. 1921, pp. 15–16.

28. "The Bahaists," *Survey*, 12 Nov. 1921, p. 257.

29. Mr. Frankland was advertising manager for the *Gazette* and a close friend of the owner, Mr. Dunscomb. While the Franklands lived in Berkeley (and long after) the *Gazette* gave much space to Bahá'í activities.

30. See letter dated 17 January 1922 in Chapter 4.

31. Shoghi Effendi to Bahá'ís of Berkeley, 7 January 1923, Letters of Shoghi Effendi, National Bahá'í Archives, Wilmette, Ill. (We have used house style for spelling and the transliteration of Persian and Arabic words. Obvious typographical errors have been corrected.—ED.) The address "Care of the members of the Spiritual Assembly" does not refer to the official Local Spiritual Assembly that was formed in 1925.

32. 'Abdu'l-Bahá to Rasmussen, 8 January 1919. For the full text of the Tablet, as translated by Shoghi Rabbani, see "Recent Tablets from Abdul-Baha to American Bahais," *Star of the West*, 10 (2 Mar. 1920), 340.

33. From a letter written on behalf of Shoghi Effendi, with a section in Shoghi Effendi's handwriting, to Kathryn Frankland, 11 November 1924, Letters of Shoghi Effendi. (We have substituted "and" for ampersands.—ED.)

34. For descriptions of these two years see Chapters 9, 10, and 11.

35. An account of our marriage written by Shahnaz Waite, "Union of the East and West," was published in *The Bahá'í Magazine*, 17 (Oct. 1926), 228–29. By the time we returned to Berkeley the first Local Spiritual Assembly of Berkeley had already been formed and recognized. For details see Chapter 5.

Chapter 4: Letters Home, 1920–1923

1. The letters, from the author's personal papers, have been edited to conform to house style with regard to punctuation, spelling, the substitution of "and" for ampersands, and the transliteration of Persian and Arabic words.—ED.

2. The author uses the word "Assembly" to refer to the entire community of Bahá'ís in the Bay Area at that time. The use of the word Assembly to refer to administrative institutions of the Faith did not become customary until several years later, during Shoghi Effendi's ministry as Guardian of the Bahá'í Faith (beginning in 1921).—ED.

3. The author's letter alludes to the controversy that arose over the Bahá'í Temple Unity Executive Board's request, early in 1921, for permission to begin construction of a Bahá'í House of Worship in the Chicago suburb of Wilmette. Forces fearing the entrance into their community of a "new and undesirable cult" attempted to block the granting of a building permit by the Wilmette Village Board. The incident is mentioned in Carl Scheffler, "Extracts from Mashriqu'l-Adhkár Report," in *Bahá'í Year Book, Volume One, 1925–1926,* comp. National Spiritual Assembly of the Bahá'ís of the United States and Canada (New York: Bahá'í Publishing Committee, 1926), p. 74; and Allen Boyer McDaniel, *The Spell of the Temple* (New York: Vantage Press, 1953), pp. 38–39.—ED.

4. See Chapter 1, note 1.—ED.

5. Saichiro Fujita had come to work for the Franklands in Fruitvale in 1903 and had become a believer there; he later went to Haifa to serve 'Abdu'l-Bahá. See also Chapter 6, note 36.—ED.

6. Ali Yazdi had been with 'Abdu'l-Bahá in Ramleh and in Haifa.

7. Bosch to Ella Cooper, 5 December 1921. For part of the text of the letter, see H. M. Balyuzi, *'Abdu'l-Bahá: The Centre of the Covenant of Bahá'u'lláh* (London: George Ronald, 1971), p. 463. (For the Bosches' account of the passing of 'Abdu'l-Bahá, see Marzieh Gail, "'Abdu'l-Bahá: Portrayals from East and West," *World Order,* 6, no. 1 [Fall 1971], 40–41, 44.—ED.)

8. Shoghi Effendi and Ali Yazdi were friends in Ramleh, Beirut, and Haifa; they attended school and university together. Shoghi Effendi invited Ali to visit him at Oxford in the fall of 1920.

9. Because Mrs. Goodall was ill, she was not told of 'Abdu'l-Bahá's passing when word came from Haifa. When she heard of it later, she was calm but died soon after.

10. "A Pioneer at the Golden Gate," *Star of the West,* 13 (Nov. 1922), 203–07.

11. See Chapter 1, note 7. Mrs. Goodall first heard the Faith mentioned by Helen Hillyer, but Lua Getsinger was her first Bahá'í teacher.

12. From 1921 through 1923 my sister, who had moved to Berkeley, and I lived together. Hence I was no longer staying at the Franklands.

13. Shoghi Effendi and Lady Blomfield, *The Passing of 'Abdu'l-Baha* (Haifa: privately printed, 1922). Excerpts from this booklet, which has long been out of print, were published with emendations as Lady Blomfield and Shoghi Effendi, "The Passing of 'Abdu'l-Bahá," in *Bahá'í Year Book, Volume One, 1925–1926*, comp. National Spiritual Assembly of the Bahá'ís of the United States and Canada (New York: Bahá'í Publishing Committee, 1926), pp. 19–31. An abridged version of the booklet was published in *World Order* as "The Passing of 'Abdu'l-Bahá: Extracts Compiled by Shoghi Effendi and Lady Blomfield," *World Order*, 6, no. 1 (Fall 1971), 6–18.—ED.

Chapter 5: "Cause Welcomes Berkeley Assembly"

1. Elmer had been adopted by his grandmother, Mrs. Dearborn.

2. The plan in 1925 was to build a first story. However, this was changed, and by 1930 the entire superstructure was begun. See Allen Boyer McDaniel, "A Superstructure Is Built," in *The Spell of the Temple* (New York: Vantage Press, 1953), pp. 53–61.

3. "Hokuk" (Ḥuqúqu'lláh, lit. "The Right of God"): refers to the system ordained by Bahá'u'lláh of tithes or payment of a fraction of the monetary value of a believer's possessions to The Universal House of Justice, the supreme governing body of the Bahá'í Faith.—ED; Ali Yazdi to Marion Carpenter, 13 October 1925, author's personal papers. (We have used house style for punctuation and for the transliteration of Persian and Arabic words, with the exception of "hokuk."—ED.)

4. Ali Yazdi to Marion Carpenter, 1 November 1925, author's personal papers. (We have used house style for punctuation, spelling, and the transliteration of Persian and Arabic words.—ED.)

5. Shoghi Effendi to Frankland, 20 November 1925, Letters of Shoghi Effendi, National Bahá'í Archives, Wilmette, Ill. (Obvious typographical errors have been corrected.—ED.)

6. From a letter written on behalf of Shoghi Effendi, with a section in Shoghi Effendi's handwriting, to Frankland, 24 November 1925, Letters of Shoghi Effendi. (We have used house style for spelling and have substituted "and" for ampersands. —ED.)

Chapter 6: Sketches of Some Early Berkeley Bahá'ís

1. Personal interview with Ella Bailey.

2. Ibid.

3. The following paragraphs are from Ella Bailey, "Memories of 'Abdu'l-Bahá," TS, pp. 1–2, 5–7, author's personal papers. (We have used house style for spelling and punctuation.—ED.)

4. For the text of 'Abdu'l-Bahá's talk at the Feast in Oakland and a brief description of the Feast see "Abdul-Baha at the Nineteen Day Feast," *Star of the West*, 4 (16 Oct. 1913), 203–04, 209.

5. His talk was first published in "Message to the Jews: Address by Abdul-Baha Abbas before Congregation Emmanu-El, San Francisco, Cal., (Martin A. Meyer, Rabbi) Saturday, October 12, 1912," *Star of the West*, 3, no. 13 (4 Nov. 1912), 3–7, 10–11. Later it was also published in 'Abdu'l-Bahá, *The Promulgation of Universal Peace: Talks Delivered by 'Abdu'l-Bahá during His Visit to the United States and Canada in 1912*, comp. Howard MacNutt, 2d ed. (Wilmette, Ill.: Bahá'í Publishing Trust, 1982), pp. 361–70.

6. Shoghi Effendi, quoted in Robert L. Gulick, Jr., "Ella M. Bailey," in *The Bahá'í World: A Biennial International Record, Volume XII, 1950–1954*, comp. National Spiritual Assembly of the Bahá'ís of the United States (Wilmette, Ill.: Bahá'í Publishing Trust, 1956), p. 688.

7. Shoghi Effendi, quoted in "Marion Jack," in *The Bahá'í World: A Biennial International Record, Volume XII, 1950–1954*, comp. National Spiritual Assembly of the Bahá'ís of the United States (Wilmette, Ill.: Bahá'í Publishing Trust, 1956), p. 674.

8. A shorter version of this sketch appeared as an in memoriam article in *The Bahá'í World*. See 'Alí and Marion Yazdí, "Kathryn Frankland, 1872–1963," in *The Bahá'í World: An International Record, Volume XIV, 1963–1968*, comp. The Universal House of Justice (Haifa: The Universal House of Justice, 1974), pp. 337–40.—ED.

9. Personal interview with Kathryn Frankland, 17 Aug. 1943.

10. Ibid.

11. Bahá'u'lláh, *Three Tablets of Baha'o'llah Revealed at Adrianople, Acca, and Bagdad: Tablet of the Branch, Kitab-el-Ah'd, Lawh-el-Akdas*, trans. Ali Kuli Khan (M. Eshte'al-Ebn Kalanter) (Chicago: Bahai Publishing Society, 1918), p. 157. (For a more accurate translation, see Bahá'u'lláh, *Tablets of Bahá'u'lláh Revealed after the Kitáb-i-Aqdas*, comp. Research Department of the Universal House of Justice, trans. Habib Taherzadeh et al. [Haifa: Bahá'í World Centre, 1978], p. 9.—ED.)

12. The first five Tablets Kathryn Frankland received from 'Abdu'l-Bahá were published in 'Abdu'l-Bahá, *Tablets of Abdul-Baha Abbas*, 3 vols. (New York: Bahai Publishing Society, 1909–1916), I, 233–35. The Tablet that follows appears on pages 233–34 of the same book.

13. Alec Frankland, quoted in personal interview with Kathryn Frankland, 17 Aug. 1943.

14. Ibid.

15. Personal interview with Kathryn Frankland, 17 Aug. 1943.

16. 'Abdu'l-Bahá, *Tablets of Abdul-Baha Abbas*, I, 234.

17. Fujita (Saichiro Fujita—see note 36.—ED.) had great respect for Mrs. Brittingham. Kathryn Frankland said that when Mrs. Brittingham was talking his eyes were full of tears (personal interview with Kathryn Frankland, 4 Oct. 1962).

18. 'Abdu'l-Bahá to Kathryn and Alec Frankland, circa 1909, Tablets of 'Abdu'l-Bahá, National Bahá'í Archives, Wilmette, Ill.

19. 'Abdu'l-Bahá, quoted in personal interview with Kathryn Frankland, 4 Oct. 1962. (Since neither documentation nor an approved translation exists for this quote, it cannot be considered authentic.—ED.)

20. 'Abdu'l-Bahá, *Tablets of Abdul-Baha Abbas*, I, 235.

21. Frankland to 'Abdu'l-Bahá, as told to Marion Carpenter Yazdi, personal interview, 17 Aug. 1943.

22. 'Abdu'l-Bahá, quoted by Kathryn Frankland in relating details of her 1920 pilgrimage to Marion Carpenter Yazdi, personal interview, 17 Aug. 1943. (Since neither documentation nor an approved translation exists for this passage, it cannot be considered authentic and must be regarded as "pilgrim's notes."—Ed.)

23. 'Abdu'l-Bahá referred to Kanichi Yamamoto as a "youth of God" in a Tablet published in 'Abdu'l-Bahá, *Tablets of Abdul-Baha Abbas*, III, 561. A shorter version of this account appeared as an in memoriam article in *The Bahá'í World*. See Marion Yazdi, "Kanichi Yamamoto, 1879–1961," in *The Bahá'í World: An International Record, Volume XIII, 1954–1963*, comp. The Universal House of Justice (Haifa: The Universal House of Justice, 1970), pp. 931–33. See also Marion Yazdi, "Kanichi Yamamoto," *Bahá'í News*, no. 556 (July 1977), pp. 4–8. The information for the sketch comes from Agnes Alexander, Ella Cooper, Kathryn Frankland, Hiroshi and Shinji Yamamoto, and my own personal recollections.

24. Agnes B. Alexander, *Forty Years of the Baha'i Cause in Hawaii: 1902–1942* (Honolulu: National Spiritual Assembly of the Baha'is of the Hawaiian Islands, 1974), p. 12.

25. Ibid.

26. 'Abdu'l-Bahá, *Tablets of Abdul-Baha Abbas*, III, 563–64.

27. Ibid., III, 559.

28. Alexander, *Forty Years*, p. 12.

29. Yúnis Khán-i-Afrúkhtih, *Kitáb-i-khátirát-i-nuhsáli-yi-'Akká* [Memories of Nine Years in 'Akká] (Ṭihrán: National Bahá'í Publishing Committee of Írán, 109 b.e.), pp.361–63. The book, to the author's knowledge, has not been translated into English. The excerpts quoted were translated for the author by Nura Mobine Ioas. (We have used house style for the transliteration of Persian and Arabic words.—Ed.)

30. 'Abdu'l-Bahá, *Tablets of Abdul-Baha Abbas*, III, 560–61.

31. Alexander, *Forty Years*, pp. 12–13.

32. 'Abdu'l-Bahá, *Tablets of Abdul-Baha Abbas*, III, 563.

33. Ella Cooper, "Early Days of the Cause in the West,"

Geyserville Bahá'í School, Geyserville, Calif., 7 July 1942.

34. Alexander, *Forty Years*, p. 13.

35. Mariam Haney, "Mrs. Helen S. Goodall," ed. Ella Cooper and Bijou Straun, TS, p. 7, Ella G. Cooper Papers, National Bahá'í Archives, Wilmette, Ill. (We have used house style for punctuation and the transliteration of Persian and Arabic words.—ED.)

36. In 1903, when he was thirteen, Saichiro Fujita had begun work for the Franklands in Oakland as a houseboy. Later he went to Wilmette to serve in the home of Mrs. Corinne True. From there he journeyed in 1912 with 'Abdu'l-Bahá to California to serve Him. In 1920 Fujita went to Haifa to serve, dying there in 1976. See H. M. Balyuzi, *'Abdu'l-Bahá: The Centre of the Covenant of Bahá'u'lláh* (London: George Ronald, 1971), pp. 266–67, and Ramona Allen Brown, *Memories of 'Abdu'l-Bahá: Recollections of the Early Days of the Bahá'í Faith in California* (Wilmette, Ill.: Bahá'í Publishing Trust, 1980), pp. 25, 129.—ED.

37. Frances Orr Allen, "Abdul-Baha in San Francisco, California," *Star of the West,* 3, no. 13 (4 Nov. 1912), 13.

38. Telephone conversation with Yamamoto family. For Shinji Yamamoto's account of life in the relocation camps see "Conversations with Americans," *World Order,* 10, no. 2 (Winter 1975–76), 53–58.

39. 'Abdu'l-Bahá, *Tablets of Abdul-Baha Abbas,* III, 560–61.

40. This sketch is taken from Ali Yazdi, Remarks at Memorial Service for Berdette Matteson, Mountain View Cemetery Chapel, Oakland, Calif., 29 Jan. 1971.

41. Cooper, "Early Days of the Cause in the West."

42. Ibid.

43. The author is very grateful for this sketch ("Some Notes on the Life of J. V. Matteson," TS, pp. 1–3, author's personal papers), which was written by Lorne Matteson, J. V.'s and Berdette's son. (We have used house style for spelling, punctuation, and the transliteration of Persian and Arabic words.—ED.)

44. J. V. Matteson, untitled and undated statement on how he became a Bahá'í, TS, p. 2, author's personal papers. (We have used house style for capitalization and the transliteration of Persian and Arabic words.—ED.)

45. Bahá'u'lláh, *The Hidden Words of Bahá'u'lláh,* trans. Shoghi Effendi (Wilmette, Ill.: Bahá'í Publishing Trust, 1939), p. 40.

Chapter 7: Postscript

1. René Dubos, *Beast or Angel? Choices That Make Us Human* (New York: Scribners, 1974), p. 7.

Part Two
Early Days of the Bahá'í Faith at Stanford University

Chapter 8: 'Abdu'l-Bahá's Visit to Stanford University and Palo Alto, 8–9 October 1912

1. Ella Cooper, "'Abdu'l-Bahá in California," n.p., n.d.
2. The Assembly Hall in which 'Abdu'l-Bahá spoke became later the Business School and then the Sociology Department. The building has now been fully renovated to house once again the Sociology Department.
3. See Chapter 2, note 3.
4. Cooper, "'Abdu'l-Bahá in California."
5. *Palo Altan,* 1 Nov. 1912, p. 1.
6. Ibid., p. 2. (Excerpts from Dr. Jordan's speech are also found in the Diary of Mírzá Maḥmúd-i-Zarqání, 25 March 1912 to 5 December 1912, TS, p. 359, entry for 8 October 1912, National Bahá'í Archives, Wilmette, Ill., and in "Address by Abdul-Baha: At Leland Stanford Junior University, Palo Alto, California, October 8, 1912, 10:15 a.m.," *Star of the West,* 3, no. 12 [16 Oct. 1912], 10.—ED.)
7. 'Abdu'l-Bahá, *The Promulgation of Universal Peace: Talks Delivered by 'Abdu'l-Bahá during His Visit to the United States and Canada in 1912,* comp. Howard MacNutt, 2d ed. (Wilmette, Ill.: Bahá'í Publishing Trust, 1982), p. 348.
8. Ibid., pp. 354–55.
9. "Abdul Baha Speaks at Stanford University," *Daily Palo*

Alto Times, 11–14 Oct. 1912, n. pag.; "To the World of Science: Address Delivered by Abdul Baha at Stanford University, Palo Alto, Cal., Oct. 8, 1912, 10:15 A. M.," *Palo Altan,* 1 Nov. 1912, pp. 2, 4; "Address by Abdul-Baha: At Leland Stanford Junior University," pp. 10–14; 'Abdu'l-Bahá, *Promulgation,* pp. 348–55.

10. "Abdul Baha Speaks at Stanford University," n. pag.; "To the World of Science," p. 4. (The wording in "Address by Abdul-Baha: At Leland Stanford Junior University," p. 14, and in the Diary of Mírzá Maḥmúd-i-Zarqání, p. 359, entry for 8 October 1912, differs slightly.—ED.)

11. Cooper, "'Abdu'l-Bahá in California."

12. *Daily Palo Alto,* 8 Oct. 1912, pp. 1, 3.

13. Ibid., p. 1.

14. Recently, while at Stanford on a walking tour, I wanted to stand where 'Abdu'l-Bahá had stood and read that inscription. I asked the guide about the plaque, but there seemed to be none. When I wrote the Stanford University Archives, which has been interested in my project and very helpful, I received this reply (Margaret Coesfeld [Stanford University Archives] to Marion [Carpenter] Yazdi, 19 June 1980, author's personal papers): "There is an inscribed stone plaque on the lower left corner of the Memorial Church facade that reads:

> Memorial Church
> erected by
> Jane Stanford
> to the glory of God and in
> loving memory of her husband
> Leland Stanford.

Perhaps you missed it in your recent visit because it is the same color as the surrounding building stones, and so doesn't stand out." The place before which 'Abdu'l-Bahá stood had been built "to the glory of God."

15. Ella Bailey gave me the photograph forty years ago, noting, though I later forgot this, that the American in the photo was Dr. Ray Lyman Wilbur. Recently, when I wrote the Stanford Archives about the photograph, I received this reply (Coesfeld [Stanford University Archives] to Marion [Carpenter] Yazdi, 19 June 1980, author's personal papers):

Thank you for sending the photo of Abdul Baha at Stanford with your last letter. The entire Archives staff found it very interesting. . . .

I was not able to identify the American man in the photo. He somewhat resembles Ray Lyman Wilbur, at that time Dean of the Medical School, but that's only a guess. . . .

Best wishes with your project.

I then remembered clearly that the man was indeed Wilbur. For further verification I asked Ray Lyman Wilbur, Jr., who wrote me: "I have looked carefully at the picture several times. The person in question could be my father, but I wouldn't swear by it. I feel you could be safe in so identifying the person as my father as many features look familiar. He was Dean of the Medical School at that time and was 37 years old" (Wilbur to Marion [Carpenter] Yazdi, 24 August 1980, author's personal papers).

16. Personal interview with Mrs. David Starr Jordan conducted by Joyce Dahl and May Stebbins, 26 Sept. 1950.

17. Personal interview with a member of the Spiritual Assembly of the Bahá'ís of Palo Alto, 8 Oct. 1950; Spiritual Assembly of the Bahá'ís of Palo Alto to Marion [Carpenter] Yazdi, 22 May 1952, author's personal papers; and Ella Cooper, "Addresses by 'Abdu'l Baha in California," TS, p. 1, Ella G. Cooper Papers, National Bahá'í Archives, Wilmette, Ill. From the first two sources I also learned that the Waverly Street home was a two-story English-type frame house surrounded by shrubbery, with two palm trees in front. (It has since been torn down.) It belonged to Mrs. Merriman's daughter, Mrs. Fredrica Marriott. Mrs. Merriman herself lived at 235 Melville Avenue. She died 13 June 1920.

18. For photograph see *Palo Altan*, 1 Nov. 1912, p. 1. From information I received from a member of the Spiritual Assembly of the Bahá'ís of Palo Alto on 8 October 1950 and from a letter from that Assembly dated 22 May 1952, I learned that Reed later went from Palo Alto to Oakland and then after his retirement to Carmel. He died at the age of seventy-three in 1945.

19. According to a 22 May 1952 letter I received from the Spiritual Assembly of the Bahá'ís of Palo Alto this church, on the corner of Cowper and Channing Streets, was later bought by the Glad Tidings people.

20. *Palo Altan,* 1 Nov. 1912, p. 4.

21. Ibid.

22. Personal interview with Seward, 14 Feb. 1924. (See Chapters 9, p. 137, and 10, pp. 166–69.—ED.)

23. Diary of Mírzá Maḥmúd-i-Zarqání, p. 360, entry for 9 October 1912. (We have used house style for the transliteration of Persian and Arabic words.—ED.)

24. David Starr Jordan, *The Days of a Man: Being Memories of a Naturalist, Teacher and Minor Prophet of Democracy* (Yonkers-on-Hudson, N.Y.: World Book Co., 1922), II, 414.

25. David Starr Jordan, in Willard P. Hatch, "Dr. David Starr Jordan," in *The Bahá'í World: A Biennial International Record, Volume IV, 1930–1932,* comp. National Spiritual Assembly of the Bahá'ís of the United States and Canada (New York: Bahá'í Publishing Committee, 1933), p. 516.

26. *Palo Altan,* 1 Nov. 1912, p. 1. This quotation from the article in the *London Chronicle* (published before Jordan knew 'Abdu'l-Bahá) has unwittingly been attributed to David Starr Jordan for many years.

'Abdu'l-Bahá's Tablet to Simkins as well as Simkins' editorial "The New Evangel," which were part of the 1 November 1912 issue of the *Palo Altan,* were reprinted in *Star of the West,* 3, no. 13 (4 Nov. 1912), 8–9.

Many years later at a commemoration of 'Abdu'l-Bahá's Stanford visit held in Palo Alto, Molly King recalls that a person then living in the house formerly belonging to H. W. Simkins presented to those in charge a file containing a number of copies of the 1 November *Palo Altan.*

27. See *Auguste Forel and the Bahá'í Faith: With a Commentary by Peter Mühlschlegel* (Oxford: George Ronald, 1978), pp. 6, 59.

28. 'Abdu'l-Bahá, quoted in *Christian Commonwealth,* 1 Jan. 1913, p. 1.

29. 'Abdu'l-Bahá to the Bahá'ís of East and West, 22 September 1914, trans. Mirza Ahmad Sohrab, TS, p. 2, author's personal papers. (We have used house style for capitalization, spelling, punctuation, and the transliteration of Persian and Arabic words. An approved translation of this Tablet does not yet exist; consequently, this translation cannot be considered authentic.—ED.)

30. Shoghi Effendi, *God Passes By*, rev. ed. (Wilmette, Ill.: Bahá'í Publishing Trust, 1974), p. 291.
31. Ibid., 291, 289.
32. Ali Yazdi, Shoghi Effendi's classmate, recalled this.
33. Personal interview with Mrs. David Starr Jordan conducted by Joyce Dahl and May Stebbins, 26 Sept. 1950.
34. Personal interview with Mrs. Percy Martin, 8 Oct. 1950.
35. Guérard to Horace Holley, 1 September 1959, author's personal papers.
36. Guérard to Horace Holley, 4 October 1959, author's personal papers.
37. Guérard to Arthur L. Dahl, Jr., 4 October 1959, author's personal papers.

Chapter 9: In the Wake of the Master—
Experiences of the First Stanford Bahá'í Student

1. Majnún is the title of the celebrated lover of ancient Persian and Arabic lore, whose beloved was Laylí, daughter of an Arabian prince. Their story is the theme of many Persian romantic poems and is mentioned by Bahá'u'lláh in the Seven Valleys. See Bahá'u'lláh, *The Seven Valleys and the Four Valleys*, trans. Ali-Kuli Khan and Marzieh Gail, 3d rev. ed. (Wilmette, Ill.: Bahá'í Publishing Trust, 1978), p. 6.—ED.
2. The author refers to a number of Bahá'í books that are today no longer in print: Bahá'u'lláh and 'Abdu'l-Bahá, *Bahai Scriptures: Selections from the Utterances of Baha'u'llah and Abdul Baha*, ed. Horace Holley (New York: Brentano's, Inc., 1923); 'Abdu'l-Bahá, *Tablets of Abdul-Baha Abbas*, 3 vols. (New York: Bahai Publishing Society, 1909–1916); Mirza-Abul-Fazl, *The Bahäi Proofs (Hujaj'ul Behäyyeh): Also a Short Sketch of the History and Lives of the Leaders of This Religion*, 2d ed. (Chicago: The Grier Press, 1914); Mary Hanford Ford, *The Oriental Rose: Or the Teachings of Abdul Baha Which Trace the Chart of "The Shining Pathway"* (Chicago: Bahai Publishing Society, 1910); Myron H. Phelps, *Life and Teachings of Abbas Effendi: A Study of the Religion of the Babis, or Beha'is Founded by the Persian Bab and by His Successors, Beha Ullah and Abbas Effendi* (New York & London: G. P. Putnam's Sons, 1903).

Three of the books she mentions, however, exist today in different editions: Bahá'u'lláh, *The Kitáb-i-Íqán: The Book of Certitude,* trans. Shoghi Effendi, 3d ed. (Wilmette, Ill.: Bahá'í Publishing Trust, 1974); 'Abdu'l-Bahá, *Some Answered Questions,* comp. and trans. Laura Clifford Barney, 5th ed. (Wilmette, Ill.: Bahá'í Publishing Trust, 1981); and 'Abdu'l-Bahá, *The Promulgation of Universal Peace: Talks Delivered by 'Abdu'l-Bahá during His Visit to the United States and Canada in 1912,* comp. Howard MacNutt, 2d ed. (Wilmette, Ill.: Bahá'í Publishing Trust, 1982).—ED.

3. "Prayers of the Báb," in Bahá'u'lláh and 'Abdu'l-Bahá, *Prayers and Meditations,* comp. National Spiritual Assembly of the Bahá'ís of the United States and Canada (New York: Bahá'í Publishing Committee, 1929), p. 1.

4. Marion Carpenter to Haney, quoted in *National Baha'i Bulletin,* 17 Dec. 1923, p. 8.

5. Jordan to Marion Carpenter, 8 November 1923, author's personal papers.

6. *National Baha'i Bulletin,* 17 Dec. 1923, p. 8.

7. Marion Carpenter to Haney, quoted in *National Baha'i Bulletin,* 17 Dec. 1923, p. 8.

8. Quoted in *National Baha'i Bulletin,* 17 Dec. 1923, p. 8.

9. Part of one of my mother's letters to me expresses very well our delight whenever Ella Cooper spoke: "I know you must enjoy hearing Mrs. Cooper. Whenever I think of her it is like sounds of sweet music, or a wonderful sunset. Something that just thrills me. I never met a Christian who inspired me as Bahais do." (A. Elizabeth Carpenter to Marion Carpenter, 22 January 1921, author's personal papers.)

10. Jordan to Marion Carpenter, 25 April 1924, author's personal papers.

11. See Chapter 1, note 22.—ED.

12. Marion Carpenter to Haney, quoted in *National Baha'i Bulletin,* 15 Sept. 1924, p. 8.

13. See Chapter 8, pp. 117–18, and Chapter 10, pp. 167–68.

14. See Chapter 10, pp. 167–68.

15. George J. Peirce, "In Memoriam—Samuel Swayze Seward, Jr.," *Stanford Illustrated Review,* Oct. 1932, p. 18.

16. It was Gray who helped me fulfill my English history

requirement for my master's degree. Instead of my taking English History, he suggested that I borrow a book of his and read it. This I did rather casually, making an outline and returning the book to his office. As a result, I was totally unprepared to be given a grueling in-depth oral examination on events and dates in English history. Perhaps Gray was teasing, for he looked at me with mock sympathy and said, "You poor little chicken!" Somehow, miraculously, that was the end of the English history requirement.

17. See Chapter 10, p. 171.—ED.

18. Probasco to Marion Carpenter, 1 July 1924, 11 July 1924, 25 July 1924, 2 September 1924, author's personal papers. (We have used house style for punctuation and the transliteration of Persian and Arabic words.—ED.)

19. The most popular pamphlet on the Faith in the early 1920s was a small blue book that contained basic Bahá'í principles, excerpts from the Writings of Bahá'u'lláh and 'Abdu'l-Bahá, and a list of nineteen Assemblies in the United States and Canada. For a short time there was also a postage-size blue pamphlet. Roy Wilhelm [a prominent early American Bahá'í who was later designated a "Hand of the Cause of God" by Shoghi Effendi] humorously dubbed these "Big Ben" and "Little Ben."

20. National Spiritual Assembly of the Bahá'ís of the United States and Canada, Randall, pres. and treas., to A. Elizabeth Carpenter, 22 October 1923, author's personal papers.

21. National Spiritual Assembly of the Bahá'ís of the United States and Canada, Randall, pres. and treas., to A. Elizabeth Carpenter, 30 November 1923, author's personal papers. (We have used house style for the transliteration of Persian and Arabic words.—ED.)

22. Haney to Marion Carpenter, 6 December 1923, author's personal papers. (We have used house style for the transliteration of Persian and Arabic words. Obvious typographical errors have been corrected.—ED.)

23. A. Elizabeth Carpenter to Marion Carpenter, circa 22 November 1924, author's personal papers. (We have used house style for spelling and punctuation and have substituted "and" for ampersands.—ED.)

24. A. Elizabeth Carpenter to Marion Carpenter, circa 22 November 1924, author's personal papers. (We have used house style for spelling and punctuation and have substituted "and" for ampersands.—ED.)

25. A. Elizabeth Carpenter to Marion Carpenter, circa 22 November 1924, author's personal papers.

26. Howard Carpenter, Barbara Probasco, and Marion Carpenter, "The Larger Vision: How Three University Students See the Needs," *The Bahá'í Magazine: Star of the West,* 15 (Mar. 1925), 369–72.

27. See Chapter 10, pp. 174, 176, and 178–82.—ED.

28. From a letter written by J. E. Esslemont on Shoghi Effendi's behalf, with a section in Shoghi Effendi's handwriting, to Marion Carpenter, 3 May 1925, Letters of Shoghi Effendi, National Bahá'í Archives, Wilmette, Ill. (We have substituted "and" for ampersands.—ED.)

29. The Kitáb-i-Aqdas (the Most Holy Book of Bahá'u'lláh, containing the laws and ordinances of His Faith) had not yet been translated into English, and this Bahá'í law was scarcely known in the United States. But we knew it and applied it in our own requirements for marriage.

30. Ali Yazdi to Marion Carpenter, 21 October 1924, 5 November 1924, 6 February 1925, 25 February 1925, 10 March 1925, 31 July 1925, author's personal papers. Marion Carpenter to Ali Yazdi, 28 July 1925, author's personal papers. (We have used house style for spelling and for the transliteration of Persian and Arabic words.—ED.)

31. Some of the articles in the *Stanford Daily* about the Jináb-i-Fáḍil lectures erroneously referred to his translator, Mírzá Aḥmad Sohráb, as a "Persian prince."

32. "The Farm" is an informal name for the Stanford campus, a picturesque 8,800 acre estate, which is separate from Palo Alto and has its own identity.

33. See Chapter 10, pp. 185–86.—ED.

34. Ali Yazdi to Marion Carpenter, 4 August 1925, author's personal papers. (We have used house style for spelling.—ED.)

35. Marion Carpenter to Ali Yazdi, 11 August 1925, 17 August 1925, author's personal papers. Ali Yazdi to Marion Carpenter, 14 August 1925, author's personal papers.

36. I had asked Howard Hurlbut, an early believer in San Francisco, to speak. He had a system of "devining" oil; he was always promising to make me rich one day!

37. I had signed a teaching contract at Chico High School in Chico, California. The customary salary for beginning teachers at that time was all of $1,800 a year. I held out for a handsome $1,900 and got it.

38. From a letter written by J. E. Esslemont on Shoghi Effendi's behalf, with a section in Shoghi Effendi's handwriting, to Marion Carpenter, 3 May 1925, Letters of Shoghi Effendi.

39. From a letter written on Shoghi Effendi's behalf, with a section in Shoghi Effendi's handwriting, to Marion Carpenter, 28 May 1926, Letters of Shoghi Effendi. (We have substituted "and" for ampersands.—ED.)

Chapter 10: Letters Home, 1923–1925

1. Marion Carpenter to A. Elizabeth Carpenter, November 1923, November 1923, 17 January 1924, 5 February 1924, 14 February 1924, 22 February 1924, 26 February 1924, 4 March 1924, 10 January 1925, 25 January 1925, 8 February 1925, 10 February 1925, February 1925, 14 February 1925, 20 February 1925, February 1925, 26 February 1925, 3 March 1925, 15 March 1925, 18 March 1925, 2 May 1925, May 1925, 6 August 1925, author's personal papers. (We have used house style for spelling, punctuation, and the transliteration of Persian and Arabic words.—ED.)

2. At this time our weekly Bahá'í meeting was being held on Thursday evenings. Occasionally, however, we adjusted the date to a speaker's or inquirer's particular requirements, as was the case for the meeting at which Leroy Ioas spoke.

3. Bahá'u'lláh, *The Seven Valleys: Revealed by Baha'u'llah at Baghdad, in Answer to Questions Asked by Sheik Abdur Rahman, a Great Mohammedan Mystic Sufi Leader*, trans. Ali Kuli Khan (Ish'te-âl, Ebn-Kalânter) (Chicago: Bahai Publishing Society, n.d.), p. 38. For a more accurate translation see Bahá'u'lláh, *The Seven Valleys and the Four Valleys*, trans. Ali-Kuli Khan and Marzieh Gail, 3d rev. ed. (Wilmette, Ill.: Bahá'í Publishing Trust, 1978), p. 29.—ED.

4. 'Abdu'l-Bahá, "The True Spiritual Teacher: Compiled from the Words of Abdul Baha," *The Bahai Magazine: Star of the West*, 14 (May 1923), 60–61.—Ed.

5. Ibid., p. 60.—Ed.

6. For explanations of the terms "Nineteen Day Feast" and "Assembly," see Chapter 1, note 22, and Chapter 4, note 2, respectively.—Ed.

7. Juliet Thompson, "Abdul-Baha's First Days in America: From Diary of Miss Juliet Thompson," *Star of the West*, 8 (28 Apr. 1917), 32–33, 37–38.

8. Marjory Morten, "Segments of the Circle," *Star of the West*, 13 (Sept. 1922), 153–55; "Message to the Jews: Address by Abdul-Baha Abbas before Congregation Emmanu-El, San Francisco, Cal., (Martin A. Meyer, Rabbi) Saturday, October 12, 1912," *Star of the West*, 3, no. 13 (4 Nov. 1912), 3–7, 10–11. The address can also be found in 'Abdu'l-Bahá, *The Promulgation of Universal Peace: Talks Delivered by 'Abdu'l-Bahá during His Visit to the United States and Canada in 1912*, comp. Howard MacNutt, 2d ed. (Wilmette, Ill.: Bahá'í Publishing Trust, 1982), pp. 361–70.—Ed.

9. In January 1925 we changed the time of our weekly Bahá'í meetings to Wednesday evenings.

10. "The Divine Revelators," in *Abdul Baha on Divine Philosophy*, comp. Isabel Fraser Chamberlain (Boston: The Tudor Press, 1918), pp. 33–78.

11. On 6 February 1925 Shoghi Effendi had cabled the American National Spiritual Assembly asking that the American Bahá'ís come to the assistance of the Bahá'ís of Nayríz, Persia, where a flood had destroyed the homes of five hundred Bahá'ís. See "Relief for Bahá'ís at Nayriz, Persia," *Baha'i News Letter: The Bulletin of the National Spiritual Assembly*, no. 3 (Mar. 1925), p. 2. The incident is also mentioned in Shoghi Effendi, *Bahá'í Administration: Selected Messages 1922–1932*, 7th rev. ed. (Wilmette, Ill.: Bahá'í Publishing Trust, 1974), p. 82.—Ed.

12. The author uses "assemblies" to refer to communities, not to administrative bodies. See Chapter 4, note 2.—Ed.

13. Marion Carpenter to Ali Yazdi, 31 August 1925, author's personal papers. (We have used house style for punctuation.—Ed.)

Chapter 11: Down the Years

1. See Howard Luxmoore Carpenter, "A Scientific Approach to Religion," *World Order*, 7, no. 6 (September 1941), 189–97.

2. Grace B. Holley, "Notes on the First Bahá'í Summer School at Geyserville, California, August 1927," TS, p. 3, author's personal papers. (We have used house style for punctuation and for the transliteration of Persian and Arabic words.— ED.) In 1927 the Bahá'í House of Worship in Wilmette was little more than an "ugly tanklike structure" as funds were not yet available to build the "Temple of Light." For a photograph see Allen Boyer McDaniel, *The Spell of the Temple* (New York: Vantage Press, 1953), between pp. 42–43.

3. Bosch to Howard Carpenter, 1 September 1932, author's personal papers. (We have used house style for punctuation and spelling and have substituted "and" for ampersands.—ED.)

4. Shoghi Effendi, *God Passes By*, rev. ed. (Wilmette, Ill.: Bahá'í Publishing Trust, 1974), p. 386.

5. Marzieh [Carpenter] Gail to Marion [Carpenter] Yazdi, 23 October 1979, 15 June 1981, author's personal papers. See also Marzieh Gail, "With Martha," Introductory Essay, *Ṭáhirih the Pure*, by Martha Root, rev. ed. (Los Angeles: Kalimát Press, 1981), pp. 1–16.

6. Root to Cooper, 28 November 1935, Ella G. Cooper Papers, National Bahá'í Archives, Wilmette, Ill. Martha had no knowledge that Howard had died that very day. Later she came to Berkeley for the express purpose of visiting Howard's grave. She and six others read the prayers for him. On hearing that Ella Bailey was having a yellow rosebush planted on his grave, Martha asked to have a part in it. In Howard's memory she gave us the book *Eternal Life*, inscribed:

Martha L. Root
Tenderest Bahá'í love to   Charles Marshall
Ali and Marion Yazdi   Lucy Marshall
[signed]   Ella M. Bailey
R. Marshall   May 15, 19 . .

7. Marzieh [Carpenter] Gail to Marion [Carpenter] Yazdi, 23 October 1979, 15 June 1981, author's personal papers. See also "The Unity of East and West: American Bahá'í Sacrifices Her Life in Service to Persian Believers: Mrs. Keith Ransom-Kehler's Mission," in *The Bahá'í World: A Biennial International Record, Volume V, 1932–1934*, comp. National Spiritual Assembly of the Bahá'ís of the United States and Canada (New York: Bahá'í Publishing Committee, 1936), pp. 389–400.

8. Marzieh [Carpenter] Gail to Marion [Carpenter] Yazdi, 23 October 1979, 15 June 1981, author's personal papers. (In some of the extracts from this correspondence that follow we have used house style for punctuation.—ED.)

9. Ibid.

10. While on pilgrimage to the Bahá'í World Center in July 1981, as I was about to leave the Pilgrim House in Haifa after an evening meeting, I was approached by a gentle and sweet lady— Mrs. Gloria Faizi, the wife of the late Hand of the Cause of God A. Q. Faizi. "Are you the sister of Dr. Howard Carpenter?" she asked me. "I knew him when I was a twelve-year-old girl; he stayed in my home. My stepmother had attended a school which the missionaries had set up; she was one of the first group of graduates, and she was able to help. I remember Howard and his radiance and his patience under his trial." Putting aside her own grief at the recent death of her husband, she had come to tell me this. I was deeply affected.

11. Marzieh [Carpenter] Gail to Marion [Carpenter] Yazdi, 23 October 1979, 15 June 1981, author's personal papers.

12. Florence [Breed] Khánum to A. Elizabeth Carpenter, 14 June 1935, author's personal papers. (We have used house style for punctuation and the transliteration of Persian and Arabic words and have substituted "and" for ampersands.—ED.)

13. Marzieh [Carpenter] Gail to Marion [Carpenter] Yazdi, 23 October 1979, 15 June 1981, author's personal papers.

14. Quoted in Marzieh [Carpenter] Gail to Marion [Carpenter] Yazdi, 23 October 1979, 15 June 1981, author's personal papers.

15. *San Francisco Call Bulletin,* 24 July 1935, Second News Section, front page.

16. Howard Carpenter, quoted in Edith Bristol, "Stanford

Man in Gamble with Death Wins: Young Doctor Gaining in S.F.
Hospital," *San Francisco Call Bulletin*, 24 July 1935, Second News
Section, front page.

17. Ibid.

18. Leroy Ioas, Remarks at Memorial Service for Howard
L. Carpenter, Berkeley, Calif. (We have used house style for capi-
talization and the transliteration of Persian and Arabic words.
—ED.)

19. Ioas to Marion [Carpenter] Yazdi, 10 January 1936, author's personal papers. (We have used house style for the transliteration of Persian and Arabic words.—ED.)

20. "Howard Luxmore [sic] Carpenter (1906–1935)," in
*The Bahá'í World: A Biennial International Record, Volume VI, 1934–
1936*, comp. National Spiritual Assembly of the Bahá'ís of the
United States and Canada (New York: Bahá'í Publishing Committee, 1937), p. 492. See also the entire article on pp. 491–93.

21. From a letter written on behalf of Shoghi Effendi, with
a section in Shoghi Effendi's handwriting, to A. Elizabeth Carpenter, 18 December 1935, Letters of Shoghi Effendi, National
Bahá'í Archives, Wilmette, Ill. (In this section of the letter, written on behalf of Shoghi Effendi, we have substituted "and" for
ampersands.—ED.)

22. Ibid. (In this section of the letter, written by Shoghi Effendi, we have used house style for spelling and have substituted
"and" for ampersands.—ED.)

23. Marion Holley [Hofman], Emma Lou Weaver, and I
were youth speakers at this convention. I recall very clearly that
at the noon recess Ali took me to Shreve, Treat and Eacret to
choose between two beautiful engagement rings. Although
nothing was said, everyone seemed to know what had happened.

24. Marzieh [Carpenter] Gail to Marion [Carpenter] Yazdi,
23 October 1979, 15 June 1981, author's personal papers.

25. For Marion Holley's account of this event see Marion
Holley, "Religion and the World Council of Youth," in *The Bahá'í
World: A Biennial International Record, Volume V, 1932–1934*, comp.
National Spiritual Assembly of the Bahá'ís of the United States
and Canada (New York: Bahá'í Publishing Committee, 1936), pp.
384–87.

26. Marion [Holley] Hofman to Marion [Carpenter] Yazdi, 7 January 1980, author's personal papers. (We have used house style for spelling and the transliteration of Persian and Arabic words and have substituted "and" for ampersands.—ED.)

27. "Prayers and Meditations for the Most Great Peace: Bahá'u'lláh, Tablet of Victory," *Baha'i News,* no. 48 (Feb. 1931), p. 1.

28. See Eunice Braun, "Farru<u>kh</u> Ioas (1920–1960)," in *The Bahá'í World: An International Record, Volume XIII, 1954–1963,* comp. The Universal House of Justice (Haifa: The Universal House of Justice, 1970), pp. 919–21. Farru<u>kh</u> (1920–1960) was a Phi Beta Kappa and graduated with distinction in 1945.

29. Yazdani to Marion [Carpenter] Yazdi, 16 June 1981, author's personal papers.

Chapter 12: Triumph

1. See Ella Goodall Cooper, "'Preparing the Way' in California," *Star of the West,* 2, no. 16 (31 Dec. 1911), 13.

2. For a description of his visit to the United States see Horace Holley, "Survey of Current Bahá'í Activities in the East and West," in *The Bahá'í World (Formerly: Bahá'í Year Book): A Biennial International Record, Volume II, 1926–1928,* comp. National Spiritual Assembly of the Bahá'ís of the United States and Canada (New York: Bahá'í Publishing Committee, 1928), p. 26. Marion [Holley] Hofman refers to this talk in Chapter 11, on p. 199.

3. Martha L. Root, "The Bahá'í Movement and North American University Circles," in *The Bahá'í World: A Biennial International Record, Volume IV, 1930–1932,* comp. National Spiritual Assembly of the Bahá'ís of the United States and Canada (New York: Bahá'í Publishing Committee, 1933), p. 467.

4. Natalie Owen to Ali Yazdi, 28 October 1962, author's personal papers.

5. From a letter written by J. E. Esslemont on Shoghi Effendi's behalf, in the section in Shoghi Effendi's handwriting, to Marion Carpenter, 3 May 1925, Letters of Shoghi Effendi, National Bahá'í Archives, Wilmette, Ill. (The letter is printed in full in Chapter 9, pp. 148–50.—ED.)

6. Faramarz [Yazdani] to Marion [Carpenter] Yazdi, 2 April 1981, author's personal papers. (We have used house style for punctuation and spelling.—ED.)

7. *National Baha'i Bulletin,* 17 Dec. 1923, pp. 7–8.

Index

Index

Back notes are indicated by "p.– n.–." Bold figures are used for photographs.